DISPATCHES FROM THE WEIMAR REPUBLIC

DISPATCHES FROM THE WEIMAR REPUBLIC

VERSAILLES AND GERMAN FASCISM

Morgan Philips Price

Edited by Tania Rose

Pluto Press
LONDON • STERLING, VIRGINIA

First published 1999 by Pluto Press
345 Archway Road, London N6 5AA
and 22883 Quicksilver Drive, Sterling,
VA 20166–2012, USA

British Library Cataloguing in Publication Data
A catalogue record for this book is available from the
British Library

ISBN 0 7453 1425 2 hbk

Library of Congress Cataloging in Publication Data
Price, M. Philips (Morgan Philips) 1885–1973
Dispatches from the Weimar Republic : Versailles and German
fascism / Morgan Philips Price ; edited by Tania Rose.
p.   cm.
Includes bibliographical references and index.
ISBN 0 7453 1425 2
1. Germany—Politics and government—1918–1933. 2. National
socialism—History. 3. Political culture—Germany—History—20th
century. 4. Political parties—Germany—History—20th century.
5. Nationalism—Germany—History—20th century. 6. World war,
1914–1918—Influence. I. Rose, Tania. II. Title.
DD240.P755 1999
943.085—dc21   98–52780
                                                                   CIP

Designed, typeset and produced for Pluto Press by
Chase Production Services, Chadlington, OX7 3LN
Illustrations printed by The Witney Press
Printed and bound in the EC by T J International, Padstow

CONTENTS

ACKNOWLEDGEMENTS

I should like to thank Nancy Armstrong, Rob Atton, Nick Jacobs, Kindred Rose, John Saville and Eve Zawadski for their help, and Pluto's anonymous reader for much good advice as well as encouragement.

My thanks are also due to staff at the British Library, the Public Records Office, the German Historical Institute, the Institut Francais and to ABZ Berlin.

LIST OF ILLUSTRATIONS

Plates

CHRONOLOGY

1918

29 September	German Army High Command calls for armistice
2 October	Prince Max appointed Chancellor
3 October	German government proposes armistice
3 November	Kiel Mutiny
8 November	Bavaria declares Republic
9 November	Germany declares Republic Kaiser abdicates
10 November	Formation of Provisional Government: Ebert appointed Chancellor; Gröner–Ebert Pact
16 December	National Congress of Workers' and Soldiers' Councils meets in Berlin
23 December	Ebert besieged in Chancellery by People's Naval Division
24 December	Troops fire on sailors; Independent Socialists resign from Provisional Government
31 December	Foundation of German Communist Party (KPD)

1919

3 January	Dismissal of Eichhorn (Berlin Police President)
7–17 January	Spartacist uprising in Berlin
15 January	Murder of Luxemburg and Liebknecht
19 January	Elections to National Assembly
6 February	National Assembly meets at Weimar
11 February	Ebert elected President of Germany
13 February	Scheidemann elected Chancellor
21 February	Murder of Eisner in Bavaria
2–9 March	Renewed street fighting in Berlin

2 March	Foundation of Third International (Moscow)
21 March	Soviet Republic declared in Hungary
7 April–2 May	Soviet Republic in Bavaria
7 May	Allies publish peace terms
16 June	Allied ultimatum to Germany
20 June	Scheidemann Cabinet resigns; new government formed by Bauer
28 June	Germany signs Treaty of Versailles
11 August	Weimar Constitution comes into force

1920

10 January	Versailles Treaty comes into force
13 January	Demonstration outside Reichstag ends in bloodshed
13–16 March	Kapp *putsch*; general strike Reichswehr sent to Ruhr when strike continues
27 March	Resignation of Bauer Cabinet; new government formed by Hermann Müller
6 June	Reichstag elections. New government formed by Fehrenbach
5–16 July	Spa Conference (disarmament and reparations)
16 October	Halle Conference: Independent Socialists (USPD) split

1921

24–29 January	Paris Conference (reparations)
21 February–14 March	London Conference (reparations)
20 March	Plebiscite in Upper Silesia Attempted Communist *coup* (March Action)
5 May	Allied ultimatum re reparations
10 May	Resignation of Fehrenbach; Wirth becomes new Chancellor; 'policy of fulfilment'
26 August	Murder of Erzberger
12 October	Partition of Upper Silesia
5 November	Wirth forms new Cabinet

1922

| 6–13 January | Cannes Conference |

18 January	Poincaré becomes Premier of France
10 April–	
19 May	Genoa Conference
16 April	Treaty of Rapallo
24 June	Murder of Rathenau
18 July	Law for the Protection of the Republic passed
7–14 August	London Conference
August	Accelerated inflation begins
24 September	Reunification of Social Democrats and Independent Social Democrats
28 October	Mussolini's 'March on Rome'
14 November	Resignation of Wirth; new Cabinet formed by Cuno

1923

10 January	Germany declared in default of reparations payments
11 January	French and Belgian troops occupy the Ruhr
13 January	Germany declares policy of 'passive resistance'
12 August	Fall of Cuno government; Stresemann forms 'Great Coalition'
26 September	Passive resistance ended; state of emergency declared
16 October	Establishment of *Rentenbank*
8–9 November	Attempted *putsch* by Hitler and Ludendorff; executive authority of Reich conferred on von Seeckt
11 November	Hitler arrested
15 November	Introduction of *Rentenmark*
23 November	Fall of Stresemann government; Wilhelm Marx appointed Chancellor; Stresemann remains in government as Foreign Minister
30 November	Reparations Commission appoints Committee of Experts to look into reparations

1924

13 February	End of state of emergency in Germany
1 April	Hitler sentenced to five years' detention
9 April	Publication of Dawes Plan
16 April	German government accepts Dawes Plan

4 May	Reichstag elections; Nationalist parties gain ground but Marx remains Chancellor
7 December	Reichstag elections
17 December	Hitler released

1925

15 January	New government formed by Luther
27 February	Refoundation of NSDAP (Nazi party)
28 February	Death of Ebert
26 April	Hindenburg elected President
14 July	Evacuation of Ruhr begins
5–16 October	Locarno Conference
1 December	Treaty of Locarno signed in London

1926

19 January	Luther reconstructs his Cabinet
24 April	Treaty of Berlin (with Soviet Russia)
12 May	New government formed by Marx
8 September	Germany joins the League of Nations
17 December	Fall of third Marx government

1927

| 29 January | Marx forms fourth Cabinet |
| 31 January | Inter-Allied Military Commission withdraws from Germany |

1928

20 May	Reichstag elections
29 June	Hermann Müller forms new government
August	League of Nations discussions on final reparations settlement and evacuation of Rhineland

1929

11 February– 7 June	Paris Conference on revision of Dawes Plan chaired by Owen D. Young
7 June	Young Plan signed
3 October	Death of Stresemann
end October	Crash of New York stock exchange
22 December	Failure of Nationalist referendum against acceptance of Young Plan

1930

27 March	Müller Cabinet resigns
29 March	Brüning appointed Chancellor
30 June	Allies complete evacuation of Rhineland
16 July	Dissolution of Reichstag
14 September	Reichstag elections; large gains by NSDAP; Brüning remains Chancellor

1931

11 May	Failure of Austrian *Credit-Anstalt* bank followed by bank failures all over Europe
20 June	President Hoover proposes moratorium on all international debts
9 October	Brüning forms new Cabinet

1932

February	Unemployment in Germany stands at over 6 million
10 April	Hindenburg re-elected President
24 April	NSDAP gains in *Landtag* elections throughout Germany
29 May	Hindenburg dismisses Brüning
30 May	New government formed by von Papen with von Schleicher as Minister of Defence
4 June	Reichstag dissolved
20 July	von Papen dismisses Prussian *Landtag* government
31 July	Reichstag elections; NSDAP largest party
12 September	Vote of no confidence in von Papen; Reichstag dissolved
6 November	Reichstag elections; NSDAP remain largest party
17 November	von Papen Cabinet resigns
3 December	New Cabinet formed by von Schleicher

1933

4 January	von Papen and Hitler hold secret talks
28 January	von Schleicher resigns
30 January	Hitler appointed Chancellor

NOTE ON GERMAN POLITICAL PARTIES DURING THE EARLY WEIMAR PERIOD

The main political parties which will be referred to in this text are:

DDP (*Deutsche Demokratische Partei*: German Democratic Party)

DVP (*Deutsche Volkspartei*: German People's Party)

DNVP (*Deutschnationale* Volkspartei: German National People's Party)

Zentrum: Centre Party

NSDAP (*Nationalsozialistische Deutsche Arbeiterpartei*: National Socialist German Workers' Party)

SPD (*Sozialdemokratische Partei Deutschlands*: German Social Democratic Party: Social Democrats)

USPD (*Unabhängige Sozialdemokratsiche Partei Deutschlands*: Independent Social Democratic Party; Independent Socialists)

KPD (*Kommunistische Partei Deutschlands*: German Communist Party)

BVP (*Bayerische Volkspartei*: Bavarian People's Party)

The *DDP* was originally a liberal party; its members were largely drawn from the pre-war Progressive People's Party but it came increasingly under the influence of the big industrialists and was further weakened by its own lack of coherence in the Reichstag.

The *DVP* were former National Liberals. The party lost support because its more progressive wing was also alienated by the influence upon it of the industrialists; moreover, its Right wing disapproved of the leadership's willingness to enter into the so-called Great Coalition in 1923.

The *DNVP* was nationalist, monarchist and anti-Semitic. The special interest groups supporting it were mainly drawn from the landowning classes and the military. It was further weakened by the emergence of smaller special-interest parties, such as property owners, victims of inflation, peasants.

The *Zentrum* was, as its name suggests, a Centre party but it was also essentially the party of the Roman Catholics. It would have been impossible to govern Germany at all during the years of the Weimar Republic without the Centre Party. Although weakened by the formation of the specifically regional Bavarian Centre Party (*BVP*) and by the apostasy of the Right-wing Catholics who switched their allegiance to the DNVP, the consistency of its liberalism ensured its survival throughout the Weimar period.

The *NSDAP* will forever be remembered as the Nazi party. The success of the Nazis was originally based on their appreciation of the importance of organisation and of the value of propaganda. Moreover, they offered social cohesion in the face of social cleavage as represented by the special interests which dominated many of the other parties.

The *SPD* was founded in 1869 and survived Bismarck's anti-socialist legislation. Because it voted for war credits in the Reichstag in 1914 the Left wing of the party became increasingly disaffected and in 1917 broke away and founded the *USDP*.

The *USPD* itself developed a Left wing: the Spartacist movement.

The *KPD* was founded at the very end of December 1918, its membership largely drawn from the Spartacists and the Revolutionary Shop Stewards' movement. It was later briefly split by a group calling themselves the Communist Workers' Party of Germany (*KAPD*) and was then reunited as the VKPD (*Vereinigte Kommunistische Partei Deutschlands*).

Plate 1: The Italian, Belgian, Bulgarian, Dutch and British correspondents reporting from the German National Assembly, Weimar, 1919. Morgan Philips Price, reporting for the *Daily Herald*, stands far right.

Straßenkämpfe in Berlin.
Barrikaden vor dem Zeitungsverlag
Rudolf Mosse.

Plate 2: 'Organising White Guards from officers and sons of bourgeoisie.' (page 29) (photo: Willy Römer, Agentur für bilder zur Zeitgeschichte, Berlin)

Plate 3: '... Mown down before machine guns against the walls of Berlin prisons.' (page 38)
(photo: Alfred Gross, Agentur für bilder zur Zeitgeschichte, Berlin).

Plate 4: Morgan Philips Price (centre) at the Conference of the Independent Socialist Party of Germany, Halle, October 1920.

Plate 5: Walter Rathenau, Foreign Minister and one of the most respected German politicians of the early Weimar days.

Plate 6: Friederich Ebert (left), the last Imperial Chancellor and first President of the Weimar Republic, and Philip Scheidemann, the first Prime Minister of the Weimar Republic.

Plate 7: The 'Red Army' in the Ruhr.

Plate 8: Adolf Hitler, 1923.

Plate 9: French troops outside the Paul
Gerhardt school, Gelsenkirchen, 1923.

M.P. Price
(Daily Herald
Correspondent
in Berlin)

Gedye
(Times
correspondent
in Cologne)

Mrs Gedye

in Rhineland near Bonn
Sept 1923

Plate 10: Morgan Philips Price (left) with C.E.R. Gedye (*The Times* correspondent in Cologne) and L.M. Gedye, near Bonn, September 1923.

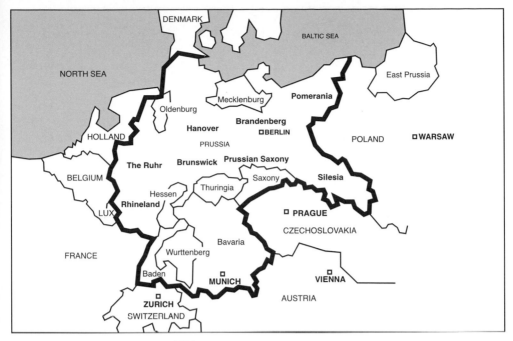

Map 1: Germany and its provinces in 1920.

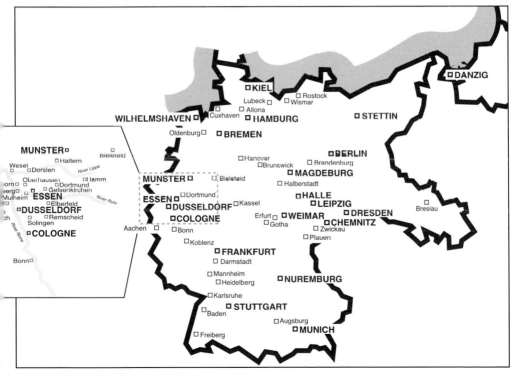

Map 2: Main towns in Germany – 1920.

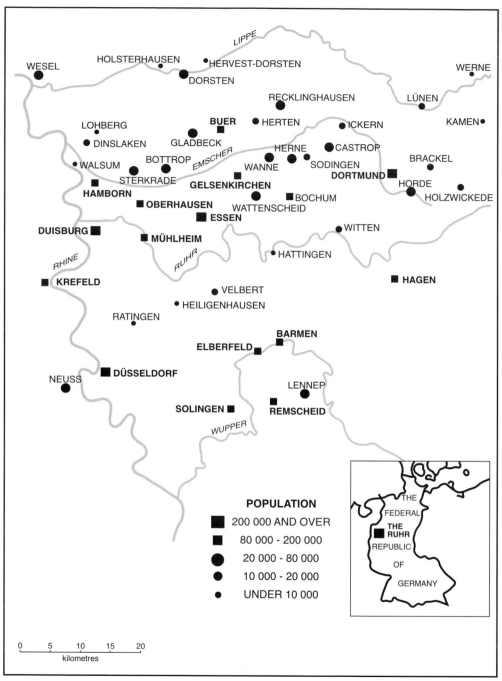

Map 3: Cities of the Ruhr Valley

INTRODUCTION

Any account of the Weimar Republic, if only of its first few years, must benefit from some understanding of German history in the century that preceded its foundation. What follows is a series of reports from Germany which appeared in one British newspaper between 1919 and 1924, put together in such a way as to form a more or less continuous narrative. The reporter was Morgan Philips Price, who had just emerged from Russia, where he had been special correspondent for the *Manchester Guardian* from 1914 to 1918 and who had, in the end, identified himself with the ideals and fortunes of the Bolsheviks. The British newspaper for which he then began to write was the Labour *Daily Herald*. The reader will soon become aware that Price was writing with a considerable Left-wing bias during these years. Yet the analysis of the events he described was largely corroborated by information reaching London through official channels and continues to be confirmed in many subsequent histories of the period. In 1918 the fate of Germany was determined by the terms of the Versailles Treaty which followed the end of the First World War.

The history of Germany in the preceding century was shaped by the post-war settlement agreed at the Congress of Vienna in 1815, after the defeat of Napoleon. The Congress of Vienna set up a federation of 39 German and German-speaking Austrian states, the chief function of which was mutual defence, although it was probably expected that the very existence of the Federation would deter any more experiments in 'Jacobinism'. A Federal Diet consisting of an Upper and a Lower House, with purely consultative functions, was set up in Frankfurt. But Austria had the casting vote in both Houses and Austria held an as yet unchallenged hegemony over the other states. Most of them had their own Diets but these, too, had a consultative rather than a representative role, and government was carried on by an assortment of systems which included kings, princes, dukes, electors and free cities: arrangements which had barely altered since the Middle Ages. Provincial Diets had also existed in Prussia since the Middle Ages, but they were organised on a caste system, with no pretensions whatsoever to democracy. The Kingdom of Prussia was, in any case, an artificial creation which was held together by its military and bureaucratic sub-structures, and these had long been dominated by the Junkers or great landowners of East Prussia.

In the course of the 1840s new ideas began to circulate in the Federation. Ironically perhaps, the advance of railway construction and the more or less universal determination of the state governments to build and own the railways within their territories, necessitated a degree of consultation with the various Diets of the Federation to enable the state governments to increase their borrowing. The middle classes began to feel more important and to notice that even such citizens' rights as had been provided under the federal constitution were being disregarded. Liberal ideas began to spread, and so did the notion that it would be advantageous if the Federation could be transformed into a federal state under the leadership of the largest one: Prussia. Unrest began to grow throughout the Federation, aggravated by bad harvests in 1846 and 1847. The French Revolution of February 1848 triggered popular uprisings in all the states of the Federation including Prussia, and in Austria political upheavals were accompanied by a nationalist revolt in Hungary.

On 31 March 1848 a preliminary representative body, the *Vorparlement*, met in Frankfurt and demanded elections on a manhood suffrage basis throughout the states for a National Assembly. The new Assembly which met (in Frankfurt) on 18 May was drawn entirely from the middle and professional classes and its members took their political labels, Right or Left, from the positions in which they sat in the house of Assembly. They set about drawing up basic laws (*Grundrechte*) and elected a Regent, the Habsburg Archduke John. Although their laws were not recognised in either Austria or Prussia the Assembly itself was recognised, for a time and if not with enthusiasm, by most of the states of the Federation. But by the end of 1849, when both the popular and the nationalist movements in the Austrian Empire had been put down, the governments of the states gradually withdrew recognition and the Archduke resigned. However, the desirability of creating a German federation with the King of Prussia at its head continued to be widely canvassed. The then King of Prussia, Frederick William IV, refused even to consider such a proposition. He would not accept any post based on a democratic constitution; and he had too well-developed a sense of the divine right which he claimed for himself to do anything which might undermine the position of a fellow-monarch, that is, the Austrian Emperor. Nonetheless, new elections to the Frankfurt Assembly were held in January 1850 and it continued to sit. Since he could not entirely ignore it, William IV now dispatched Bismarck as ambassador to Frankfurt and Bismarck began to see for himself the extent to which Austria continued to dominate German affairs.

In the period of reaction which set in after the end of the revolutionary waves of 1848 the people who gained the most were the Prussian Junkers, both in terms of re-establishing their feudal rights and in their domination of government circles. Bismarck came from a Junker background and what he saw in Frankfurt left him determined to see Austria driven out of the German Federation. In order to bring about such an ambitious project he needed the assurance of absolute power behind him; he therefore welcomed the authoritarian and almost mystical concept of monarchy held by Frederick William IV and his successor in 1861, William I. Despite the repressive atmosphere of the state, elections to the Prussian Diet in 1858 had produced a Liberal majority in the Lower House and this was repeated in 1862. William I now put Bismarck in charge of forming a government and, when the Lower House struck out of his budget the costs of the King's cherished proposals for army reform, Bismarck simply ruled without a budget: something which the Reichstag held against him for a long time.

A long-standing irritant in the field of foreign policy at that time was a conflict in the duchies of Schleswig and Holstein, where Austria, Denmark and Prussia were all competing for the right to rule. In 1863 the King of Denmark attempted to annex the duchies and Austria and Prussia collaborated to defeat him in the field. It was then agreed that Prussia should rule in Schleswig and Austria in Holstein. Three years later Bismarck invaded Holstein, defeated the Austrian army at Königgraz, set up a new North German Federation without Austria and concluded a series of secret alliances with the South German states. The new Federation was provided with a Lower House, the Reichstag, and a second House, the Bundestag, representing the governments of the component states. A common policy affecting all military, foreign policy and economic affairs was instituted. The first new Reichstag met in February 1867 and the new constitution was adopted in April of that year.

Having defeated Austria in 1867, Bismarck turned his attention to Napoleon III's France, from which he believed the next threat to the new German Federation must come. A pretext for war was provided when a distant relative of the Hohenzollern King of Prussia was offered the then vacant throne of Spain. The offer was refused but the French government, through its ambassador, put an intolerable degree of pressure on the King to ensure it would never be accepted in future. The wording of the King's refusal to grant further interviews to the ambassador was made public in such a way as to infuriate the French who immediately declared war. Although France was the first to mobilise, the army reforms which William I had succeeded in carrying through ensured an overwhelming German victory and lost France the provinces of Alsace and Lorraine. The North German Federation had been supported, in the Franco-Prussian war, by the South German states of Bavaria, Baden and Wurtenburg. The next step was their incorporation in a German Empire, which was proclaimed at Versailles in January 1871. Bismarck went on to secure the Empire's position as a power by a series of interlocking treaties involving – in the course of the next 20 years – Russia, Austria, Italy and Turkey, and culminating in the Congress of Berlin in 1887, at which an attempt was made to settle all outstanding issues in south-eastern Europe and the Balkans.

The acquisition of Alsace and Lorraine brought rich deposits of coking coal and potash, as well as a thriving textile industry, into the German economy. The industrial revolution had arrived late in Germany. Until the last third of the nineteenth century the German economy had been predominantly agrarian. The railway boom was followed by a late industrial revolution and commerce benefited from the *Zollverein*: a customs union between almost all of the component states of Germany. The abolition of tariffs had begun in 1818, initially between the territories of the Kingdom of Prussia, but the Prussian example was followed by the other German states and by 1833 nearly all of them adhered to the union. After the Franco-Prussian war French reparations had been fed into a rapid expansion of industry, and the larger industries, notably metal and construction, flourished. Above all, banking thrived and in Germany the relationship between banking and industry was closer than in the other countries of Western Europe. The fact that the heads of most of the leading banks were, at that time, Jewish, aggravated an endemic tendency to anti-Semitism, the consequences of which hardly need to be emphasised here. National associations of heavy industry began to be formed to fight against the very principle of free trade upon which Germany's former prosperity had been founded, and competition from imported grain brought the interests of the landowners together with those of the industrialists. By 1879 Bismarck himself had become a convert to protection and tariff walls began to be erected around Germany. The restriction of trade which followed resulted in a crisis of overproduction, since the home markets could no longer absorb the whole of the gross national product. Protection enhanced the position of the large landowners and thus of the officer class and the higher bureaucracy, thereby further increasing the influence of Prussia throughout the machinery of state. Industrialists began to find it necessary to acquire figureheads from among this sector of society. By the early 1880s, the accelerating needs of industry convinced influential members of both the governing and the industrial classes that the acquisition of colonies was now a necessity.

Since the 1850s German traders and missionaries in Africa and the Pacific Islands had been proposing German protectorates in the areas in which they were working. The practical need to acquire overseas markets coincided with a widely felt impulse to find ways of emphasising the fact that Germany had become a

major power. In the 1880s protectorates were set up in West and
East Africa and in the Pacific Islands of Fiji, New Britain and
New Guinea. Personally, Bismarck would have been content to
leave their management to purely commercial interests, but the
banks and syndicates involved did not want sole responsibility
for the territories. In 1890 an agreement was made with Britain
regarding the control of considerable territories in Central and
East Africa, but in 1894 disputes developed over conflicting interests in North Africa, the Sudan and the Portuguese colonies.
Britain began to be seen as a natural enemy. Germany had enormous interests in the Transvaal, involving iron, steel, chemicals,
machinery, dynamite, whisky and banking. Germans owned 20
per cent of all the foreign capital invested in the Transvaal. When
the Kaiser sent a message of support to President Kruger at the
time of the Jameson Raid (an unsuccessful attempt by a rogue
group within the British South Africa company to overthrow the
government of the Transvaal), continued friction between
Germany and Britain was ensured. During the Boer War
Germany openly sympathised with the Boers.

The 1890s were years of strenuous military and naval
rearmament in Germany, the latter being undertaken under the
influence of Admiral von Tirpitz, who had become convinced,
during postings in the Far East, that Britain was the enemy and
that the only way to constrain Britain was – quite literally – with
battleships. Moreover, it was no longer a question of simple
status-seeking: an influential school of thought proclaimed that
Germany had a mission to civilise the world. In the 1880s
patriotic societies were formed to popularise that mission. The
Navy League and the Colonial League promoted policies concerned with their titles. The Pan-German League, formed in the
following decade, had similar objectives: expansionist, colonial-
ist and militarist, but appealed to a more influential following.
Its adherents were drawn largely from among Junkers, industrialists, the bureaucracy and the academic professions. It was also
overtly class-based and anti-socialist. But the more populist
movements, known in less respectful circles as *Hurrapatriotis-
mus*, proved to be a useful way of distracting minds from the
social issues now surfacing in a society which had suddenly
developed a large industrial working class.

In 1869 a Social Democratic Party, primarily concerned with workers' interests, had been founded after two earlier attempts had ended in schism. In 1878 a so-called Socialist Law, introduced by Bismarck, banned any kind of political or social activity 'designed to subvert the existing political and social order'. The law was not repealed until 1890, although it was unable to prevent twelve Social Democrat deputies from being elected to the Reichstag in 1881 and from steadily increasing their numbers in subsequent elections. Jingoism proved capable of diverting a certain amount of attention away from domestic politics and Bismarck was clever enough to disarm a good deal of political opposition by introducing unemployment and other forms of social insurance which were then well ahead of their time in Europe. But neither Bismarck, the Pan-German League nor the Conservatives in the Reichstag succeeded in preventing the growth in influence of the German Social Democrats who had become, before the end of the century, the most influential socialist party in Europe. When, in 1889, Bismarck had wanted to make the Socialist Law a permanent feature he was frustrated by an *ad hoc* majority in the Reichstag. In 1890 he found himself increasingly at odds with a new young Kaiser, William II, who was at that time under the influence of a school of thought which believed that enlightened social welfare policies were the best defence against socialism. Increasingly at odds with his monarch in both domestic and foreign policy matters and having become an aggressively authoritarian old man, Bismarck was dismissed.

By the end of the century the German military mind had begun to brood on the possibility of Germany having to face a war on two fronts: one against a vengeful France and one against Russia. The formation of the British *Entente Cordiale* with France in 1904 and the Anglo-Russian Treaty of 1911, with Britain as the common factor, did nothing to diminish this obsession. A plan – the Schlieffen Plan – was devised to pre-empt the feared encirclement by attacking France first in a flanking movement and thereafter attending to the frontier with Russia. In 1908 Austria annexed Bosnia-Herzegovina from the crumbling Ottoman Empire, ignoring the claims of Serbia to that territory. Germany now assured the Austrian government that in the event of an attack upon it by Serbia and the consequent and predictable support of Serbia by its historic protector, Russia, Germany would come to the aid of Austria. It was regarded as axiomatic that if Russia were then to mobilise France would do the same. Any future war would have to be a general European war. The unknown quantity was Britain. What was not known was that since 1912 the British government considered itself bound, by secret naval understandings, to come to the aid of France if the Schlieffen Plan was put into effect.

In retrospect, after an interval of more than 80 years, the war of 1914–18 appears to have been inescapable. It is as though the scenario for it had been deliberately written. What was not inevitable was that Germany would be defeated. Until America came into the war in 1917 on the side of the Entente and Associated Powers (Belgium, Italy and Japan) Germany's confidence in her own victory appeared to be well founded. All the plans made for the demobilisation of the German army were based on the assumption of victory. At the end of 1917, Allied strategists were thinking in terms of the war lasting at least two more years. But 1917 proved to be a turning point for more than one reason, although coincidence is as likely an explanation for all that happened in that year as any suggestion of cause and effect.

The first Russian Revolution took place in March 1917. The Tsar abdicated and a more or less Social Democratic Provisional Government was put in his place. But Russia remained in the war. A disastrous summer offensive was undertaken by the Russian armies as the result of Allied pressure. The failure of the offensive, accompanied with terrible losses and combined with the failure of the Provisional Government to realise any of the hopes which had been placed upon it, made it glaringly obvious, by the autumn of 1917, that Russia could not remain a combatant in the war. A second revolution – the Bolshevik Revolution – took place in November and by the end of the year the new government had secured an armistice with Germany. The vicious treatment of the Soviet government by the military dictatorship which then passed for government in Germany, by the terms of the Treaty of Brest–Litovsk, exemplified the worst national characteristics now attributed to Germany. But the harsh provisions of the treaty raised little sympathy for Russia in the West. The French and British governments felt militarily betrayed and ideologically threatened. A German spring offensive in 1918 was at first alarmingly successful, yet the Allies still managed to find enough troops with which to invade North Russia in August, using an assortment of justifications which included bringing Russia back into the war on the side of the Allies and liberating the 'real Russia' from its new government.

At this time the *Manchester Guardian* newspaper had a correspondent in Russia, Morgan Philips Price, who had gradually become convinced that the Bolshevik government represented the only hope of holding Russia together and preventing its total disintegration. Counter-revolutionary armies (financed by the Allies) were advancing on the centre from the south and east and the Allies themselves had landed troops at Archangel and Murmansk. Price decided to employ his journalistic skills by writing pamphlets for distribution among the Allied troops arguing against the Allied intervention in Russia and on behalf of the Soviet government. His dispatches to his paper were in any case being totally suppressed by the Official Press Bureau – the British censorship agency – in London. By the time the war in the West looked like coming to an end Price knew that he was considered a dangerous subversive in his own country and that he had better not try to return. The German 'revolution', which took place almost simultaneously with the end of hostilities, raised expectations of the imminence of world revolution in some circles in the Kremlin, although they were not shared by Lenin: a fact which Price learned in the course of a personal interview with him around that time. He now had only one idea, which was to try to get out a more accurate picture of what was going on in Russia than the mixture of malignant fantasy and rumour which was appearing in the British press. After some discussion with the Russian Foreign Minister, Tchicherin, it was agreed that he should apply for permission from the new Provisional Government in Berlin to cross into Germany and see what he could do from there. He also planned to make contacts with other foreign correspondents in Berlin and to continue his propagandist activities on behalf of the Soviet government.

By now Price considered himself a Marxist. He came from a wealthy family, with money made from cotton and timber and subsequently invested in land. But on both sides there was a long tradition of involvement in Liberal and radical politics. Between 1832 and 1914 five of his relatives had been or were Liberal Members of Parliament and he himself, at the age of 29, was the Liberal candidate for his native city, Gloucester. Believing – with others – that Britain need not and should not have become involved in a general war he resolved to take no part in it. In the autumn of 1914 the British press appeared to be suffering from the delusion that Russia, by virtue of her alliance with Britain and France, had become a democracy. Price had travelled extensively in Russia before the war and spoke the language fluently. He felt that the one thing that he could do, and that made sense to him, was to find out the truth about what was really going on in Russia. He had access to C. P. Scott, the editor of the *Manchester Guardian*, and Scott authorised him, as *'correspondent particulier'*, to go to Russia for a few months and write not necessarily articles for publication, but letters briefing Scott personally for use as background to his editorials. Price arrived in Russia in December 1914 expecting to stay there for a few months; in the event he remained in Russia as special correspondent of the *Manchester Guardian* for four years. Until the first Russian Revolution he acted mainly as a war correspondent, having soon discovered that articles or even letters about Russian politics did not often get past the Russian censors. Between the spring of 1915 and the spring of 1917 he spent most of his time on the Polish or the Caucasus fronts, and 141 of his articles about the war in those areas were printed in the *Manchester Guardian*. After April 1917 he wrote mainly from St Petersburg and Moscow, although he travelled about as much as he could, given the state of public transport in Russia in those years. His articles of 1917 and 1918 form a coherent account of the revolutions and have already been published as *Dispatches from the Revolution* (Pluto Press, 1997).

When Price left Russia, although he did not yet know it, he had been sacked by the *Manchester Guardian*, Scott's gentle reproof being that 'it did not do' for one of his correspondents to have so completely identified himself with the government of the country from which he was reporting. For a short time after his arrival in Berlin he continued to file dispatches to his old paper and two of them surprisingly got past the British censor. But by the end of 1918 he realised that he would have to find another outlet for his journalistic activities. It was not long before he was approached, via an intermediary, by the editor of the *Daily Herald*, George Lansbury.

The following account of the first years of the Weimar Republic is largely composed of his articles for the *Daily Herald* between May 1919 and January 1924. Having been written for a much less well-endowed and a smaller newspaper than the *Manchester Guardian*, they were necessarily much shorter than the extensive articles he wrote from Russia. The present writer has therefore been obliged to contribute a good deal more background material than was necessary in the case of the previous volume in order to maximise the value of the information contained in the original texts.

Where the texts of articles have been abridged, the passage omitted was either repetitious or a digression. All datelines refer to the date of publication in the *Daily Herald*. All copy was filed in Berlin unless otherwise stated.

Tania Rose
London

1918

Germany begins to lose the war – Kaiser appoints Prince Max of Baden to negotiate with Wilson – government and parties in Imperial Germany – the armistice – the German Revolution of November – Workers' and Soldiers' Councils – the German army and the Freikorps – Price arrives and interviews members of the Provisional Government – Congress of Workers' and Soldiers' Councils – street fighting in Berlin – Rosa Luxemburg and the founding of the Communist Party of Germany

By the beginning of September 1918 the Allied armies had at last gained the initiative in the Great War. For the past six months the Germans had driven them further and further back. In August the Allies began to reverse the tide of hostilities and now not only in France but in Bulgaria and Turkey the Central Powers were retreating and the Austrians were already suing for peace. Ludendorff, the Commander-in-Chief of the hitherto victorious German armies, was now directing their withdrawal. Lloyd George wasted no words in describing the situation: 'On September 28th Ludendorff and Hindenburg took stock of the outlook and reached the despairing conclusion that the war was lost, and that there was nothing for it but to appeal at once to the enemy for an armistice.'[1]

After a day of urgent meetings between military and political leaders at Spa, on 29 September Germany applied to the American President for an armistice and for peace to be negotiated on the basis of the Fourteen Points contained in his message to Congress on 8 January 1918. These contained not only a blueprint for the future settlement of Europe, including the liberation of all occupied territories, but also a declaration of intent as to how international relations should be managed in future.[2] The negotiations that followed were at first confined to Germany and the USA. A series of exchanges in the form of Notes took place between the German and the American governments. In his Note of 23 October Wilson pointed out that neither he nor the powers with whom he was associated (the Allies, consisting of France, Belgium, Italy and Britain, and the Associated Powers: Japan and America) were convinced that the government with which they were dealing in Germany had any serious claim to be considered a democracy. 'The military masters and the monarchical autocrats of Germany', as he put it, appeared still to be in control. As matters stood the Allies and the Associated Powers would be demanding not negotiations but surrender. The hint was unmistakable. Germany stood to get a better deal if the Kaiser was no longer on the throne of Germany.

The German constitution – 'a monarchical executive co-operating or quarrelling with representative institutions without any organic relationship existing between the two'[3] – gave the Kaiser and the army virtually dictatorial powers. There was indeed an elected Parliament – the Reichstag – but the Kaiser had the sole right to appoint his prime minister – the Chancellor – without having to pay the least regard to the political complexion of the Reichstag. The Reichstag, moreover, had only minimal powers over taxation, most of them being delegated to the provincial governments; foreign and military affairs were conducted entirely over the head of the Chancellor by the Kaiser together with the Supreme Command. Indeed it had been the German Supreme Command, and Ludendorff personally, who had insisted, in the course of the meetings on 29 September, that the appeal to Wilson must be made by a democratically constituted government. The then Chancellor, Hertling, refused to have anything to do with such a proposal and resigned. Prince Max of Baden, a man with a reputation for liberalism in most things, was appointed Chancellor in his place. For the first time a Cabinet was constructed which bore some relationship to the composition of the Reichstag.

Since the elections of 1912 the greatest number of seats in the Reichstag had been held by the Social Democrats and the Left Liberals, although not enough to constitute an overall majority. The Centre Party had co-operated with the parties of the Right to support the Conservative government until the passage of the Reichstag resolution in favour of a negotiated peace in July 1917.[4] From then onwards, the Centre co-operated with the parties of the Left. On the eve of the appointment of Prince Max as Chancellor (2 October) the Interparty Committee of the Reichstag set out a Four Point Programme of constitutional reforms which, it demanded, the next Chancellor should at least discuss with them. The Committee also demanded a voice in the selection of ministers. Thus the numerical majority in the Reichstag – Social Democrats, Liberals and Centre Party – was able for the first time to influence the composition of Prince Max's Cabinet, and that Cabinet now contained for the first time a Social Democrat, Friedrich Ebert.

The German Social Democratic Party (SPD) was the oldest socialist party in Europe, having been founded in 1869. Suppressed under Bismarck, it nonetheless won adherents in terms of the popular vote, and in 1890 it was legalised. The first Congress of the SPD was held at Erfurt in 1891. Already the party was beginning to divide between its Right and Left wings; foremost in the latter group were Rosa Luxemburg, herself a political refugee from Poland, and Karl Liebknecht. The Left Socialists demanded that the party adopt the principles of political action laid down in the Communist Manifesto, which was in theory – though only in theory – the basis of the SPD programme. The main body of the party was content to work for socialism by parliamentary means.

Ebert had been chairman of the parliamentary party since 1912 and was largely responsible for the fact that nearly all the Social Democrats had voted for war credits in 1914 and had generally observed the *Bürgerfrieden* or civic armistice which had taken the place of politics during the war. But as the war went on the Left wing of the party became increasingly restive. In March 1916, 18 members were expelled from the party. In January 1917 the executive of the main body of the party announced that dissident groups within the Social Democrats must no longer consider themselves members. The party now fell into two groups, the Majority Social Democrats (SPD) and the Independent Social Democrats (USPD) who were determined to carry on an active struggle against the continuation of the war. The question then arose whether the extreme Left of the USPD – known as the Spartacists – should form a third party or remain within the USPD. Under the guidance of Luxemburg the Spartacists, for the time being, decided to remain within it. The two groups were, she said, 'two complementary heirs to the inheritance of the German and the interational social democracy' and the problem of tactics 'can only be solved in open, constant and systematic struggle between the two tendencies'.[5] The fragmentation of the German Left even then was not complete. Outside the Reichstag industrial action had begun to be co-ordinated by the Revolutionary Shop Stewards, who were to become an influential factor when, at the very end of 1918, the Spartacists called their first Congress and the German Communist Party (KPD) was formed in one of the committee rooms of the Prussian Diet.

The armistice negotiations dragged on throughout October. The Allies were understandably wary. The armies were still fighting and German submarines were still sinking passenger ships without warning. It was not immediately apparent that anything had changed. Until this time there had been little evidence of any strong republican feeling in the country at large. But the slow pace of the negotiations and the fear that the constitutional reforms initiated at the end of September would not be considered adequate by the Allies combined to radicalise public opinion. The Kaiser appeared to be incapable of recognising that he could have influenced the progress of the armistice negotiations by abdicating. Instead, on 28 October, he took himself to the army headquarters at Spa, where he was out of reach of the civil power. On the same day the German Naval High Command, without informing the Chancellor, ordered the fleet at Kiel to put out to sea. The mutiny that followed, although generally considered to be the beginning of the German Revolution, was not originally political at all in character but 'a set of enlisted men's grievances'. It gave rise to a movement which characterised the almost theological debate about the nature of government which was to preoccupy and paralyse the parties of the German Left for the next five years.

The sailors formed a Council and sent delegations first to the other Hanseatic ports and then to most of the major cities of Germany, and in the atmosphere of collapse which overtook the country in the last days of the war, Workers', or Workers' and Sailors', or Workers' and Soldiers' Councils were set up in many of them. The idea of government by Soviet or Council was of course borrowed from revolutionary Russia, but it was not altogether new in Germany. In January 1918 there had been a massive strike wave in the course of which local Workers' Councils had briefly existed in many cities. But in November as in January, the Councils were more concerned with the preservation of law and order than with the promotion of socialism, and they were overwhelmingly controlled by the cautious Majority Social Democrats. Even so, the appearance of the Councils was enough to play a significant part in bringing down the government.

On 9 November, as soldiers from the Berlin barracks joined demonstrators in the streets of Berlin, Prince Max resigned and announced – some hours before he was authorised to do so – that the Hohenzollerns had relinquished their rights to the throne. He said nothing about a republic. He transferred the office of Chancellor to Ebert and, as Ebert was already a member of the government, the appearance of an orderly transfer of power was maintained. It was intended that he should form a caretaker coalition Cabinet to govern pending the convening of a National Assembly to decide on the future constitution of the state, which would of course include the question of the future of the monarchy. But already Ebert's party colleague, Philipp Scheidemann, aware that public opinion was now increasingly tending to republicanism, and possibly meaning to pre-empt a similar declaration by the Workers' and Soldiers' Councils, had on the same day proclaimed a republic before the vast crowd which assembled outside the Reichstag. Shortly afterwards, the Spartacist leader Karl Liebknecht, who had only recently been released from prison, declared publicly that it would be a *socialist* republic (his emphasis).

The Berlin Soldiers' Councils had already called for elections to Workers' and Soldiers' Councils to be held the next morning (10 November) to form an assembly and appoint a provisional government. In the meantime Ebert had appointed his Cabinet, consisting of three Majority and two Independent Social Democrats and one Revolutionary Shop Steward. This was to be known as the Council of People's Representatives (*Rat der Volksbeauftragten*). Thus on the eve of the armistice two theoretical centres of executive power had been created, although when the Berlin Assembly of Workers' and Soldiers' Councils met it recognised the *Rat der Volksbeauftragten* as the legitimate Provisional Government of Germany.

During the night of 10 November Ebert received a telephone call from the Quartermaster General of the German Army Command, General Gröner, who had succeeded Ludendorff in that position. Gröner proposed that the services of the High Command would be placed at the disposal of the Provisional Government on condition that the Government now allied itself with the officer corps in maintaining order and discipline in the defeated and demoralised army, restoring the rule of law and rejecting the claims to authority of the Soldiers' Councils. Under the circumstances Ebert clearly felt he had little option but to accept Gröner's conditions. From that moment, any pretensions to socialism of the Provisional Government were fatally compromised.

The terms of the armistice signed on 11 November were extremely harsh. The Germans were to evacuate all the territory they had occupied in the west, the whole of the left bank of the Rhine (including, of course, Alsace) and bridgeheads over the Rhine at Cologne, Mainz and Coblenz. They were required to surrender large quantities of war materials, their submarine and High Seas fleets together with locomotives, rolling stock and motor vehicles. Moreover, the blockade of Germany would not be lifted.

The Gröner–Ebert pact had ensured the survival of the German General Staff however, and therefore – in one form or another – of a German army. On 11 November Germany had approximately 6 million men under arms and was required to demobilise them immediately. All existing plans for demobilisation had been based on the assumption of victory and of the availability of time in which to disperse the men in an orderly fashion. But in the last weeks of the war the army had begun to disintegrate. Units stationed in occupied territory had generally kept order until they reached the German frontier and some kept together until they reached their home garrisons. Others simply went to their own homes as best they could, to face unemployment and hunger. Workers' and Soldiers' Councils did what they could to help feed and house them. Where they returned in orderly units attempts were even made to give them a decent welcome. The mythology propounded by the politicians that the German army had not been defeated but 'stabbed in the back' had many different origins. No one knew as yet how much of a standing army Germany was going to be permitted to retain. But the Provisional Government was able to call upon regular army (*Reichswehr*) units which still stood at over 1 million men in January 1919. In addition volunteer units – *Freikorps* – were formed, largely composed of ex-officers, many of whom remained unregenerate monarchists. By Christmas 1918 units of the Reichswehr and some 4,000 Freikorps were stationed on the outskirts of Berlin, and a volunteer force of revolutionary sailors – the People's Marine Division – had appointed themselves to defend the Congress of Workers' and Soldiers' Councils and occupied government buildings in the centre of the city. At a time when massive street demonstrations were taking place almost daily in Berlin, the Government, afraid that the sailors might be tempted to overturn it, sent in a force of regular troops to turn them out. One result of this episode was the resignation of the two Independent Socialist members from the Provisional Government.

The first national Congress of Workers' and Soldiers' Councils met in Berlin on 16 December. It had been agreed that it would decide the date for elections to the National Assembly while the Provisional Government was to be responsible for preparing for the elections. Nearly two-thirds of the Congress were Majority Social Democrats and the Congress voted to leave to the Assembly the question of what form the future government of Germany should take. A proposal to invest supreme legislative and executive power in a system of Councils was easily defeated. At the same time the Congress called for the socialisation of industries and for measures to democratise the army: the so-called 'Hamburg Points'.[6] Those members of the Congress who had been outvoted on the question of the Assembly – Independent Social Democrats, Spartacists and Revolutionary Shop Stewards – were among those who met again at the end of December to found the German Communist Party. A prominent actor in that development was Karl Radek, the head of the Central European Department of the Russian Foreign Office, who had been sent to represent the Soviet government at the national Congress of Workers' and Soldiers' Councils. He had been refused entry at the frontier but had succeeded in crossing it later in disguise.

Radek also formed the link for Morgan Philips Price between Moscow and Berlin. As the *Manchester Guardian*'s special correspondent in Russia from December 1914 to December 1918 Price thought the Allied intervention in Russia, which had begun in August 1918, was disgraceful. From being a sceptical observer of the Bolsheviks in November 1917 he had become convinced that theirs were the only policies which stood a chance of holding Russia together. After the intervention began he became openly partisan. When the war in the West ended, Radek was his closest contact in the Soviet Foreign Ministry and, after discussions with Radek and Tchicherin (the Foreign Minister), Price decided to apply for permission to come to Berlin. His aim was not only to report on the new situation there, but also to try to project a truer picture of what was going on in Russia than the stories of anti-Bolshevik refugees in neutral countries, which were the source of much of what was being printed in the British press.

As a matter of fact the editor of the *Manchester Guardian* had written to Price, with a good deal of encouragement from the British Foreign Office, to say that the paper could no longer afford to be associated with someone so obviously pro-Bolshevik and that he would have to 'discontinue the correspondence'. Price never received the letter and after he arrived in Berlin he sent five more cables to the *Manchester Guardian*. From entries in his diary it is clear that Price was expecting to meet Radek in Berlin, but because Radek had arrived illegally it took a little time before they found each other. He interviewed Radek on the situation in Russia when he left the country, and this formed the basis of one of his cables. It was stopped by the British censor, as were another three – all of them about the situation in Germany – which he sent before he gave up trying to get through. But two of them were passed for publication. What follows consists of extracts from those which dealt exclusively with Germany. It will be noted that at this stage Price was still using the political terminology (such as, Soviet, Commissar) that he had learned in Russia.

Manchester Guardian 13 December

A fortnight ago I obtained permission from the Revolutionary [Provisional] Government of Berlin to enter Germany for the purpose of studying the conditions prevailing in that country ... On Sunday 1 December I commenced the journey westward across Russia, past Smolensk, where I saw trainloads of Russian prisoners pouring in from Germany ... I reached the first frontier post forty miles east of Minsk, where the Russian Revolutionary Frontier Commission passed me over to the German Soldiers' Soviet [Council]. I found the German soldiers mostly backward Bavarian peasants, who allowed the officers still much power and even elected them to the Soviets ... The nearer I approached the German frontier the more revolutionary I found the German Soldiers' Soviets. At Eyktunen I was passed through the German customs, which was run by common soldiers only. During the journey through East Prussia soldiers boarded the train, turned the officers out of the compartments and made them stand in the corridors. The trains were packed with troops returning home, and the atmosphere became more revolutionary as I approached Berlin, which I reached after six days' journey.

Manchester Guardian Berlin, 16 December

I had an interview this morning with one of the ministers of the revolutionary German government. I was received in the house of the former Imperial Chancellor in the great hall in which the Berlin Congress of 1878 was held. At the table before which the socialist minister of new Germany sat, Bismarck once used to write. Herr Haase began by calling my attention to the question of the fate of the ex-Kaiser about which, he said, the German government had not yet come to any decision. The German government would, he said, shortly publish a new White Book containing all the documents in the possession of the Government concerning the outbreak of the war, from the ultimatum to Serbia to the invasion of Belgium. It would then be possible for the world to judge better as to the responsibility for the war. Everything in the possession of the German government would be published ... As the armistice ends in thirty days, and as it is impossible to summon the National Assembly in that time, it is assumed that the armistice will be renewed. There could be no question of allowing the old Reichstag to claim to represent the German people, for neither Social Democrats, Poles[7] nor Alsatians would attend its sittings if it tried to assume power. 'It is an international principle', said Haase, 'that a government should be recognised if it is *de facto* in power, and we can claim this. The local disorders that have broken out in some districts are due to old reactionary officials who have not yet been got under control.'

On my question as to the relations of the German revolutionary government to the Soviet government of Russia, Haase replied that a state of war did not exist between them ... As regards the internal development of the revolution he said the German working classes were receiving their political education. The great masses of returning soldiers were foreign to politics and might not at once rise to the occasion and through apathy might assist the bourgeois parties. But the organised workers of the towns would be elements that would in the long run ensure the establishment of a socialist republic in Germany. On being asked if there was any possibility that the National Assembly would be dissolved by force, Herr Haase replied that he could say positively that this was out of the question. The Spartacus group could only obtain control of Germany if industrial and social conditions in Germany got so bad that the working masses saw their only hope in a more radical government than at present. 'In what way can the Allies help the new Germany?' I asked. 'They can help', replied Haase, 'by concluding an immediate preliminary peace and by relieving the food situation in Germany by raising the blockade. In this way orderly demobilisation will be guaranteed and a beginning made of peaceful reconstruction. The Allies need have no fear that Prussian militarism will ever again raise its head. We look to the Allies for the realisation in practice of those ideals for which they have been fighting.'

Stopped by the British Censor
Berlin, 19 December

The first All-German Congress [Congress of Workers' and Soldiers' Councils] which opened here on Monday, in respect of the balance of parties, resembles the first All-Russian Soviet Congress in June 1917. The dominant element is the Right group of [Majority] Socialists and Right-wing Independent Socialists. The Spartacists, an extreme Left group, form a small minority while Left-wing Independents occupy an intermediate position. The delegates seem to have been hastily elected from the small middle-class *intelligent-sia* and non-commissioned officers. The general atmosphere of the Congress is characterised by the absence of the revolutionary enthusiasm so noticeable at recent Russian Congresses. One feels that German revolutionary democracy has yet to receive its political baptism of fire. There seems to be a marked disinclination among the Right wing of the Congress to tackle the social and economic problems of revolutionary Germany and a general desire to throw responsibility for the future on the National Assembly. Meanwhile the cry from this quarter is 'peace at any price'. On the other hand the seed of Bolshevism is to be seen in left Independents and Spartacist delegates. The latter show, by their demand 'All power to the Soviets', that the same struggle which convulsed Russia last January on the question whether there was to be a national democratic parliament or a dictatorship of the proletariat, bids fair to be fought out shortly in Germany. Left Independents to whom I talked, while not standing openly on the Spartacist position, seem ready for the indefinite postponement of the National Assembly to a date when it will no longer be needed. The first day of the Congress was taken up with the report of the central Soviet Executive [*Volzugsrat*]. In the debate following a hot contest developed between the Scheidemannites, who mainly control the State Executive [*Rat der Volksbeauftragten* or Council of People's Representatives, i.e. the Provisional Government] and the popular commissioners and Independent Socialists who up to now mainly control the Soviet [Congress of Workers' and Soldiers' Councils] ... The former are under suspicion of sheltering in the Executive old officials of the Kaiser, who sabotage the revolution, are trying to use the army as an agent of counter-revolution, and are carrying on a provocative policy against the Allies in the occupied provinces in order to induce the latter to occupy more German territory. Ledebour openly stated in his speech that these gentry want the Allies to come in to put down the Soviets. Meanwhile the Spartacist group would welcome Allied occupation for different reasons. The influence of the Spartacist group on the soldiery was seen on the second day, when representatives of the Berlin garrison, along with workers, entered the Congress hall and presented revolutionary demands including the dismissal and disarming of officers and handing authority over the army to soldiers' Soviets. Yet I saw these same troops last week march into

Berlin with national banners and Hindenburg flags which had been given them by their officers. The Spartacist infection seems to act as rapidly on Prussian grenadiers as the Bolshevik infection did last year on Kerensky curassiers. Nor does Berlin appear to be the only place where this process is going on. A Bavarian delegate told me today that returning groups in the south are also coming under the influence of the urban workers, and that the desire in Bavaria and the Rhineland provinces to separate from revolutionary North Germany is only confined to reactionary clerical workers and the gentlemen of the heavy industries whose patriotism calls for the support of Allied bayonets.

Stopped by the British Censor
Berlin, 20 December

The close of the All-German Soviet Congress on Friday was marked by the signal victory of the Ebert-Haase government over the Independent Socialists and the Spartacist group ... Workers' and Soldiers' demonstrations in the middle of the week, while they denoted growing unrest among the proletarian masses, were no more than a protest against the attempt of the bourgeois parties to stem the tide of social revolution. The bulk of the Congress had been elected from the middle classes; workshop foremen and non-commissioned officers stood their ground and proved that the revolution in Germany has not gone beyond the stage in which the feudal monarchy is destroyed and bourgeois republicanism is left in place. It is clear that the masses, under the influence of the Right socialist and liberal bourgeois press, firmly believe that the National Assembly, which Congress decided shall be elected next month, is capable of solving the economic problems of modern Germany on a socialist basis. A member of the Independent Socialist Party and a prominent figure in the late Soviet Executive [*Volzugsrat*] admitted to me yesterday that his party would probably be badly beaten at the election for the National Assembly, which will return a moderate socialist majority in coalition with the bourgeois parties. The revolutionary movement, he said, would probably be set back temporarily, 'but as soon as the masses see that the National Assembly cannot solve the economic problems arising out of the war, and cannot socialise industries because a coalition government will be made up of people interested in preventing such changes, they will return to us and the Soviets will regain the power of which the Congress has just deprived them'. It is clear that the Right socialists who now dominate the Government hope to bring the industries of the country back on to a peace basis without serious social change, and are ready to frighten the German masses with the bogey of Allied invasion if the German Revolution touches the sacred rights of property. On the other hand the Independent Socialists and Spartacist groups are likely to gain enormously by the policy of the Allies of trying to bleed Germany white by great war indemnities. Cutting off central Germany from Alsace and Silesian coal and iron will shortly cause a great industrial crisis here and increase unemployment and hunger. These parties are therefore quietly biding their time. The only difference between the Left Independents and the Spartacist group is that the latter believe in the tactics of creating revolutionary psychology by mass demonstration while the former are ready to wait until economic conditions prepare the ground for the next stage of social revolution.

Stopped by the British Censor
Berlin, 27 December

On Christmas Eve the Marine detachment of the Berlin garrison [the People's Marine Division] resisted an attempt by the Ebert-Scheidemann government to disband them, and conflict occurred between them and some troops which the government hurried into Berlin. Then followed scenes exactly similar to what I used to see in Russia during the Kornilov rebellion before the October [November] Revolution.[8] Armed revolutionary workmen and sailors explained the political situation in street meetings to soldiers who had been sent by officials of the old regime to do gendarme work. As soon as the soldiers became aware of the situation they declared their solidarity with the more revolutionary elements. A well-dressed portion of the population attempted to arrest the process of the closing of the revolutionary ranks by throwing out patriotic cries, accompanied by threats that if the working classes and soldiers take power into their hands, foreign armies will come in and restore order. An inclination on the part of anti-socialist and middle-class elements to appeal to the Allied goverments is perceptibly increasing ... But the process of psychological change marking the transference from national to class consciousness is fast setting in. Among Berlin citizens the conviction that Bolshevism is a greater danger than Allied imperialism is in the ascendancy. It is not impossible that these elements of the population are hoping that in the economic vassalage under the Allies to which Germany is to be condemned, they will maintain their class privileges as agents of the foreign tribute collector. This process of closing the ranks, revolutionary and counter-revolutionary, which began in Russia during the summer of 1917 seems to be beginning in Germany now. The withdrawal of the Independent Socialists from the Government will probably be the signal for the creation of a coalition government of Scheidemann socialists and bourgeois parties. Meanwhile the political mobilisation of the masses proceeds below.

Price met both Liebknecht and Rosa Luxemburg very shortly after he arrived in Berlin; although he met them more than once, he wrote nothing about either of them at the time. Only later, in his book *My Three Revolutions* did he describe how taken aback he had been at their first meeting by the reservations Luxemburg seemed to be expressing about the nature of the class base of the government of Soviet Russia. '"Dictatorship of a class – yes," she said, "but not the dictatorship of a party over a class."'[9] He attended the meeting on 31 December at which the Communist Party of Germany was founded but took no notes. A few years later he wrote, of this meeting, that 'the elements suffering from "infantile sickness", as Lenin later called it, were strongly represented there'.[10]

In the same book Price described the events of 1918 to 1922 in Germany, from a Marxist point of view, in considerable detail. Obviously, from that point of view, the most important event of 1918 had to be the so-called November Revolution, the failure of which, by the time he came to describe it, was only too evident. But even given his openly professed bias, few subsequent historians have disagreed with his verdict, however many additional reasons for that failure have been identified: '... The real meaning of the German November Revolution was shown by the fact that, except for a few weeks, the middle classes did not let the direction of State policy out of their hands.'[11]

1919

The Berlin uprising – the Reichswehr and the Freikorps – elections to the National Assembly – the Weimar Constitution – strikes in the Ruhr – Assembly meets at Weimar – more strikes in the Ruhr and street fighting in Berlin – the Versailles Treaty – condition of Germany in May and June – recruiting for the Russian White Armies – 'German Revolution Disappearing' – USPD conference – the Comintern – Bavaria – the Reichswehr, the police and the paramilitary forces

By the beginning of 1919 Price had probably guessed that he no longer had a job. He knew that almost nothing of what he was sending to the *Manchester Guardian* was getting into print. He had a sense of mission to tell the truth, as he saw it, about what was going on in Soviet Russia. He had access to enough of his own money in England to go on living cheaply in Berlin while he did so. He spent most of his time, in the first days of the year, writing articles for Scandinavian socialist papers and pamphlets about Russia and the Council system of government, some of which were later translated into German and other languages. For the second time in less than two years he was present at what appeared to be a turning point in European history. But for the time being he had no outlet in the British press for anything he might otherwise have written about it. Between January and May 1919 therefore, apart from a handful of letters (there was as yet no postal service between Germany and Britain), the only surviving, contemporary account he wrote of the events which were unfolding before him is to be found in his diary. But he continued to function as a freelance journalist, attending press conferences given by government ministers and other public figures, interviewing politicians and talking to people in the streets.

Elections were due to take place on 19 January for the National Assembly which was to create a new constitution. At the founding meeting of the Communist Party (KPD) the question of whether its supporters should take part in the elections had been raised. Luxemburg and Liebknecht were in favour of doing so but they were outvoted. Meanwhile, following the expulsion of the People's Marine Division and the resignation from the Provisional Government of its Independent Socialist members, the Cabinet asked for the resignation of the Independent Socialist Police President of Berlin, Eichhorn. He refused to go on the grounds that he had been appointed by the Executive of the Workers' and Soldiers' Council and was therefore not answerable to the Provisional Government. Talking to the press on 4 January the Revolutionary Shop Stewards' leader, Ernst Daümig, who like Luxemburg and Liebknecht had been in favour of participating in the elections, said that he did not anticipate any kind of disorder in Berlin before they took place. Germany was too exhausted and in any case politics by demonstration was not in the tradition of German socialism.[1] Moreover, he said, demonstrations increased the risk that military units working for their own reactionary ends might be drawn into the city. Nonetheless, a Revolutionary Committee was set up and the call was issued for a mass demonstration to protest against Eichhorn's dismissal. On 5 January, 150,000 people came on to the streets and stood before the police headquarters' building. But in the absence of any attempt at leadership, having stood about aimlessly for some hours they dispersed. The same thing happened again the following day. Now Liebknecht, together with two members of the Revolutionary Committee but against the judgement of six others, including Daümig, decided to call a general strike, to resist Eichhorn's dismissal by force if necessary and to overthrow the Government. An armed group occupied the offices of the Majority Socialist newspaper, *Vorwärts*, on 6 January and issued a special revolutionary edition. Three other newspaper offices were also occupied, two of them being Berlin papers and the third the Right-wing Prussian *Kreuzeitung*. This in itself constituted a challenge to government which could hardly be ignored. Luxemburg had been against the enterprise from the start but, once it began, she felt that it had to be followed through decisively. In the Communist newspaper *Rote Fahne* (*Red Flag*) she called for elections to new Councils as a base from which to overthrow the Provisional Government.

Some years later her successor in the leadership of the Communist Party, Paul Levi, wrote that she had privately made up her mind to break with Liebknecht over the occupation of *Vorwärts*, once the issue was resolved one way or another.[2] It is usually considered to have been his idea and it was certainly his doing. But British Intelligence sources later learned that it was possible that he may have been provoked into it by a secret agent attached to Ludendorff, in the hope of increasing the disorder in Berlin so much as to increase recruitment into the paramilitary organisations assembling around the city.[3]

The diary that Price kept during the first few months of 1919 was only a pocket diary so there was not room for many words for each day. He wrote badly, hastily, in pencil and some words are indecipherable. Nonetheless, the diary gives as graphic an account of the events that followed as many written at much greater length.

7 January

Great demonstrations both sides again. Workers occupy some railway stations. Gov. bring in troops. Fraternisation. Some firing and casualties. Groups in streets discuss questions such as wages, hours, capitalist system. Masses appear to be realising economic issues of Revolution. Went to *Vorwärts* office.

8 January

Went to *Vorwärts* office. Chaos! Impression that no organisation exists. Wrote article. Demonstration, firing and fraternising continue. Most of the troops declare themselves neutral. Independents mediating.

9 January

General feeling of depression everywhere. Shooting begins at midday around Anhalter station and newspaper quarter. Gov. trying hold railway stations till fresh troops arrive. Hopes of Left and Red Guards depend on fraternisation. Gov. is organising White Guards from officers and sons of bourgeoisie. Kurfürstendam is full of military calling for volunteers in streets. Counter-revolutionary front is slowly uniting.

10 January

Wrote all morning. Same atmosphere as yesterday. Towards evening rumours that gov. troops will attack *Vorwärts* building in mass. Went to *Vorwärts* and found all in readiness for attack. Parties of middle, Independent Socialists still attempting mediation but Gov. apparently intends to decide conflict by blood and iron.

In the conditions Price describes there must have been more rumours than facts in circulation, and his next entry appears to anticipate the murder of Luxemburg by several days.

11 January

Heavy fighting this morning. Gov. troops stormed *Vorwärts*. Spartacists arrested. Rosa Luxemburg. All lost! Troops apparently specially selected White Guards, mainly officers and not yet demobilised front troops who don't understand position here. Saw large bodies of them pass through city this afternoon. Looks as if reign of White Terror will begin.

12 January

Walked out to Grünewald [outskirts of Berlin]. Artillery and machine-guns going all the time. Police President taken. Reds hold out in isolated centres in north of city. How bad Red organisation is. No plan to capture centre as [word indecipherable] did. Capitalist press jubilant.

14 January

Talked with Daümig who says workers v. oppressed. Whole tactics of Spartacus he considers disastrous. Mass of soldiery not ready for next step of revolution.

15 January

Reign of White Terror. Arrests everywhere. Meanwhile railway strike for higher wages. That is when the victors will find their victory is Pyrrhic.

16 January

Stunned by appalling news of foul murder of Liebknecht and
Luxemburg. Too staggered to conceive the fact, except to feel
instinctively that this fiendish crime will do more than anything
else to unite all ranks of Revolution against this accursed hydra of
Prussian militarism which Allies cannot kill because they are
themselves brother hydras. Saw Müller Senior [Richard], who saw
Liebknecht's body and can affirm that shots were fired from front
at short distance.

17 January

A deathly quiet prevails in the city. The quiet of the grave. Military
patrols streets, artillery posted everywhere. Armed White Guards
being organised by a certain Reinhardt go about arresting and
terrorising at pleasure. Several of my friends disappeared. A fine
condition for eve of election for National Assembly. Attended
sitting of Berlin Soldiers' Soviet [Council]. Most of delegates from
garrison seem frightened at having called in spirits they cannot lay.

The day before she was killed, and knowing that the uprising
was doomed, Luxemburg had argued in *Rote Fahne* that defeat
was the necessary precondition for eventual victory in revolution, provided that the reasons for the defeat were understood.
This was a lesson that the German Communist Party never
learned.

On the day of the elections Price attended a press conference
held for foreign journalists by Noske, the Minister of the
Interior in the Provisional Government, a Majority Social
Democrat who had already acquired an ominous reputation as a
strong man when he was sent to deal with the consequences of
the mutiny at Kiel two months earlier. Noske evaded all
questions put to him concerning the deaths of Liebknecht and
Luxemburg, only insisting that justice would be done. If
military rule was necessary to protect the rule of law, then there
was no alternative to military rule. 'A country like Germany
cannot exist with machine-guns continually being set up.' The
soldiers and officers he had brought in to restore order were
loyal to him, both personally and as a socialist. He admitted

that not many of the officers were likely to be Social Democrats. 'If I could have put together an army consisting entirely of party members I should have tried to do it.' But he did not doubt that the regular army officers would do their duty. Referring to the elections he said, 'If this thing hadn't happened in Berlin our electoral chances would have been infinitely greater than they are today ... As a result of these terrorist activities ... people have begun to think and a lot of them have moved to the Right.' He blamed the Spartacists for the fact that the Majority Social Democrats were unlikely to get a clear majority in the Assembly, but 'if the majority of the German people do not vote socialist then it is my view that the will of the people must be respected'. He did not doubt that the Majority Social Democrats would be well represented in the Assembly. 'If there are Left-inclined people in the National Assembly with whom one can make a decent agreement in the general direction of socialism, we shall go with them.' But that did not include Independent Socialists. 'I could not sit at the same table with them.'

In his diary Price wrote of the impression that Noske made upon him on that occasion: 'Spirit of Bismarck breathes in every word he utters.' Yet in reply to a question as to whether he thought the fact that Germany was now a socialist republic would make any difference to the way she was treated at the Peace Conference, Noske, perhaps surprisingly, had said:

> I have no illusions that Lloyd George and Clémenceau will offer a decent peace just because we are a socialist republic. On the contrary, these English and French bourgeois are not interested in making life pleasant for the German republic so that the English and French workers can follow the example of Germany. Only unrealistic politicians ... could make such an assumption. Here we are with a completely defeated army, having to put up with the fact that the Poles are invading our country. I don't see that the conditions of peace are any better for that and I don't notice English and French workers exerting themselves to get better conditions [of peace] for us.

Noske's reference to Poland related to the fact that Polish irregular forces had, in anticipation of the peace settlement, occupied large tracts of West Prussia, Posen and Upper Silesia to which Poland was laying claim. Even before the end of 1918 appeals for volunteers for frontier protection had come not only from the commanders of several German army groups, but also from the Central Council of the Congress of Workers' and Soldiers' Councils.[4] The Central Council and the Cabinet agreed basic regulations for the command and discipline of such troops, and a number of formations were constituted. The officers tended to be monarchists and the other ranks to consist not of veterans but of adolescents with little direct experience of war and students. The most notorious of these formations was the *Freikorps*, but the Reinhardt Brigade and the Garde Kavallerei Schutzen division, although all notionally raised for frontier protection, were all to be similarly and deliberately used – under the pretext of keeping order – against the Left.

The result of the elections (which were held on 19 January), as Noske had predicted, did not give the Majority Socialists an overall majority, although they got the largest number – 38 per cent – of the votes. A coalition was inevitable. Its components were the Centre Party (*Zentrum*) with 19 per cent, and the German Democratic Party (DDP) with 18.5 per cent. The conservatives – German National People's Party (DNVP) – got 10 per cent and the German People's Party (DVP) 4 per cent. The DVP was composed of former National Liberals, who were constitutional monarchists by tradition, but who were prepared to support a republic. The DNVP was openly monarchist, nationalist, anti-Semitic, and tied to both heavy industry and the landowning classes. The term Pan-German – meaning in this connection irredentist – was also often applied to them. The National Assembly formally assumed authority on 4 February, Ebert was elected President on 11 February and Scheidemann Chancellor. A Cabinet was in place two days later.

The Weimar Constitution was the product of a compromise between two drafts, both influenced by the need to avoid the defects of the Wilhelmine Constitution. One draft was the work of an academic lawyer with impeccably democratic credentials: Professor Hugo Heuss. The other was put together by a committee of the Cabinet of the Provisional Government containing members of the Majority Socialist, Centre and Democratic Parties. Both drafts had aimed at reducing the powers of the federal states while yet ensuring that the central government of the Reich could not become too mighty. A unified code of labour laws and social legislation was laid down, as well as a centralised railway, postal and tax-collecting system. The two houses of Parliament – the Reichstag or federal parliament representing the central government interest, and the Reichsrat, representing the interests of the federal states – were both to be elected by adult suffrage and proportional representation. Elaborate arrangements for maintaining a democratic balance between them were vested in the president, who was to be elected for seven years by the votes of everyone over the age of 35. Under Article 165 of the constitution a State Economic Council (*Reichswirtschaftsrat*) was set up to represent the state, employers, workers, consumers and co-operatives, with the right to be consulted by the Reichstag in all economic matters and to propose legislation to the Reichstag. After a three-day debate the Assembly referred the final form of the constitution to a committee which deliberated until July, at the end of which month it was adopted.

The January uprising in Berlin had by no means been an isolated event. In the Ruhr miners struck over Christmas 1918 for better pay, shorter shifts and more food. Mineowners made apparent concessions but then sent for troops to break the strikes. Workers' and Soldiers' Councils had been set up all over the Ruhr and, unlike the rest of Germany, tended to be dominated by the Independent Socialists, especially in the south. Düsseldorf became a centre of Left political activity. A massive demonstration there in support of the Berlin uprising ended in bloodshed. In Essen the Council occupied the headquarters of the Mineowners' Asssociation, and announced the socialisation of the coal industry. There was, of course, no legal foundation for this gesture and the Government in Berlin denounced it. On 13 January a miners' conference elected a Commission of Nine to represent them but Berlin refused to recognise it. The miners then elected more Councils and literally took over the mines. When the Government threatened to send in troops the miners formed their own Red Army. In February government troops under General von Watter and *Freikorps* units began to occupy the smaller mining towns. A delegate conference of miners, meeting at Mülheim, proclaimed a general strike which secured the support of more than half of the Ruhr miners and of some workers in other industries as well. Fighting continued. An agreement between the Red Army and the government troops to withdraw to specified points was ignored by the troops. A new Commission of Nine met at Essen and called for a new general strike. By 10 April at least 75 per cent of the miners were on strike and a state of siege was declared in most Ruhr cities. The Commission of Nine were arrested or forced into hiding and in the last week of April the strike collapsed. The *Freikorps* continued to harass the miners and a legacy of bitterness and unrest was ensured in the Ruhr for years to come.

In Bavaria, the Workers' and Soldiers' Council which had been set up in Munich on 7 November 1918, even before the proclamation of the republic in Berlin, had like most other Councils in Bavaria and elsewhere at that time been primarily concerned with maintaining order. Its leader, Kurt Eisner, an Independent Socialist, wanted to see a kind of dyarchy develop between Councils and the state Parliament or *Landtag*, but this was not radical enough for some of his colleagues. In any case he was assassinated in an apparently motiveless attack on 20 February. In the ensuing confusion no formula emerged for the reconciliation of the two systems of government and a Soviet Republic was proclaimed on 6 April, while the *Landtag* moved to Nuremburg and sent to Berlin for help. The Munich Soviet was overthrown with great loss of life. Attempts to institute government by Council were also made between January and March at Halle, Brunswick, Leipzig and Bremen, Gotha, Mannheim, Stuttgart and in Upper Silesia. In Berlin a five-day strike begun on 3 March ended in bitter street fighting between the People's Marine Division and a Republican Soldiers' Guard on the one hand, and Noske's forces on the other. Martial law was declared again and the strike was put down with great brutality.

On 3 February Price got a permit to attend the first meeting of the National Assembly and two days later he left in a special train for Weimar, together with all the other correspondents and some of the members of the National Assembly. He found the atmosphere in the town 'more fitting', as he put it in his diary, 'for a literary and scientific congress than a political assembly at the greatest crisis in its history'. He attended the opening of the

Assembly and interviewed a number of the party leaders. Erzberger, leader of the Centre Party, struck him as 'very plausible, a good talker and able ... anxious to frighten us with talk of danger of Bolshevism triumphing'. He sat with Stresemann (Democratic Party) and Noske, both of whom told him that socialisation would have to be put off indefinitely, largely because there was nothing to socialise. Price saw no difference between their respective outlooks. Scheidemann's first speech as Chancellor gave him 'the very worst impression. The whole spirit of his party and of the democrats supporting him is Prussian militarism dressed up with another sauce.' On 14 February Price moved on to the Ruhr, where as has already been described, a period of great unrest was in progress.

16 February

Went by train to Mülheim and met Spartacus leaders at Conference of Revolutionary Shop Stewards for the Ruhr. Found them decided to declare general strike to enforce withdrawal of Gov. troops advancing towards Essen. Decision appeared to me hasty, as no preparations for strike committee had been made. Still, men seem very determined.

18 February

Went to meeting of Workers' and Soldiers' Council. Majority Socialist and Mineworkers' Union members in majority, who read a resolution of protest against Mülheim Communist conference of 'armed bands'. Terrific uproar in which they decide to withdraw, leaving Communists and Independents. Latter continue and decide on general strike. Elect committee. Depressed feeling everywhere and state of immaturity. I am particularly struck with primitive organisation and lack of leadership among workers.

20 February

Went to Bochum and saw leaders of Mineworkers' Union. Found them an admirable shield to protect mineowners. They seem doubtful even about socialisation. Visited miners' meeting at pithead and found union leaders have undoubtedly great power over men, who follow them thinking *they* will bring them socialisation.

21 February

Meeting of Workers' and Soldiers' Council. Report of deputation sent to Münster to negotiate with government. General feeling that strike had collapsed through lack of organisation. Surprised to find government troops ready to withdraw under certain rather severe conditions. Only suppose bourgeoisie fear wreckage of mines by sabotage. Terrible news about Eisner's murder.

24 February

Long talk with Chief of Police Düsseldorf. Hot stuff – Communist. Düsseldorf perfectly quiet, one would never think Spartacists are ruling the town. Shops open, theatres and cafés full. Communism not such a terrible threat to Düsseldorf bourgeoisdom.

25 February

Arrived in Berlin after quite decent journey. Wrote article for Independent Socialist bureau on situation in Ruhr district.

In his book *Germany in Transition* (1923) Price briefly described the general strike which broke out in Berlin on 5 March.

The questions at issue were economic and the Majority Socialist leaders of the trade unions actually headed the strike with the Independents and Spartacists. On the following day Berlin was quivering with the thunder of artillery, shells crashed into the houses of the working-class quarters and machine-guns rattled. What had happened? The strike committee, on which all three socialist parties sat, issued a manifesto saying they had nothing to do with the disorders.

In fact, fighting between Noske's troops and the People's Marine Division had started despite the fact that the socialist parties were already negotiating with the Government on the question of the role of the Councils and the socialisation of industry.

7 March

Heavy fighting in Alexanderplatz region. The Workers' and Soldiers' Council resolves to stop the strike. Gov. replies partially accepting their demands. Council system to be inserted into constitution and socialisation to be begun at one.

8 March

Great damage in fighting in North Berlin still going on. Strike ending. The workers have nothing to do with the quarrel between the troops but the Gov. will of course try to fasten responsibility on the Communists.

Price later described the events of that day in his book *Germany in Transition*:

Noske called the Berlin press representatives on 8 March and told them that the government troops were fighting Spartacus. He gave them a long list of the names of sixty policemen said to have been murdered in most bestial manner in the Lichtenberg suburbs by 'Red Guards'. The effect was instantaneous ... within twenty-four hours the few Spartacist leaders who had survived the January week, and among whom was the able friend of Rosa Luxemburg, Leo Jogisches, were arrested and brutally murdered by agents of the secret police. The necessary atmosphere in which this murder could be shrouded had been created. Under the cover of this hue and cry against Spartacus the non-Spartacist Republican Guards were disarmed and carried off, and in large numbers mown down before machine-guns against the walls of the Berlin prisons.

In his first letter to his brother, on 16 March, Price again described the events of the previous week and concluded:

This venomous serpent, Prussian militarism, clothed now in the robe of 'Social Democracy' is rampant again in Germany and the Allies are going to make peace with it and give it food, that it may all the easier oppress the German workers. But one thing is most marked in the last week. Thousands of workers and middle-class people too, who formerly supported the Majority Socialists, have gone over to the Independents and the Communists. There is a feeling of solidarity among the workers such as I have not seen since the commencement of the revolution.

While Germany, still blockaded and still suffering from severe food shortage and malnutrition, barely kept from disintegrating, the victorious Allies sat in Paris and considered her fate. So long as the negotiations for an armistice based on the Fourteen Points had been confined to President Wilson and the German government, there was a serviceable degree of understanding between them as to the meaning of the words they were using. Wilson had made it quite clear that by the word 'restoration' (of civilian damage) he did not mean either punitive damages or the exaction of an indemnity for the whole cost of the war. But once the French became involved, between the armistice and the Peace Conference, it became clear that this was precisely what they intended to have and that they intended to ignore the Fourteen Points. In the run-up to the British General Election of December 1918, moreover, the Conservative, Liberal and Unionist parties had vied with each other as to who would deliver the more savage terms to the defeated Germans.

When the Peace Conference opened in Paris on 18 January 1919 it consisted initially of two representatives each from the USA, France, Italy, Japan and the British Empire: the Council of Ten. From March onwards the work of drafting the treaty was delegated to a Council of Four, excluding Japan. That Council was supplied with numerous subordinate specialist advisory Councils. In the course of these proceedings Lloyd George began to have doubts as to the wisdom of the extent of the retribution being planned, if only because it might increase the risk of a Bolshevik *coup* in Berlin. 'We cannot both cripple her and expect her to pay', he said.[5] But his words carried no weight with the French. The draft treaty was presented to a German delegation invited only to receive it without comment and to submit observations in writing. It had been decided not to enter any figures as yet for the amount that it was intended to demand from Germany by way of reparations (redefined by France and Britain to include the whole cost of war pensions). In his *Economic Consequences of the Peace* Keynes suggested that this was probably because any figures based on a realistic assessment of Germany's ability to pay would have fallen far short of what the French and British publics were expecting.

The draft treaty dealt primarily with frontiers, material and penalties. Germany was to return Alsace and Lorraine to France and yield the Silesian coalfields to Poland. The Saar basin was to be ceded to France for 15 years after which its status was to be determined by a plebiscite. The Rhine was to be demilitarised and Allied bridgeheads established on the right bank, with an Inter-Allied Commission to supervise the occupied areas. The whole cost of the occupation was to be borne by Germany. All capacity to manufacture arms and all forts were to be destroyed. The sizes of the future German army and navy were to be strictly limited. Germany was to admit sole guilt for the war. The Kaiser as well as war criminals were to be brought to trial. Interim payments and coal deliveries were to be made on account, pending the fixture of final figures for the reparations to be paid. Penalties were laid down for the non-observance of these or any other clauses of the treaty. No account was taken, in estimating German capacity to pay, of the losses she had already sustained in terms of territory, coal, shipping and materials handed over under the terms of the armistice, such as locomotives without which nothing could be moved. And the blockade was to continue.

In the first debate on the treaty in the Assembly (now meeting in Berlin) on 12 May, only the Independent Socialists favoured acceptance of the terms as they stood, largely because they felt that rejection would only lead to worse. A German memorandum of observations was submitted to the Allies on 29 May. They pointed out that the terms violated the pre-armistice understanding as to the meaning of the Fourteen Points and that the territorial provisions of the treaty violated the principle of self-determination. They rejected sole guilt for having begun the war. They protested against Germany's exclusion from the League of Nations and against the lack of reciprocity contained in the disarmament clauses. These observations resulted in one serious and two minor modifications. The Allies agreed that there could be a plebiscite in Upper Silesia. Germany would be admitted to the League of Nations when sufficient evidence of good behaviour had accumulated. And the period of the occupation of the Rhineland might be reduced, also after evidence of good behaviour. The draft thus amended was resubmitted to Germany on 16 June and the Government was given five days (subsequently extended to 13) in which to sign it.

The reduction in the size of the army, the occupation of the Rhineland and the war guilt clause were felt by influential senior army officers to be unacceptably insulting, but the Cabinet was persuaded, largely by the realistic Erzberger, to agree to sign the treaty if only the clauses concerning war guilt and war criminals were removed. Thereupon on 16 June the Allies issued a 24-hour ultimatum threatening invasion; rather than sign, the entire Scheidemann Cabinet resigned at midnight on 20 June. A new Cabinet under the Majority Socialist, Otto Bauer, was formed, in coalition with the Centre Party. Bauer signed, noting only that the German people were 'yielding to overwhelming force' in the face of 'injustice without parallel'. Hindenburg had carefully avoided associating himself with the decision to sign and was thus able in later years to repudiate those who had 'betrayed' the honour of the German army.

At some point in May 1919 Price became the correspondent in Berlin of the British Labour newspaper, the *Daily Herald*, which had existed as a daily before the war, been reduced to once-weekly production during the war, and was now in a position to become a daily once again. His dispatch of 26 May 1919 would appear to be his first for that newspaper.

24 May

The hopes of all those who want to save Germany from lapsing into chaos and anarchy are now centred on a favourable reply to the proposals for modifying the peace conditions which are to be handed to the Allied powers by the German delegation in a week's time.

The facts are that if Germany does not receive within a short time raw materials and food, not only will she be unable to maintain her own internal economy, but she will be unable to pay even that portion of the indemnity which the Allies naively think they are going to get from her.

Amongst the Majority Socialists with whom I have spoken opinion seems to be hardening to a determination not to sign if the Allies decline to accept modifications which will enable Germany to live and carry out reasonable obligations, including reparations for damages in France and Belgium. If, however, as in the peace terms, Germany's inland waterways are to lose a large part of their transport stock, and if the already appalling condition of the working classes in the towns due to the milk and meat famine is to be increased by handing over 150,000 head of cattle, and if no provisions are to be made to provide the raw materials with which to keep Germany alive, then the Majority Socialists and, it seems, all the bourgeois parties favour letting the Allies walk into Germany and see what they can themselves get out of the devil's cauldron which they are creating.

On the other hand, the Majority Socialists in the Berlin Workers' and Soldiers' Council brought in, at the last sitting of the Council, a resolution declaring that the Government should sign after exhausting all means of obtaining amelioration, but adding that peace under these conditions should not signify a permanent renunciation of the principle of self-determination for purely German territories or a permanent exclusion of Germany from the economy of the world ...

'Better sign the peace conditions, we don't want any more of these', I heard a pale, underfed Berlin workman this afternoon say to his mate, as he pointed to a procession of war invalids and cripples passing up the Wilhelmstrasse to demonstrate before Ebert's government offices. I think this is typical of the state of feeling among the workers in the towns of Middle Germany.

27 May

I have just had a conversation with Richard Müller, president of the Berlin Workers' and Soldiers' Council and leader of the Independent Socialists in the first two Congresses of Workers' and Soldiers' Councils of the German Republic.

'Germany's internal war debts', he said, 'amount to 200 milliard marks. She has two million war cripples and two million dependents of war cripples who must be supported. In addition there is an unknown amount of debt raised during the war by local authorities. To cover the interest and the sinking fund 30 milliard marks will be needed from the national income.

'In 1913, when German industry was working normally, the national income was 34 milliard marks. Now, without raw materials, with the railways in a state of collapse, our national income has shrunk to a fraction of the former. The few raw materials still remaining in Germany must be used to set industry on its feet again. The whole railway system needs renewal. The machinery in the factories needs scrapping and replacing. If these last reserves of raw materials are to be taken from Germany the whole economic system must cease to work. If Germany cannot pay her internal capitalists 30 milliard marks, still less can she pay the 60 milliard marks demanded by Allied imperialists. Besides, there is another point. A new spirit has come over the German worker. He will not work for the slavedrivers of capitalism any longer. The German workers did not turn out the Prussian military oligarchy in order to set up a capitalist oligarchy masquerading under the name of democracy. As long as the present Government exists there will be constant strikes and chaos and the Entente will be powerless to stop it.'

30 May

Speculation continues as to whether the Government will or will not sign the peace conditions ... In general it appears that the instinct of class preservation is forcing the German government to the conviction that it is better to bear the ills of imperialist Versailles than to fly to revolutionary Moscow or indulge in dramatic deals with the Communists as in Hungary.[6] The [German] Communists, as a matter of fact, have declared themselves for refusing to sign peace and damning the consequences, which puts them in the same boat as the Pan-Germans. Between these two extremes the mass of moderate opinion seems to be crystallising in favour of negotiations for concessions which would at least save the face of the German government and make the economic clauses capable of being carried out, which at present they are not.

As it at present stands it is almost certain that the Government would not sign ... It is perhaps not generally recognised that the peace conditions would reduce the Government's volunteer army to about one-third of its present size and would throw thousands of officers out of employment. The latter, who for weeks past have been careering over Germany, dissolving the Workers' Councils, arresting Labour leaders and closing down socialist newspapers, evidently hope that the Allies will allow them to remain part of their *cordon sanitaire* against the Eastern 'infection'.

23 June

What is happening now in Weimar is similar to what passed in Petrograd on the fateful date in January 1918 when the Russian Soviets were considering the ultimatum of victorious Prussian militarism. The same spiritual struggle is seen on the faces of everyone. It is a question of deciding whether it is better, by signing, to bear the ills one has, than to fly to others one knows not of, or whether by refusing to sign, to sacrifice immediate well-being for an abstract idea. On the other hand there is this difference between the Russian and the German Revolutions in the present predicament. Whereas the former was a revolt of the indignant Russian proletariat and the peasantry against a whole world of capitalist imperialism in arms against it, the latter was never more than a mild protest of middle-class politicians with hazy Liberal ideology against the regime which they had suffered under, but had meekly accepted, for four years. It is nevertheless good to see that in Germany today the decision to sign or not to sign is being left to the parties of the National Assembly. This indicates an advance on the old secret diplomacy and the intrigues of Court *camarillas*, high finance and military juntas, which seem to flourish in the place from which this ultimatum to Germany issued forth.

24 June

The question remains whether the new Government which is going to sign the peace terms is likely to last, or whether it will be no more than a makeshift formed for the sole purpose of signing the treaty. Everything seems to point to the fact that the Government change is nothing more than a shuffle of cards to make the signature of peace possible, while leaving questions of internal policy unaffected ... No one must lose sight of the fact that this peace will be water for the mill of the Pan-Germans, who will go to the German peasant-proprietors and other politically backward elements and say to them: 'See, we are right. The Entente meant to ruin Germany after all. Put your faith in us, who are preparing for the next national war, for only so can we escape slavery.'

On 28 June the German Foreign Minister, Hermann Müller and Johannes Bell (representing the Majority Socialist and the

Centre parties respectively) signed the treaty in the Hall of Mirrors at Versailles. The Bauer government remained in power for another nine months.

In Germany itself the summer was punctuated by strikes characterised by increasingly unsuccessful attempts to obtain control over industry through Workers' Councils in the face of renewed attempts to reintroduce pre-war management systems. Price wrote a good deal about this in the autumn of 1919, but during the summer he was preoccupied by what was apparently going on, on Germany's 'Eastern front'. He was perhaps the more inclined to dwell upon this subject because on 9 July he had been arrested and put in the Moabit prison by the Berlin police. This turned out to have been at the request of the British Occupation forces, who wanted to prevent him from trying to make contact with Allied soldiers in the occupied zones and distributing pamphlets, which the officers did not want them to read, as they gave alternative accounts of what was going on in Archangel and Murmansk. But they could find nothing with which to charge him under German law and after three days he was released.

Under the terms of the armistice Germany was to evacuate all the territory she had occupied in Eastern as well as in Western Europe. There were German troops in all the Baltic countries, formerly part of the Tsarist Empire, long after the Treaty of Brest–Litovsk had supposedly put an end to the fighting on the Eastern front. Article XIII of the Versailles Treaty, however, provided that they should be allowed to remain where they were for as long as the Allies, obsessed with their fear of Bolshevism, considered it 'desirable having regard to the interior condition of these territories'. Initially, no Allied Commission was appointed to supervise their withdrawal and, although the German Provisional Government recalled some of their regular troops in this theatre, they were easily replaced with volunteers. Field Marshal Hindenburg, appointed Commander of the so-called Eastern Front Protection Force in February 1919, announced that he saw his role as the leader of a crusade 'against our new enemy, Bolshevism'.[7]

Far from being poised to attack the West, however, the Soviet government was at that time fighting for its own survival, in a civil war on four fronts. Counter-revolutionary or White Armies were advancing under Admiral Kolchak in the east, General Denikin in the south and General Yudenich in the north, while the Allies themselves had landed troops at Archangel and the Murman peninsula. In the spring of 1919 Yudenich was about to make the first of his two unsuccessful attempts to capture Petrograd. There were, additionally, in this theatre two soldiers whose activities were less clearly intelligible: General von der Goltz and Colonel Avalov-Bermondt. Von der Goltz had originally been sent to defend East Prussia against the Red Army. Bermondt was a cossack colonel of Finnish origins, who had raised his own counter-revolutionary forces in the Ukraine but had then refused to join Yudenich and was now operating as a kind of warlord with monarchist sympathies. Von der Goltz had extracted, from some of the big Baltic landowners, promises of land for any of his troops who might prefer not to go home at the end of their service. Many of them now feared expropriation, since the Baltic states (Estonia, Latvia and Lithuania) had all declared independence in 1917 from the Tsarist Empire and had set up their own provisional governments. Von der Goltz, in fact, had ideas of more or less colonising these states as a form of compensation for the loss of Germany's overseas colonies, and the prospects were not unattractive to German soldiers with nothing much to go home for. Most of them were, moreover, strongly monarchist in sympathy, and there were still plenty of monarchists in Germany to ensure a constant flow of recruits and the diversion of war material before it had reached the breakers' yards, as required by the treaty.

Throughout the summer of 1919 the head of the British Military Mission in Berlin, Lieutenant-General Neil Malcolm, was reporting that he was receiving 'fairly reliable' evidence that German agents, or Russian agents secretly supported by German monarchists, were recruiting demobilised German soldiers and Russian prisoners of war still being held in Germany for service in Russian counter-revolutionary armies. Malcolm knew where the headquarters of the recruiting organisation was in Berlin, and the German authorities had ignored his requests to put a stop to the recruitment.[8] But he admitted, in a later report (8 August) that 'Insofar as Colonel Bermondt proposes to use his forces against the Bolsheviks he may be of service to us.' Price clearly had his own sources of information on the subject, although his object was to draw attention to rather than conceal the facts.

19 August

The evidence that Germany is becoming a recruiting ground for the armies of the Holy Alliance against Soviet Russia increases every day. On the one hand half a million Russian workmen and peasants who are prisoners of war are held back from returning to their home, and according to reliable information I have received, in West Prussia are being used by the Junkers to work on their estates at 2 marks a day as strike-breakers because the German peasants demand better conditions. On the other hand, the Allied governments have no objection to Russians, and even Germans, entering military detachments that are being formed here as reinforcements for Kolchak, Denikin and Yudenich.

Last night the *Freiheit* published further information about this public scandal. At the Russischer Hof hotel in Berlin there is a recruiting office for the Russian counter-revolutionary armies. The recruits receive 50 marks per head, uniforms and all outfit. At Jena another recruiting office is opening where recruits receive 330 marks and are promised all they can get from the Jewish population when they get to Russia. Last Saturday 110 German recruits were sent in this way to the Baltic Provinces and more are following. In Latvia the 6th German Reserve Corps are reported to have joined Yudenich. In Hamburg, according to the *Freiheit*, recruits have been supplied with outfits from German war stores.

The alliance between Russian monarchists, Prussian Junkers and British brass hats is becoming daily more impudent and shameless.

For the rest of the year 1919, despite his natural preoccupation with events in Russia, Price became the chronicler of the process to which one *Daily Herald* sub-editor gave the headline: 'German Revolution Disappearing'. The two wings of the former Social Democratic Party drew ever further apart. The Majority Social Democrats, partners in a coalition government, became more committed to the theory of parliamentary government, the Independents to government by Council. Noske, as Minister of the Interior, continued to use high-handed methods for silencing those who disagreed with him. As has already been noted, the Executive Council established in December 1918 by the Congress of Workers' and Soldiers' Councils was from the start dominated by Majority Socialists but many Councils at more local levels were more Independent-minded.

27 August

The Central Bureau of the Berlin Workers' Council was yesterday occupied by Noske's White Guards. All the money and papers found there were seized, the premises sealed up, and members of the Executive thrown on to the street. I hear, however, that the great part of the money collected from the workers was saved.

Within the last six months the change which has come over the Berlin proletariat is so great that the Majority Socialists are no longer considered as a political factor in the city and the surrounding districts, and competition for influence among the workers has passed to the Independent Socialists and Communists. The Majority Socialists, however, have their nominees everywhere in state bureaucracy and in the Executive Committee which was appointed by the last All-German Congress of Workers' and Soldiers' Councils. This body has done everything to prevent the spread of the Council idea among German workers and to hinder their industrial organisation. For this reason they have now passed through the National Assembly a law on Workers' Councils which aims at putting working-class representatives on conciliation boards, where they are to sit with employers ... Boards of course are to be purely advisory. The Majority Socialists, who are now openly a party representing the small German bourgeoisie, see their only hope of retaining power over the German masses through such laws and naturally Noske, with his White Guards, has to be called in to try to remove with bayonets any organisation which attempts to put into concrete shape the desire of the masses.

6 September

During the last week I hear the question has been much debated among Berlin workers whether a general strike should be called to force Noske's hands, but it has been finally decided that the movement is not sufficiently developed in the provinces to give much chance of success. Moreover, a certain fear seems to be coming over the masses at the catastrophe which is coming this winter. It is interesting to see how the German bourgeois press exploits the coming coal famine and the cold and famine which is awaiting that section of the population not rich enough to buy from the profiteers. Workmen are being induced to raise production in order to save the country from the fate awaiting it, and the German workman is inclined to be frightened into work, even under the old economic system, in the hope of escaping the sufferings of the coming winter.

In Berlin a metalworkers' strike began in mid-September after a wages agreement based on grading was subsequently nullified when the employers reclassified the grades. The strike was, in its turn, hampered by disagreements over the use of strike funds between the old official trade union and the Council organisation which was running the strike on the shop floor. But hardship in Berlin was not confined to workers on strike.

7 November

I have just received the following figures of the monthly budget of a Berlin tram driver who has a wife and a daughter of 12. His monthly wage is 400 marks, which is equivalent in English money at present rates to £4. The weekly wage of a Berlin tram driver, in English money, is therefore £1 a week. Against this there are the following expenses monthly.

	Marks
Rent	55
Taxes	20
School money	16
Fire and lighting	38
Washing	12
Travelling expenses	17
Clothing	25
Footwear	12
Pocket money, newspaper, odd repairs	25
Food	180
TOTAL	400

The 180 marks (36s.) for food has to last three persons for one month. The other day I went into the restaurant of the Adlon Hotel and found that a luncheon there costs 30 marks without wine. It is impossible to get through the day there without paying 60 marks for food alone. In other words, in a day in a fashionable Berlin restaurant one person spends on food as much as a member of a working-class family spends in a month. I would add that the official meat ration now is half a pound a week. No milk is obtainable except for invalids and small children. The food of the family whose budget I quote above consists on most days of black bread, potatoes and vegetables. Occasionally a pound of butter is bought at speculative prices for 28 marks a pound. That has to last for six weeks or two months.

10 November

As if to notify the world that there never was, as far as he was concerned, a German Revolution, Noske has, on the eve of the anniversary [of the Revolution] arrested the strike leaders of the Berlin metalworkers and declared the institution of Workers' Councils abolished ... It looks therefore as if the last remnants of Germany's so-called Revolution are disappearing and the land openly being ruled by the same military *camarilla* which for four years has been the curse of the world. Things would look black were it not for the fact that the bankruptcy, famine and economic collapse of Germany make it impossible for Noske with his machine-guns to maintain a dictatorship indefinitely.

The metalworkers of Berlin yesterday voted on the question of continuing the strike, and in any case they will remain out till the arrested leaders have been released. There is a general feeling among the men that a mistake was made in calling a general sympathy strike for Berlin before making sure that it would meet with a full response. The partial strike has, as events show, only given Noske the chance he was waiting for. The more experienced leaders among the Independent Socialists and the Communists whom, by the way, Noske has arrested along with the others, favoured the metalworkers going back last Monday on a compromise, thus conserving their funds and energy for another effort later.

During the summer of 1919 the Independent Socialists had begun to identify a role for themselves in opposition. In the course of the year membership had more than doubled (from 300,000 to 750,000) and the party now owned 55 newspapers. At the end of November they held their second party conference. At their first one, in March 1919, the Independents had attempted to square the circle, adopting mutually exclusive ideas which would combine the Council with the Parliamentary system of government, yet with the formal objective of securing the dictatorship of the proletariat. At their second conference, they accepted the logical consequences of adhering to the theory of government by Council.

Leipzig, 3 December

While the Majority Socialists are rapidly disappearing as a political factor in Germany, the parties of the two extremes are increasing, on one side the monarchist Pan-Germans and on the other the revolutionary Marxian groups of the Left. The change in psychology of the working classes has also affected the tactics of the Independent Socialist Party ... On the first day of this conference I was struck with the change that has come over the party since March ... The opening speech on the subject of tactics by Crispien brought out the fact that even the members of the Central Executive had come over to the view that there is no such thing as a political democracy so long as there is no industrial democracy ... This speech was followed by a lively debate in which it became clear that the bulk of the delegates reject parliamentary action as a method for realising the socialisation of industry. At the same time they do not intend to withdraw their members from the National Assembly, the tribune of which they intend to use as a platform for making revolutionary appeals to the masses and for discrediting bourgeois parliamentarism. The economist Hilferding made an interesting exposition of his views on socialisation, from which it appeared that he considers the present state of chaos in the capitalist system favourable for laying the foundation of a socialist society, but he seems to regard the present moment as in many respects less favourable than last winter, when the German middle classes were crushed and cowed by military defeat.

Leipzig, 10 December

The Independent Socialist Conference has now taken two decisions likely to be of historical importance. The first decision is embodied in the new party programme passed unanimously on Thursday evening. The kernel of this programme is found in the following passage:

> The Independent Socialist Party stands for the Soviet [Council] system and aims at the building up of Councils of hand and brain workers as organs for realising the dictatorship of the proletariat.

The new programme also contains passages on trade unions which are regarded as part of the fighting organisation of the Soviet system. Parliamentary action is permitted only with a view to destroying the capitalist system of which parliaments are a part. Thus since the November Revolution of last year the German Independents have undergone a process of mental evolution which brings them, in all but a few details, to the same general position as that of the Russian Bolsheviks and the German Communists ... The second decision of the party, which is the natural corollary of the first, was taken yesterday. It was decided by an overwhelming majority to leave the Second International and to declare that the party stands wholeheartedly for the Third International in Moscow.

The Third (Communist) International had been founded in Moscow in March 1919. It had been difficult for many would-be delegates from Communist parties in other countries to get there, owing to the travelling conditions of the time, and under the circumstances the International was inevitably both organisationally and doctrinally Russian-dominated from the start. The foundation of the Comintern gave those Western Allies who were supporting the various counter-revolutionary forces operating in and around Soviet Russia, a good reason for continuing to do so. But the need for discretion began to be felt. The Allies' insistence that von der Goltz must be recalled from the Baltic fronts had finally resulted in a definite order from Noske on 4 October; moreover, his troops were told that if they remained on that front, it would be without pay. The German government had to ask for the appointment of an Inter-Allied Commission to supervise the withdrawal. But another general, Eberhardt, was sent out to take the place of von der Goltz as Commander of the 6th Frontier Reserve Corps.

28 November

News has reached here from the Baltic States that the German Iron Division and some other detachments are withdrawing towards the East Prussian frontier. Bermondt has, according to official communications, put himself under the command of the German General Eberhardt. Whether this means that the German Baltic adventure is finally liquidated it is too early to say. Much will depend on the work of the Inter-Allied Commission. Many things point to the fact that the French government is running a policy in the East which is not in accordance with that of the British ... This interpretation is supported by the fact that Niessel, the French Commissioner sent to the Baltic, is credibly reported to be working to retain German troops there on the condition that they come under the direct command of the Allies and advance against the Bolsheviks.

In the album in which Price pasted cuttings of the above and the following articles, he wrote beside them: 'These telegrams were based on reports given to me by Radek who was, though in prison in Berlin, in direct touch with Moscow. I saw him frequently during those days.' Radek had been arrested in March 1919 on account of his illegal entry into the country in December 1918 and he remained in prison until the end of 1919, enjoying almost diplomatic status in the later stages of his confinement.[9] Price had known him well in Russia, was in frequent contact with him in Germany until his arrest and had been given a permit to visit him regularly while in prison.

2 December

It has come to my knowledge that three persons have recently met at a place in East Prussia. The first is Freiherr von Maltzahn, head of the Russian department of the German Foreign Office, a Junker who is connected with the German metal industry. The second is

Guchkov, a Russian monarchist, a prominent Octobrist, president of the second Imperial Duma under the Tsar. The third is General Niessel, the French Commissioner in the Baltic. Guchkov has been working for some weeks past in the salon of Countess Kleinmichel, who through the war gathered round her in Berlin those pro-Russian Germans and pro-German Russians who were ready to make a separate peace between their two countries at the expense of England and France. The presence of Guchkov in these circles means, therefore, a gathering of the clans in Berlin in support of Denikin and Kolchak. Before, however, anything like the active intervention of Germany can take place in support of the Russian counter-revolution, it is necessary to prepare the German *petits bourgeois* who, since the revolution, have been wavering between Pan-Germans and Majority Socialists. The *Berliner Tageblatt* has been mobilised, and on Tuesday there appeared in this organ of Berlin respectability an interview with Guchkov from the pen of Hans Vorst, who comes from a Baltic Baron's family but poses as the representative of so-called 'Democratic Russia' in this country. Guchkov, in this interview, emphasises the necessity for supporting Denikin and Koltchak and pleads for the mutual co-operation both of Germany and of the Allies in this task ... All this further confirms my former report that the French government is trying to suppress the border democracies of the former Russian Empire, to create a big anti-Bolshevik front with the aid of German troops, and after removing Prussian generals to put these troops under French officers.

Price travelled rather less in 1919 than was his habit as a journalist. He had visited the Ruhr in the spring but that was before his appointment to the *Daily Herald* and he only wrote about what he saw in his diary. In the summer the main events that any correspondent would have needed to report had taken place in Berlin. In the autumn he began to visit some of the other big cities: Frankfurt, Munich and Leipzig. In Bavaria he was surprised to see open recruiting for the German army.

Munich, 21 October

Bavaria is essentially a country of small peasants. Of the 670,000 agricultural holdings, roughly 240,000 are under five acres and

250,000 between 12 and 50 acres. In the whole state there are not more than 535 holdings over 250 each. And yet the presence of these smallholdings does not seem to have done much to solve the social problem.

There are throughout Central Europe two economically opposing elements among the working population. The small Bavarian peasant with his cottage, ten acres and a cow, interested in selling his produce at the market square at his own price, is an example of the one. The hungry urban proletariat needing fixed food prices to guarantee its starvation rations is an example of the other.

The smaller peasants here suspect that the larger peasants and landlords all over Germany and particularly in Prussia are escaping their share of the burden of supplying the towns at fixed prices, by their influence upon the state and local food administration. They have therefore organised a Bavarian *Bauernbund* (Peasants' Union), in its way a form of Soviet or economic Council with a political programme. The *Bauernbund* is the middle party in the Bavarian village. To the right and left of it two bitterly hostile groups are mobilising themselves – the Independent Socialists and the Clericals: the Red and the Black Internationalist forces. The Black International in the Bavarian villages of course has concluded a Holy Alliance with Noske. In most villages you can see posters calling upon the youth to enlist for the Reichswehr. 'All young men urgently needed', I read on the walls of the post office in Immanstadt last week. 'Particularly required are those who have served in the war and are ready to give a long term of service to the Fatherland. Conditions – absolute discipline and obedience to superiors.'

Under the terms of the Treaty of Versailles the size of the Reichswehr was to be limited to 100,000. In May 1919 it still stood at 400,000, demobilising fast but also reorganising for the future. Many British military and diplomatic observers at the time recorded their concern that the ceiling on the Reichswehr might have been placed so low that there would not be enough troops to 'keep order': a danger which preoccupied the Allies for obvious reasons. There was a nationally organised armed constabulary – the *Sicherheitspolizei* – also known as the Blue Police, under the control of the Ministry of the Interior. But the Allies did not object to the formation of two voluntary but more or less paramilitary organisations to supplement both the Reichswehr and the *Sicherheitspolizei*. These were the *Zeitfreiwilligen* (Volunteer Army) and the *Einwohnerwehr* (Home Guard) which were both also under the control of the Ministry of the Interior. The *Zeitfreiwilligen* acted as a kind of reserve, to be called on by the Reichswehr for help only in emergencies, at which time they would temporarily come under military control. It was thought by some observers that the Ministries of Defence and the Interior might have been colluding at the secret transfer of some regular army officers due for demobilisation to the *Zeitfreiwilligen*.[10] When they were not helping the regular army the *Zeitfreiwilligen* were supposed to revert to the status of the other voluntary organisation, the *Einwohnerwehr*. These were at all times locally organised, controlled and armed. Recruitment for the *Zeitfreiwilligen* by poster or in the press was not allowed. Price's reference to recruitment posters must therefore have been not for the Reichswehr or the *Zeitfreiwilligen* but for the *Einwohnerwehr*.

Traditionally Bavarians were much given to forming common-interest or profession-based associations which often took the form of shooting clubs, the members owning their own weapons, often wearing some kind of uniform, and taking part in frequent open air rallies and festivals. Members of such organisations were obviously predisposed to enrol in the *Einwohnerwehr*. Moreover, several Allied observers reported that they had been told by local government officials in Bavaria that thousands – the figure of 400,000 was mentioned by one – of rifles were concealed in private homes. It would have been literally impossible to call them all in. In any case, it is clear from the reports that they sent in that these observers – members of visiting British military or diplomatic missions all over Germany – were obsessed at the time with the fear of a 'Bolshevik' *coup*.

Although Price saw no evidence of it in October 1919, a former Forestry Commissioner in Bavaria, Herr Escherisch, had already begun to try to affiliate his local *Einwohnerwehr* – to which he had given the sinister-sounding name of 'Orgesch' – with similar bodies in other parts of Germany as, in his own words, 'a strong barrier with which to oppose the Red flood from the East'. He failed to win official approval from Berlin for this project, but it is difficult not to see it, in retrospect, as anything other than a portent. It is significant that Allied observers did not appear to be at all worried by this development.

The dominating event of 1919 was, of course, the Treaty of Versailles, but a number of other developments are also to be noted: the role of the councils, in any constitutional sense, was diminishing while the proliferation of paramilitary organisations had already begun. For more than half the year Germany had still been blockaded and hardship and hunger still afflicted the working- and lower-middle-class sectors of the population. The Allies, by tolerating recruitment in Germany for the White Armies in Russia showed that they were still more afraid of Bolshevism than of German *revanchism*. But the event that ensured that war would break out again, even if not for another 20 years, was the signature, in 1919, of the Treaty of Versailles.

1920

Russo-German relations – Workers' Council Bill – the Reichstag demonstration, bloodshed and martial law – the reduction of the Reichswehr – food situation – the Kapp putsch and the general strike – The 'Red Army' in the Ruhr – elections and a new government – the Spa Conference and reparations – the Russo-Polish war – the second Congress of the Comintern and the 21 conditions – realignment of the German Left – Bavaria and the Einwohnerwehr – Organisation 'Consul' – the trustification of German industry

Diplomatic relations of a sort had been established between Soviet Russia and Germany in March 1918 after the Treaty of Brest–Litovsk. They were strained but not broken when the first German Ambassador to Russia, Count von Mirbach, was murdered in Moscow in July 1918 by Socialist Revolutionary extremists. The Soviet Ambassador in Berlin was asked to leave Berlin on 5 November, in the last days of Prince Max's Chancellorship, when it was discovered that he was involved in distributing pro-Bolshevik propaganda. And as Workers' and Soldiers' Councils began to spring up all over Germany at the end of the war, inflammatory appeals were beamed at them by wireless from Moscow, exhorting them not to choose the parliamentary, but rather the Council route to democracy. The predominantly Majority Socialist Provisional Government of Germany was of course hoping that the future National Assembly would choose a parliamentary form for the future government of the country. Yet both the Soviet and the German provisional governments insisted that diplomatic relations were still intact.

The Soviet government wanted to be formally recognised by the new German government. They were also anxious to ensure that the German troops left behind in the Ukraine – and seen by the Entente powers as potential allies for the White Armies in the ongoing civil war – should not become embroiled with the Red Army. But the German government could not afford to appear too eager to make friends with Soviet Russia if there was to be any hope of more food for the German people, let alone any chance of mitigating the harshness of the Armistice terms. The Ebert government was forced to adopt a policy of 'dilatoriness', but not outright hostility, to direct its relationship with Soviet Russia.

A complicating factor was that Germany was in no hurry to withdraw troops from its 'rimland' – Estonia, Latvia and Lithuania – all of which were now occupied, if not wholly governed by the (Russian) Red Army. The German government was in any case bound by Article XII of the armistice agreement to leave troops in the Baltic theatre, although by the end of 1919 it suited them to argue that they had offered to do so in the first place. The Allies, who had given limited – and ineffectual – naval assistance to the provisional governments of the Baltic States during the advance of the Red Army early in 1919, had positively welcomed the arrival of the German *Freikorps* and other units in that theatre in the course of the year. The troops had also been made welcome by the provisional governments which were precariously subsisting in those countries. The anti-Bolshevik crusade made a useful screen with which von der Goltz could conceal his personal territorial ambitions in the area. And the British, as has been shown above, knew all about the recruitment for the Russian White Armies of Russian prisoners of war and German soldiers that had gone on throughout 1919.

In his first dispatch to the *Daily Herald* in 1920 (2 January) Price reported that the German Foreign Office 'according to official organs here' had petitioned the Entente on behalf of Bermondt to allow him to transfer half his troops to the Petrograd front. Bermondt had been obliged to withdraw to East Prussia in September 1919, but according to a British intelligence report he had since secured financial aid from 'leading German business houses'.[1] But the French Prime Minister, Clémenceau, together with those whom Price described as 'his English supporters in the Northcliffe Press' did not, he understood, want Germans in a position from which they might make territorial claims in the Baltic area. On the other hand they had no objection to German troops being used against the Red Army. In a letter to the British Foreign Minister, Lord Curzon, early in 1920 the British chargé d'affaires, Lord Kilmarnock, reported what he was hearing in German military/ monarchist circles. Something like a Napoleonic adventure, it was believed, might now to be expected from the triumphant Red Army. The Allies should not therefore be too insistent on the reduction of the German army to the level prescribed in the Versailles Treaty, because an invasion of Poland by the Red Army was very likely. Kilmarnock also reported that the former Russian Foreign Minister, Guchkov, on whose presence and activities in Germany Price had reported on 2 December, was 'giving it out' that he had Allied approval for his enterprise.[2]

15 January

Germany is now as she was during the Thirty Years' War, a recruiting ground for any duke, prince, bishop or other robber bandit who possessed a bludgeon and plenty of impudence. So now she is a recruiting ground for the twentieth-century robber bandits in top hats or brass helmets who possess machine-guns and bags of paper money. It is not surprising, therefore, to hear that conversations have taken place between Herr Mankewitz, director of the Deutsche Bank, and unofficial agents of the French Mission, at which a 600 milliard rouble loan was discussed, to be taken up by England, France and Germany and guaranteed by the future counter-revolutionary government of Russia, on the railway and mineral wealth of the country. Rumour has it that Germany is to supply the cannon meat (led by French officers) and England the bulk of the cash.

So far, however, I am convinced that the matter has not gone beyond the stage of unofficial discussion, because among these international counter-revolutionaries the spirit indeed is willing but the flesh unfortunately is weak. Nevertheless, these symptoms deserve to be carefully watched. For it should not be forgotten that the Deutsche Bank, the Dresdner Bank and the Disconto Bank had all three, before the war, considerable French, English and American capital invested in them, and anything in which they got their fingers is sure to have at its back high international finance that knows no fatherland and only one enemy – socialism ...

On the other hand, there are groups in the [German] Foreign Office, the War Office, and among the big business bosses, who are opposed to supporting the Russian counter-revolution and are quite ready to enter into business relations with the *de facto* government of Russia. The existence of these people provides part of the armoury for the Churchill–Northcliffe campaign about a so-called Bolshevik–German conspiracy.

Talks were about to start, in fact, between the Russian and the German governments concerning the exchange of prisoners of war and supposedly limited to that. But in his letter to Curzon, Lord Kilmarnock reported that it was widely believed that economic, though not political, matters would also be discussed and that there was considerable scope for the exchange of raw materials (from Russia) in exchange for machinery, coal, medicines and, above all, skills.

Article 165 of the Weimar Constitution provided a statutory role for Workers' Councils, but it was never properly defined or implemented. On 12 August 1919 Price had reported that a conference of representatives of Workers' Councils of the chief industrial centres of Germany had taken place at Halle, and a new system for their direct election at factory level in future was being set up. But he had warned that it was likely to come into conflict with the old Central Executive (*Volzugsrat*) set up at the two earlier Congresses of Workers' and Soldiers' Councils, which consisted mainly of Majority Socialist nominees. Within a week he was reporting that the Berlin Council had been closed down by Noske (see p. 48). The Government then introduced its own Workers' Council Bill which, although falling far short of the original Russian model, nonetheless provided for the election of Councils by all employees and for the right, among other rights, of workers' representatives on factory management boards to inspect the books annually. In the course of discussion in the Reichstag during the autumn of 1919 amendments dismantling some of these rights had been moved, so that the bill, in the words of an Independent Socialist critique, was 'simply anchored to the existing private capitalistic system without any regard to the interest of the community in general'.[3] The bill so amended was then discussed in the Reichstag on 13 January 1920. The Central Committee of the Berlin Workers' Council had issued leaflets reiterating the rights which they wanted to see restored. Price was outside the Reichstag.

15 January

The pavements round the Reichstag buildings last night were covered with blood, following on a struggle between the soldiers and the crowd ... In order to press their views on the Reichstag the workers of Berlin and district: metal, transport, water, gas, railway and shop industries – in fact the greater part of the working-class population of the city – struck work yesterday morning for one day. Great processions began, towards midday, to move from all parts of Berlin towards the centre of the city. By two o'clock the scene round the Reichstag resembled those of the revolution in 1918. Certain delegates of the Workers' Councils tried to get access to the Reichstag to hand the President a memorandum and resolutions passed at meetings held outside. A force of Noske's White Guards posted round the building, however, allowed no one inside. After some jostling a number of workers' delegates succeeded in pushing through into the building but were ejected by reinforcements of troops sent in three automobiles. These troops then began to drive back the crowd from the Reichstag. It was difficult to see what followed, but I witnessed a number of serious collisions between workers and troops between the Bismarck Monument and the Reichstag steps. A number of the Noske troops were disarmed by the crowds, but I did not see any of them assaulted or injured at this stage. About three o'clock the troops suddenly opened fire from the steps of the Reichstag and a terrible pandemonium followed. A large number of demonstrators fell, and isolated detachments of troops were set on by the crowd and seriously handled. The tumult lasted some time, but the troops ultimately succeeded in driving the demonstrators away. The sitting of the Reichstag was suspended.

16 January

This morning all Prussia was declared under martial law, and executive power has been handed over to the Prussian military authorities. Noske's first act has been to announce that all public meetings will be dispersed by force, and the Berlin Independent Socialist and Communist newspapers have been suppressed. The situation is not unexpected. The Communist *Red Flag* last week published a secret memorandum from General Lüttwitz to the Cabinet in which he demanded, under a veiled threat, martial law for all Germany ...

In West Germany the movement among railwaymen is growing daily. *Vorwärts* reports today a general railway strike in the whole coal district of Ruhr, the men demanding satisfaction of their wage claims. The miners in several of the Ruhr districts have given notice that after 1 February they demand a six-hour day ... It is clear that another big mass movement is affecting the German proletariat. The increasing misery of high prices, insufficient wages, insufficient food and the political persecution of the Noske regime is forcing them into resistance. Unemployment is increasing. In Berlin alone nearly half a million are idle. While the economic situation here can be partly traced back to the result of the blockade and the Versailles Peace, it cannot be too strongly emphasised that the chief cause is the industrial anarchy of the capitalist system, which is attempting to make good the material losses of war by a merciless exploitation of the German proletariat.

28 January

The coal crisis and the miners' movement for a six-hour day is, along with the attempt on Erzberger, the central point of interest here. The continued suppression of all Independent Socialist and Communist newspapers throughout the whole of Germany, and the systematic campaign of the capitalist press against the miners are phenomena which are clearly connected. In general, it can be observed that the capitalist press ... is anxious to drive a wedge between the miners and the workers in other industries which consume coal and are threatened with closing down through coal shortage. Even Herr Hue, who represents the Majority Socialists at the Congress of German Miners now sitting at Bochum, admitted the justice of the six-hour day principle. But he and other spokesmen of the government tried to prove its impossibility at present by alluding to the obligations imposed on Germany under the treaty's coal indemnity clauses.

Among the obligations under the treaty which were now causing considerable concern was the limitation of the size of the Reichswehr. Early in 1920 it seemed that there was only one figure which everybody could agree upon: that the regular army now stood at 400,000 men but that this was a gross underestimate of the number of effectives which could be called upon. The British General Staff thought that with the various paramilitary formations added the total might be over 700,000.[4] An estimate used by Churchill as Minister for War would have doubled that total.[5] Under the terms of the Treaty the Reichswehr was variously supposed to be reduced to 100,000 by 31 March 1920 and 200,000 by 10 April 1920, but no decision had yet been reached as to which figure was to apply. The British General Staff thought that the lower figure entailed a serious danger that the German government (which they thought was honestly trying to hold the country together and fulfil its treaty obligations) might be overthrown by successive *coups*, first by the Junkers and then by the Communists.[6] The Allied Military Committee at Versailles, on the other hand, perhaps reflecting more the anxieties of the French, wanted not only to see the lower figure adhered to, but in addition wanted the *Sicherheitspolizei*, the nationally organised and armed Security Police, disbanded and replaced by an enlarged, regionally organised civil police. One officer, reporting on the *Sicherheitspolizei* in Prussia, noted that whole units of the old Reichswehr were believed to have transferred to them intact.[7] Concerns were also beginning to be expressed about the motives and political affiliations of those who had joined the paramilitary units. Even Noske, writing in *Vorwärts*, admitted that whereas these formations had begun simply as groups of men known to and vouched for by their officers, who had held together because they believed they were needed to maintain order, this was now no longer the case.[8] Indeed at the end of 1919 the headquarters of the Majority Socialists had appealed for more working-class volunteers to join the *Einwohnerwehr* to counteract its known reactionary tendencies.[9] And it was not long before reports reached London that the Bavarian model of the *Einwohnerwehr*, *Orgesch*, did not 'recruit far outside the Right'.[10] The figures used by Price in the following account of the state of the army at the beginning of February 1920 should be treated with reserve, although in some respects they tally with other estimates.

4 February

The coming into force of the Versailles Treaty creates a situation in which the Allied governments will have to show whether they intend to disarm the Prussian militarists, or whether the clauses in the treaty providing for this disarming were only meant for the gallery. The present strength of the German armed forces is stated to be roughly one million of men, of which 400,000 are in the Reichswehr, or the regular army. Information, however, which has come into my possession leads me to believe that this is, if anything, an underestimate. It would appear that the total number of persons in Germany either directly under arms, or else in reserve, engaged in regular drilling, is as follows:

Reichswehr	750,000
Zeitfreiwilligen	150,000
Einwohnerwehr (for Bavaria)	270,000
Einwohnerwehr (rest of Germany)	500,000
TOTAL	1,670,000

The nucleus of this army is the Reichswehr, formed in January 1919. I well remember at this time the street meetings, addressed by speakers from the Pan-German and Majority Socialist parties. People with a 'stake in the country' were called upon to enlist in the Reichswehr and save the land from the Spartacists. Shortly after this passers-by in the Berlin streets saw placards everywhere, portraying appalling Bolshevik monsters creeping across Europe and eating human flesh. During the course of the summer the Reichswehr rose to three-quarters of a million on the pretext of 'preserving order' and of protecting the 'Fatherland' from the danger in the East. Now by the terms of the treaty Noske's army will have to be reduced from 750,000 to 100,000. Officially a 'reduction' in the Reichswehr is in progress ... but soldiers who are discharged from this force are virtually compelled to enter the Zeitfreiwilligen. I have seen an order, signed by the Commander-in-Chief of the Reichswehr in Bavaria, giving instructions to his commanders to regard all refusals on the part of soldiers being discharged from the Reichswehr to enter the Zeitfreiwilligen as acts of insubordination. The result is that if the Reichswehr has on paper been reduced to 400,000 men, the Zeitfreiwilligen is in actual fact automatically increased from 150,000 to 500,000. This force thus becomes a reserve for the

Reichswehr ... The powers beind the German Reichswehr are under the influence of the Eastern school of German imperialism, which is inclined to abandon the West and look to the East. Their aim is sooner or later to re-establish the *'Deutschtum'* in the Baltic Provinces, and in return for this concession they would offer the Allies German cannon fodder for any future attempt to overthrow the present regime in Russia.

14 February [11]

... It is believed here [Berlin] that the British War Office has taken steps to let it be known that the British government will not insist on the immediate carrying out of the clauses in the Versailles Treaty providing for the reduction of the German army to 100,000 men. According to the treaty this reduction should take place on 1 March, but its postponement will give Noske a free hand to continue his work of building up a huge mercenary White Guard army of a million and a half of men in order to make Europe safe for capitalism. Signs are increasing that with the coming spring this army is not going to confine itself to Central Europe only. There are signs, however, that German capitalists' interests are divided on the Russian question, and these signs have been increasing of late. In consequence the German Foreign Office has become a shuttlecock between the two competing forces in the German industrial world. One of these forces is a group round the so-called *Export Verband*, which is a combine of the metal industries and engineering firms. Before the war these firms catered for the Russian market, and it is a matter of small importance to them what form of government there is in Russia so long as they regain the market. On the other hand the German heavy industries are throwing their weight in the scale against relations with Soviet Russia and are carrying on secret negotiations with those financial interests in Entente countries who are ready to include Germany in the new anti-Bolshevik alliance. Such giant coal and iron trusts as Thyssen, Stinnes and the Kali syndicate are now interested in the export of machinery. Before the war they exported pig-iron, rails and other manufactured products to the West and were the chief competitors of British manufacturers in the British colonies and South America. Now they have largely changed the nature of their business and have become exploiters of mineral wealth. They are therefore ready to come to an agreement with Entente capital and to renounce the manufactured export trade in the British colonies in return for the right to exploit sources of raw materials in Russia.

During his correspondence for the *Daily Herald*, Price would return many times to what might be called the Stinnes factor in German politics. Hugo Stinnes came from a family which had been prominent in the Ruhr coal industry for generations. He had already built up an industrial empire long before the war and he acquired, and used, considerable political clout via the People's Party (DVP). Many more extracts from what Price wrote about Stinnes will appear in the following pages, but in February 1920 his influence on events had only begun to be noticeable, and as a then Marxist Price was probably quicker to draw attention to it than some of his journalist colleagues. Most observers, whether diplomats, soldiers or journalists were, at the beginning of 1920, primarily concerned with describing the only too obvious phenomena of unemployment and hunger – the blockade had only been lifted in July 1919 – and their invariable concomitants: social and industrial unrest. It was now also becoming clear that the consequences of having quite deliberately financed the war by inflation would have to be dealt with equally deliberately.

24 February

Since the New Year there has been a steady deterioration in food conditions in Germany. Not only have all rationed foods risen in price, but the bread ration has been reduced from 2,350 grammes to 1,950 grammes per week.

I know in Berlin unskilled working-class families who are trying to keep their heads above water on wages of 600 marks per month, equivalent in English money to about 10s. a week. These families get horseflesh sausage about once a fortnight, and their midday meals consist of potatoes and cabbage without fat. On the other hand the rural population of Germany is living as well as before the war, and in the towns the prosperous bourgeoisie and profiteers can dine at expensive hotels and restaurants.

The country is flooded with paper money, which has made the rural population refuse to part with their food products. As the result of all this, there is general demoralisation leading to, firstly, the German capitalists exporting all available manufactures in order to get paid in foreign gold currencies, in spite of the fact that the home markets are starving; and secondly the Government is failing to establish efficient public control over production and distribution.

It is clear that in order to tackle the economic problem of Central Europe a number of measures are necessary, some of which depend on the Allies, but others on the Germans themselves. First, much stricter control over the agrarian interests is needed. Second, it is necessary to enable production to be raised by opening up foreign commercial exchanges. One difficulty in the way of this is the absurd economic clauses of the Versailles Treaty. It is essential to restrict Germany's liabilities to restore Northern France and Belgium to the amount she is capable of paying. Further, it is necessary to guarantee the German industries with certain raw materials. But in view of the state of foreign exchanges, it is impossible for Germany to receive a loan for raw materials from America without mortgaging the national assets and the German proletariat to Wall Street.

The British General Staff's fear that the German government could be overthrown first by a *coup* from the Right and then by one from the Left looked like being realised in the middle of March 1920. General Malcolm had been made aware on four separate occasions between September 1919 and March 1920 that elements within the army were contemplating a *putsch*. He had more than once been asked what the British government's attitude to such a development would be. He had always said that his government would never countenance such an act and that no change in the government of Germany would be recognised except as the result of a democratic process. Moreover, he had always seen to it personally, after such an approach, that the German government had been warned. But on the night of 12–13 March Berlin was taken completely by surprise. The *putschists* themselves were not quite ready either. Lüttwitz, the commanding general in Berlin, ordered by Noske to disband two brigades in compliance with the Treaty of

Versailles had refused to obey the order and had accompanied his refusal with demands for a number of political and even constitutional changes.

The British chargé d'affaires in Berlin later reported to Curzon that he understood that the *coup* had been planned originally to take place in June but that the government had got wind of it and had searched the houses of two of the conspirators on 10 March, when a quantity of compromising material had been found. Noske then dismissed Lüttwitz and thought he had pre-empted the *coup*.[12] But just before midnight on 12 March, one of the brigades threatened with disbandment, the *Erhardt*, or Naval Brigade, began to march on Berlin. The Chief of Staff of the Reichswehr, von Seeckt, refused to allow the regular Reichswehr units under his control to fire on them and Berlin was thus undefended. The Government, realising that it would not be able to organise opposition to the *coup* if in captivity, moved out of Berlin, first to Dresden and then to Stuttgart, where it summoned the National Assembly to meet. The next day the *Erhardt* Brigade entered Berlin and a civil servant, Wolfgang Kapp, a man distinguished in nothing except his extreme Right-wing nationalist views, together with Lüttwitz, issued proclamations and made as if to govern. The civil service, even the telegraph clerks, refused categorically to collaborate with them. On the other hand neither the German People's Party (DVP) nor the National Party (DNVP) came out in opposition to the *putsch*. And a group of representatives of German shipowners who were visiting London at the time let it be known that they could 'answer for the loathing borne by the capitalist class in Germany for the Noske government', that they 'would throw in [their] lot at once with any anti-socialist government ... and bore the present movement no ill will'. The state governments of Bavaria, Saxony and Wurtemburg declared for the Reich government, but those of East Prussia and Pomerania supported Kapp. A summary of Intelligence sent to the War office on 16 March reported that the Reichswehr and the *Sicherheitspolizei* were both believed to be on the side of the 'revolution'.

The Kapp adventure was defeated by a general strike called jointly by the Government, the Majority Socialists, the Independent Socialists and the trade unions acting, for once, unanimously. The Communist Party took a doctrinaire line, refusing to support one capitalist regime against another. After three days the *Erhardt* Brigade withdrew, pausing only to fire twice on bystanders. Pending the return of the government from Stuttgart the Minister of Justice, Schiffer – a Democrat – assumed the role of head of state and von Seeckt was appointed Chief of the Army Command. But the socialist unions refused to call off the strike, which was by now nationwide, until the Government conceded an Eight-Point programme of reforms which included their right to be involved in the reconstruction of the Government, the disbandment of reactionary military formations and the socialisation of industry. They also insisted on the resignation of Bauer as Chancellor and Noske as Minister of the Interior. The Majority Socialist Hermann Müller became the next Chancellor.

In the Ruhr, where the strikers had organised themselves into an army – again calling themselves the Red Army – representatives of the socialist parties signed an agreement with the Government at Bielefeld on the basis of the Eight Points, but the Red Army, which consisted mainly of ex-soldiers, would not accept it. The British Commissioner at Coblenz reported on 25 March that the 'taking up of arms' in the Ruhr had been directed against the *putsch* and was not 'a purely Bolshevik movement'.[13] The strikers were not extremists, but members of the socialist parties, acting in unison 'to beat down the reaction'. But the restored Government now decided that its writ must run in the Ruhr and, against British advice, troops were sent to enforce it. General von Watter, who commanded the Reichswehr in the Ruhr, had been an active Kapp supporter until it was obvious that the *putsch* had failed. The Red Army may have numbered as many as 80,000 but was without central leadership and was now held together more by hatred of the Reichswehr than by any political or social objective.

As the Reichswehr advanced, the Red Army broke up into small units and began to live by plunder. The Government now asked – and received – permission from the French government to reinforce its troops in the Ruhr above the number permitted by the treaty. It made the mistake of announcing this in the Reichstag whereupon the French immediately denied it. By then, German reinforcements had arrived in the Ruhr and the French, alleging breach of the treaty, occupied five German towns which had not been included in their original zone of occupation. Many thousands of the Red Army fled into the British zone. And the British responded by withdrawing their representative from the standing conference of Ambassadors in Paris until they received 'adequate assurances' against further unilateral action by the French.[14]

The Kapp 'government' had imposed a drastic censorship on outgoing foreign telegrams and Price sent very little from Berlin until the *putsch* was over. His first dispatch, written while the *putsch* was still in being, appeared two days later.

18 March

We are living now in Berlin without light, gas or water. The new Government is caught like a rat in a trap. It is increasingly clear that it is not only up against the Labour, Socialist and Democratic parties, but that large sections of the middle and lower bureaucracy are passively resisting. I hear that yesterday union was attained between the Scheidemann Socialists and the Independents in Berlin, both deciding upon common action against the new regime. A prominent Scheidemann Socialist told me this morning that reversion to the old state of affairs after the overthrow of the Kapp government is impossible. I have just seen a proclamation for a general strike in Silesia signed by middle-class men and Socialists, by Catholic Centrists and Communists. On the other hand, it is not to be expected that the new Government will give up without a struggle, and it has considerable support among the uneducated middle classes and peasantry in Pomerania, North Germany and East Prussia. Anti-Semitic propaganda is a method by which it is trying to make itself popular among the dark and ignorant elements of the population. In the street where I live is a notorious Jew-baiter who has been engaged for some time past in manufacturing rubber batons for use in pogroms.

30 March

This morning the Government issued an ultimatum to the workers of the Ruhr to disarm and dissolve the Worker's Councils within 24 hours. In a speech in the Reichstag today the new War Minister, Gessler, justified this action by alluding to the 'Red Terror' in Duisburg and other Westphalian towns. According, however, to Legien, who spoke on behalf of the All-German Trade Union Executive, the Majority Socialists and Independents of the Ruhr have decided to take joint action against the anarchist and syndicalist elements who are trying to declare a Soviet Republic there. 'The workers of the Ruhr', said Legien, who is a most conservative trade union official, 'demand only one thing – the disarming of the Reichswehr and the counter-revolutionary White Guards.' This corresponds with a report I have just received from the Ruhr that the workers of all political parties there will not lay down their arms without absolute guarantees that the Reichswehr and the Security Police [*Sicherheitspolizei*] shall not be sent into the coalfields.

6 April

Information from the Ruhr shows that in most of the towns peace and order reign, but in some parts of the neutral [unoccupied] zone there are irresponsible bands against whom the local Socialists of all shades are taking action. The existence of these bands gives the Junker junta just the excuse it wants to march into the Ruhr. The Berlin government is in a state of helpless indecision and its official spokesmen are making contradictory statements according as they are to a greater or lesser degree under the influence of General von Watter's headquarters. Negotiations with France over the occupation of the neutral zone continue. Already Watter's troops have reached Duisburg and the French government is making use of this advance to secure the right to extend its own area of occupation.

15 April

There has been a steady consolidation of the forces of reaction of Germany during the Kapp week. The people behind the Kapp adventure, though defeated on the surface, have gained below. This is particularly the case in South Germany. In Bavaria even the Majority Socialists have been excluded from the Government, which relies now solely on the parties of the Right. The newly created Bavarian Centre and the Peasants' Party are separatist in tendency and working with Pan-Germans in Prussia, who prefer a small reactionary Germany to a large revolutionary one.

According to my information the centre of the reaction is now Pomerania, which is the spiritual Mecca and Vendée of Junkerdom to which have flocked the leaders of the Kapp adventure, quite undisturbed by orders issued by Hermann Müller's government for their arrest for high treason. The landlords and their retainers here are well armed, and many Baltic regiments are scattered on their estates, the soldiers having brought all their arms with them. There is a strong Socialist and Communist movement among the agricultural labourers of these parts, but as the workers are completely disarmed the whole countryside is at the mercy of the Junkers.

Cologne, 27 April

I have just returned from the Ruhr Valley and must state my belief that the Ruhr is ripe for another workers' uprising, better organised, more united and more desperate in character than the one overwhelmed by the Reichswehr. In Münster, Wesel, Dorsten, Essen, Bochum, Dortmund and half a dozen other industrial centres, the machine-guns and bayonets of the Reichswehr maintain a precarious truce. Here and elsewhere the Red Army has ceased to exist as a visible force. But the organisation which called it into being in the early days of April is stronger than ever and beyond the reach of the military. In many small towns south of the Ruhr the workers are today practically controlling local government ... A central committee, with representatives in all the cities of the Ruhr Valley, is functioning here and biding its time ... German military authorities estimate that less than 10 per cent of the weapons in the possession of the workers have been surrendered as the result of the recent fighting. This estimate is substantiated by individual workers, who told me without hesitation that they have rifles secreted ... The morale of the Reichswehr in the Westphalian cities is bad ... Privates pass their officers in the street without saluting – something almost unbelievable in Germany. A majority of the workers enrolled in the Red Army could not by any stretch of imagination be called Bolsheviks ... Captain Otto Schwink, former bridgehead officer at Cologne for the German General Staff, told me that, without doubt, the last revolution started merely as a working-class protest against the Kapp–Lüttwitz *coup*. Since then, however, sentiment among the Ruhr workers has swung far towards the Left, partly because of the brutality shown by the Reichswehr in putting down the uprising, partly because of the feebleness shown by the Ebert government in resisting the present encroachments from the Right ... There is every indication that another Junker *coup* in Germany will bring that country nearer to real Bolshevism than anything so far.

In fact the German Communist Party was at this time split and less likely than ever to achieve an effective *coup*. The first general elections to the Reichstag were due to take place in June and the KPD had issued an appeal to German workers to participate in them on the understanding that this would be a purely tactical move towards the party's strategic end. But the extreme Left of the party now formed itself into the Communist Workers' Party (KAPD) in the interests of doctrinal purity. In an uncanny fulfilment of what he had earlier called the Churchill–Northcliffe Bolshevik–German conspiracy, Price reported on 27 April that secret agents of Kapp and Lüttwitz had approached both wings of the Communist Party with a view to involving them in yet another conspiracy. This would deliberately create a Red Terror, after a few weeks of which it would be easy to establish a dictatorship under Hindenburg. The old Communists would have nothing to do with it, but members of the KAPD had apparently toyed with the idea for a while, under the delusion that they might be able to turn the tables on the officers concerned and convert them to socialism.

The Reichstag elections were held on 6 June. The Democratic and Centre parties both lost seats and the Majority Socialists lost even more in a swing to the Right of which the main beneficiaries were the Nationalist Party (DNVP) and the People's Party (DVP). The Majority Socialists, preferring the freedom of opposition, withdrew from the Government and, with the exception of two brief reappearances in 1923 and 1928–30, effectively removed themselves from politics for 25 years. The new Government was a coalition of the Democratic, Centre and People's parties under Konstantin Fehrenbach.

10 June

The situation thus created is characteristic of the instability of bourgeois parliamentary institutions in Germany. As *Rote Fahne* said yesterday, 'The ballot box has shown that the new Parliament can decide nothing and can only deepen the class struggle.' The Majority Socialists, in their sitting yesterday, discussed the situation thus created. I hear that although it was decided to announce that no coalition with the Right parties was possible, nevertheless there was a strong current of opinion holding that this was the only solution ... The official organs of the Majority Socialists continue to hold out olive branches to the Independents, and *Vorwärts* talks of the impossibility of a new government without the latter. I can, however, say with some confidence that the rank and file of the Independents have too clear a conception of the present situation in Germany from the point of view of revolutionary socialism to allow themselves to be sidetracked ... The growth of class consciousness in the German workers is also seen by the fact that in spite of the persecution and murders of Communists by the Noske regime, the Communists have got over 400,000 votes.

18 June

Germany seems to have entered on a period of permanent Cabinet crisis. All the attempted combinations of the middle-class parties have not yet succeeded in improving the invalid's constitution ... In general it may be said that Germany presents today a picture of complete political confusion and a blur of meaningless colours. The parliamentary system is becoming daily less able to hide the real rule of finance-capital and heavy industry, and this is preparing the ground for a dictatorship from the Right or Left. But as the Left has neither armed force nor moral enthusiasm, the immediate future can only rest with the Right, which will probably rule under a thin veneer of a makeshift parliamentary coalition. The Majority Socialist leaders seem to be preparing for the role of independent critics from the outside, thereby robbing the Independents of the monopoly of opposition. The triumph of reaction behind the scenes in Germany, together with the growing counter-revolution in Austria and Hungary[15] and the flirting which has been going on in Paris between Hugo Stinnes and the French financial interests, all point to a steady strengthening of the White Capitalist International.

24 July

One of the German representatives in Spa, who remains anonymous, declares in *Freiheit* that he there heard Hugo Stinnes, the great Westphalian coalmaster, express himself indifferent whether the Entente occupied the Ruhr or not, because the Allied troops would enforce an increase in the miners' working hours. The writer adds that Stinnes and Millerand [the French Commissioner General for Alsace and Lorraine] are aiming at exploitation, by a co-partnership of French and German capital, of the coal and iron resources of West Germany, northern France, Lorraine and Normandy.

Price was here drawing attention for the first time to a theme which would recur again and again in his dispatches for the next three years. The fact was that French heavy industries needed the Ruhr coke, the only coke with which Lorraine ore could be smelted. Saar coal was unfit for coking. The desirability of some kind of economic union between the coal-producing areas of the Ruhr and the Saar and the ore-producing areas of Lorraine and northern France was recognised by the magnates of both French and German heavy industries. This was to complicate the German government's response to the French occupation of the Ruhr in 1923 and lead to secret and not-so-secret negotiations in that year between members of the German Alliance of Heavy Industries, its French counterpart, the Comité des Forges, and MICUM, the Inter-Allied Mission for the Control of Factories and Mines (see p. 166).

It was now nearly a year since Germany had signed the Treaty of Versailles, but the decisions of the Reparations Commission as to the amount of reparations to be demanded and the form they were to take were not expected until May 1921. Nonetheless payments on account had been required since August 1919. The German government was already falling into arrears in their shipments of coal to France: hardly surprisingly in view of the Kapp *putsch* and its consequences in the Ruhr. In the spring of 1920 the Allies showed some willingness to consider alternative plans for payment. The Germans were invited to make their views known at Spa on 5 July. The question of the future size of the German army was due for consideration at the same time. The impression made by the German delegation on this occasion was extremely unfortunate. The military representatives arrived in uniform and wearing all their medals, conforming exactly to the Prussian military stereotype. The economic delegation included Stinnes, supposedly in the role of expert, who behaved with such catastrophic arrogance that the Allies lost all inclination to be more accommodating. The best the Germans could obtain was a six months' extension for the fulfilment of the disarmament conditions. Price now systematically began to record Stinnes' activities.

15 July

Particulars which I am able to send of the newly founded 'Union of German Employers' are of great interest. It is peculiarly significant to note that the Foreign Minister, Dr Simons, who has been prominent at Spa, is a president of the *Reichsverband der Deutschen Industrie* (Alliance of German Industries),[16] which is one of the most influential members of the union, and that another important man on the union is Stinnes himself. According to my information the plan for the creation of this Employers' Union originated last May from the Hanseatic League, a body which was formed in 1910 to protect the interests of home and foreign trades in the North German ports. But the League has now itself a much wider task, for it aims at nothing less than uniting the whole capitalist world of Central Europe against socialism and Labour. A circular which I have before me shows that the originators decided to act after the success of the last general strike in March against the Kapp *coup d'état*. That strike undoubtedly frightened the captains of industry in Germany, for then, for the first time in history, the conservative German trade union leaders, pushed by their rank and file, were compelled to use the industrial weapon for political ends. The union will aim at 'influencing the Government against socialist experiments' and will secure its own nominees in the government departments, who, under the name of 'business ministers' will do the bidding of their masters.

On Germany's eastern borders a new crisis began to develop in June 1920. Having advanced into Russia for two years after the end of Russo-German hostilities, the Polish army had reached Kiev. The [Soviet] Red Army now regained the initiative and drove the Poles back into Poland, reaching the outskirts of Warsaw in August. With the Red Army in Poland, the Allies and Associated Powers became even more than usually afraid that Germany might fall victim to Communism and there was warlike talk of going to the rescue of Poland. The parties of the Left seriously began to suspect that their governments wanted to declare war on Soviet Russia, leading in Britain to the formation of a Council of Action to mobilise opposition to any such development and in Germany to the refusal by some workers to handle war materials bound for Poland. Polish soldiers were also involved in disorders in Silesia, where the promised plebiscite was due to take place shortly under Allied supervision.

9 August

The Russian northern army is making a big encircling movement round Warsaw from the north. The Red troops have very various uniforms, and are sometimes in civilian clothes with a red band on the cap. All are perfectly disciplined and respect the German frontier. They appear also to be well equipped with the artillery so considerately supplied by the Allies last year to Denikin and Kolchak. The Central Committee of the Workers' Council in Berlin, which is incorporated with the Berlin Trades Council, has issued instructions to all its members to watch and inspect all cases of suspicious war material for Poland. The Independent *Freiheit*, referring to Robert Williams' telegram to German transport workers,[17] writes: 'The decision of the British trade unions to prevent arms and munitions from passing to Poland is a most satisfactory symptom of the determination of English Labour to put an end by direct action to the intrigues of the militarists. We hope and believe that English and French workers will do their duty if the Entente militarists try to tamper with the neutrality of Germany and use her as a transit place for war plans in the East.'

25 August

There is no foundation for the German story that Polish regular troops have crossed the frontier in force, with the object of occupying the province [Upper Silesia] and anticipating the plebiscite. On the other hand, the assertion of General Lerond, who is chief of the Inter-Allied Commission, that the disorders were of Bolshevik origin is quite as nonsensical. Just a year ago there was a rising which was put down with such appalling brutality by the German regular troops, that thousands of Upper Silesian workmen became pro-Polish through sheer fury against the Berlin government. The Inter-Allied Commission that now governs the province is acting much more wisely. Where there are armed bands of pro-Poles the Security Police is kept in the background by its order. Allied officers are going from place to place, sometimes alone, sometimes accompanied by a few soldiers, trying to persuade the relcalcitrants to give up their arms ... The Upper Silesian proletariat, I may add, is the most wretched, worst exploited and most backward in all Germany ... A short while ago there was no real antagonism between Polish and German-speaking workers ... but nationalist agitation has split them into two hostile armies. The Upper Silesian capitalists are all German-speaking and they are united. The disorders do not mean a victory either for the pro-Polish or the pro-German movement, but they certainly mean a lamentable setback for social revolutionary progress in one of the world's greatest mining areas.

In July 1920 the second Congress of the Third International met in Moscow. Only three days before her death Rosa Luxemburg had argued against the foundation of the new Communist International on the grounds that no strong mass revolutionary parties had as yet come into existence in the West. She feared that a Bolshevik-dominated International would alienate the movement elsewhere. The first Congress (in March 1919) had indeed set up an Executive Committee consisting entirely of Russians. Although Lenin's theses (*Left-Wing Communism: an Infantile Sickness*) which accepted parliamentary work as an interim stage towards revolution, had been published in May 1920, the second Congress set out to prevent 'dilution' by groups which had not yet completely discarded the ideology of the old Second International. Communist parties from 36 countries were represented at the second Congress of the Third International, but it was decreed that these were now no longer delegates from national parties, but merely 'member sections' of the Comintern. The Central

Executive Committee, sitting in Moscow, was given almost unlimited powers. Twenty-one conditions for membership of the Comintern were laid down, most of which were designed to concentrate power and decision-making ever more firmly in the hands of the Executive and to drive away any merely reformist elements.

18 September

German Independents are at present passing through a crisis as the result of the demands – which are in fact an ultimatum – of the Moscow International regarding the conditions of entry to the latter. Moscow's tactics are clearly to get the goat to swallow the dynamite and to gather up the pieces that remain. There is reason to believe that the conditions given to the Independents are severer than to other Western socialist parties and the reason is not difficult to understand. During the supreme crisis of Soviet Russia last year, when Yudenitch was at the gates of Petrograd and Denikin at Orel, certain Independent leaders could find nothing better to do than to open a pamphlet offensive of their own against the Russian Communists. The latter will not easily forgive this. The situation thus created is likely to lead to a definite split in the Independent Party ... There is a group led by Daümig and Stöcker which is working for the unconditional acceptance of Moscow's demands. At present it is too early to forecast the result, which will be decided at the National Party Congress at Halle next month.

18 October (Halle)

By 237 votes to 156 a resolution by Daümig and Stöcker in favour of joining the Third International was passed. The defeated moderates then left the hall and held a secret meeting elsewhere. Yesterday for the first time an official representative of the Communist International appeared on the tribune of a Western European socialist party. Zinoviev's speech on the 21 conditions for the entry of Independents to the Moscow International was epoch-making. To the consternation of those who were prepared to break up the Congress on the question of acceptance or non-acceptance, he said he was commissioned by the Third International to say that the 21 points were not a catechism and that they would be tolerant in their application. 'We want no hierarchy in Moscow', he said, 'any more than you, and we should be glad to transfer the seat of the Third International either to the country where Karl Marx was born or to the city of the Paris Communards, if either the French or the German capitalist governments will give us the necessary facilities.'

Passing to another theme he referred to the phenomenon observed in socialist parties in every country, which centred round the prospects of world revolution. The Right-wingers said the revolutionary wave had passed; the Left-wingers said that it was only now coming. 'We have never called on anyone to go out into the streets and make a revolution tomorrow. We have demanded that all parties calling themselves socialist and revolutionary should prepare the ground for the revolution by keeping ahead of the masses, showing them clearly the issues before them. But that is what the Right-wingers do not do. On the contrary they drag behind the masses and damp down their revolutionary enthusiasm and confuse the issues by pacifist phrases. We say that the world economic situation is driving the masses to social revolution through hunger, misery and unemployment, and that only the psychological initiative is lacking on the part of the leaders. Hence the capitalists of all lands are able to retain their hypnotic influence over the masses by their hold on the press – their monopoly of propaganda by which they lull the masses to a sense of impotence.' At the end of Zinoviev's speech, all the Left delegates, which represent about two-thirds of the Congress, rose and sang the *Internationale* and cheered for the Third International.

Halle, 19 October

This afternoon the long-expected split in the Independent Socialist Party of Germany took place ... Amid cheers for the Independent Socialist Party and counter-cheers for the Third International, the minority of the Congress, numbering 156, left the hall and reopened a congress of their own in another hall. The significance of the event which has happened today in Germany cannot be overestimated. It is not likely for the present that the new Left Independent Socialist Party will fuse with the Spartacists. Many tactical as well as technical reasons speak against this. Nor is it likely that the new Right Independent Party will join up with the

Scheidemann Socialists at once. Nevertheless the inexorable logic of history is driving these two elements together, just as it is driving the Left Independents towards the Spartacists.

The revolution devours its children, and just as Danton was swept away by Robespierre because he failed to speak the decisive word in the hour of danger, so now those elements who shrink from facing the consequences of the final reckoning with capitalism in Germany are faced with the question whether they will continue to co-operate with those who have just been their deadly enemies or disappear from the scene. One may regret this new division in the ranks of the German socialists, but it was as inevitable as the setting of the sun. The days of isolated centrist groups who don't know what they want and won't be happy till they get it, are gone.

A few days before the Halle conference the Majority Socialists had held their own conference. For the first time since the end of the war they were not burdened with the responsibility of government.

Kassel, 15 October

When the National Congress of the German Majority Socialists opened here yesterday, the secretary reported that the party now numbered 1,180,000 members, an increase of 15 per cent over last year. It has over 150 provincial press organs. The atmosphere of the Congress was one of confidence in the future of the party, and I observed fewer signs of opposition groups than in last year's Congress. In Weimar this is probably accounted for by the fact that the party is now out of the Government. The party seems, however, to be gradually changing its character and to be becoming a recruiting ground for organised brain workers. The lower grades of government officials, while coming over in increasing numbers to socialism, are frightened of going very far. The general attitude of the leaders was seen in a speech by Wels, who spoke against the Bolsheviks of the Left and against the Right. Their party, he said, would not enter the Government with the People's Party, which was intriguing secretly with the monarchists. Socialism could only come by means of democratic voting.

Wels' speech contained three important demands which may be regarded as the official view of the Majority Socialist Party. 'We demand', he said, 'the revision of the Versailles Treaty in accordance with socialist principles. We ask that the International Bureau at Amsterdam[18] should secure for Germany that the contribution for restoring the wasted areas in France should be made mainly in labour and only in second degree in materials. We demand peace and the re-establishment of normal relations with the *de facto* government of Russia.' In general it may be said that the Majority Socialists are marking time and waiting in the hope that the break-up of the Independents into two camps will enable them to unite with the Right wing of the party, and thus form the basis for a pure Labour government in Germany.

The final stage in the realignment of the Left which took place in Germany in the course of the autumn of 1920, was the fusion of the Left Independents with the old (original) Communist Party.

7 December

The Communist Unity Congress opened yesterday in Berlin. The day before the Left Independents and the old Communist Party held separate conferences which decided on fusion. The report of the Left Independent delegates showed that they had 438,000 paying members, which is considerably more than half of the old Independent Party. On the other hand, the Right Independents have carried with them most of the party machinery and the press. The Lefts claim that they could get the remainder, who are still with the Right, once fusion with the old Communists is effected and they are in possession of a strong press. The old Communists number about 20,000, thus bringing the total organised workers represented at the Unity Conference to half a million. The new German Communist Party ranks after the Russian as the second largest in the world.

In Bavaria, where a year earlier Price had been surprised to see recruiting going on openly for the *Einwohnerwehr*, the Majority Socialist Chancellor, Hoffman, had been replaced at the time of the Kapp *putsch* by the anti-republican conservative Gustav von Kahr. The *Einwohnerwehr* had now become a factor in Bavarian politics. In a letter to Lord Curzon, the British Consul-General

in Munich described a ceremony which had taken place in
Munich on 25 September, when 'some 70,000 *Einwohnerwehr*
men arrived in Munich from all over Bavaria and marched,
under flying colours and with bands playing' in 'a parade
obviously intended to stimulate the idea of the *Einwohnerwehr*
and to intimidate the radical sections of the population. Each
man had been supplied with ten rounds of ammunition and it is
not improbable that a counter-demonstration would have been
welcome as an opportunity for showing the metal of the "Wehr"
men.'[19] In a piece printed a few days earlier, which incidentally
referred to the parade as forthcoming, Price mentioned rumours
of an impending monarchist *coup* in Bavaria and drew attention
to another aspect of Bavarian affairs which gave grounds for
concern. France appeared to be giving tacit encouragement to
long-established Bavarian separatist tendencies by turning a
blind eye to the *Einwohnerwehr* rifle competitions and parades,
which were illegal under the Versailles Treaty. Rumours were
also circulating that France intended to occupy the Ruhr.

22 September

France seems already to look on Bavaria as officially freed from the
military conditions of the Versailles Treaty, for she has definitely
permitted the continuance of the Bavarian White Guard organisations, which make no secret of the fact that they exist for the
purpose of creating a reactionary ring round the industrial cities of
Prussia and North Germany. Moreover, it is stated in well-
informed circles that the French government is giving financial
assistance to the Bavarian White Guards, thus bringing Hindenburg and Ludendorff indirectly into its service. Up to now the
Bavarian reaction has feared to break away openly from Prussia
because of Bavaria's dependence in the coming winter on the coal
from the Ruhr. The plan for a *coup*, therefore, must be taken
together with French intentions in the Ruhr.

Increasingly, as 1920 wore on, Price appears to have been
looking for evidence of the involvement of German heavy
industry in politics and government. Obviously any such
evidence fitted his own preconceptions, but it is remarkable how
often an event reported or a connection made by him, involving

'the industrials', was also reported by British military or diplomatic observers in their dispatches to London. Even the slightly improbable discovery of a 'Lie Factory' in Magdeburg, which he reported in mid-August, was also reported to Curzon by Kilmarnock.

16 August

A favourite method of discrediting the German working class, scaring the bourgeoisie and strengthening reaction has been to invent elaborate stories of Spartacist conspiracies to upset the government and establish Bolshevism in Germany. In spite of their obvious absurdity, these stories always received prominence in the reactionary press and were widely believed. Sceptics naturally wonder in what lie factory they were made. It has at last been discovered at Magdeburg, where the police have unearthed a secret service of spies, propagandists and *agents provocateurs*. Many arrests have been made and incriminating evidence has been found ... The Magdeburg service and its branches, it is now clear, were financed by the German 'heavy' industries, although only one or two names of individual donors have been discovered. The object of this vast and evil conspiracy is, of course, to discredit the German Revolution and impress the Allies with a sham Bolshevik menace, so that they will allow Germany to keep a big army and prepare the way for militarist reaction.

In September, in a report on the Government's plans to socialise the coal industry, he discovered a capitalist conspiracy again.

27 September

It is to be expected that Stinnes, who is the big man behind the People's Party, will withdraw his support from the Government, and there have been sufficient indications for some time past that he would welcome a French occupation of the Ruhr rather than give way on socialisation. Indeed I find it is believed in trade union circles here that the French will use the attempt of the German government to socialise the mines as an excuse for an occupation. Already the coalowners in the Ruhr are preparing to pick a quarrel with the miners on the question of the dismissal of certain men, and the latter are convinced that this is part of the scheme to get a French occupation.

Towards the end of the year he found yet another example of the manipulation of production for profit at the expense of output.

26 November

The position in the Ruhr now is that the coalminers, although working on insufficient food, are actually raising output. On the other hand, among the heavy industries dependent on coal, works are closing down. The directors of two big smelting concerns with whom I spoke put this down to the Spa Agreement and to the forcible export of 2 million tons of coal to France. But representatives of the Workers' Councils whom I met told me a different story. The giant trustification of coal and iron concerns which Stinnes is carrying out, they said, has started a policy of restricting production in order to get under their control the purchasers of the finished iron products, the textile works and other consumers of their key industry goods. They do this by starving these industries and thereby the public. I was assured that there is enough coal in the Ruhr to keep more furnaces going than are actually going now, and that there is sufficient iron, if it were rationed and if those who are deliberately holding back the stocks were dealt with. Colour is lent to this view by the fact that most coal and iron trusts, in spite of the fall in production, have been making giant profits. I obtained figures which showed that the Phoenix Trust has produced 32 million tons less finished products than last year and yet is paying a dividend of 20 per cent instead of 16 per cent. I have also other similar figures.

These key industry trusts have so watered their capital by reckless expansion that they can only maintain their profits by squeezing increasing surplus values off their products; in other words, by continually screwing up prices. Since high production decreases prices, production must be kept down on the home market, and as much as possible sold abroad at world prices. Thus I spoke with the director of a big engineering firm who, though full of complaints about Spa, informed me in the same breath that he was

offering locomotives in Holland 40,000 guldens cheaper than the
Dutch engineering firms. It is a significant fact, also, that certain
textile factories in the South Ruhr, engaged in luxury trades, are
working overtime.

The year 1920 saw the emergence of a number of elements
which would become increasingly important in German politics: reparations; separatism and monarchism in Bavaria; the
realignment of the Left, accompanied by the withdrawal of the
Social Democrats from active participation in government for
nearly a generation; the increasing influence of what British
diplomats called 'the industrials'. But if there was one event
which exemplified the state of the post-war settlement in
Germany it was the Kapp *putsch*, from which the Right gained
no advantage but the Left appeared to learn no lesson either.

1921

Reparations: the Cannes and London Conferences – Wirth and Rathenau – the food situation, housing and health statistics – the March Action and its aftermath in Saxony – Max Hölz and his 'army' – Levi expelled from the KPD – result of the plebiscite in Silesia: Korfanty – murder of Erzberger – Bavaria shifts to the Right – Majority Socialists discuss coalition with People's Party – conditions in occupied areas of Rhineland and Ruhr – reparations: Germany declares inability to pay – industrialists offer help under stringent conditions

In July 1920, at Spa, the Allies had decided that final determination of the amount to be extracted from Germany in reparations required still further study. A special Reparations Commission was set up and ordered to report to the Allies by May 1921. But without waiting for the report to be delivered, they met again in Paris in the last week of January 1921 and made their own interim decisions. They fixed the amount of reparations to be paid over 42 years at 2 billion gold marks rising to 6 billion per annum; the first payment was to be made on 1 May 1921. In addition, they demanded 26 per cent of the proceeds of German exports. The German government counter-proposed a total liability of 30 billion gold marks, claiming that they had already paid two-thirds of this amount. The Allies met again in London on 21 February, dismissed the German counter-proposals and alleged that Germany was now in deliberate default. They demanded payment on the lines they had set down in Paris, on pain of sanctions. To emphasise the point, they occupied three more towns in the Ruhr and impounded the customs receipts of the occupied territories.

At the end of April the Reparations Commission produced its report, setting the total sum of German indebtedness at 132 billion gold marks. This figure was considerably modified, in effect, by the method of payment proposed, which was to be by three sets of bonds, the first to be delivered in July 1921 and the other two in November 1921. The result of this formula would have been to reduce the debt to 50 billion. At a third conference in London, which lasted from 3 April to 10 May, the reparations bill was finally fixed at the 132 billion figure, bearing interest at 6 per cent. An immediate payment of 1 billion was required and regular quarterly payments of 2 billion were to begin in January 1922. Moreover from November 1921 the Germans were to hand over 26 per cent of the proceeds of their exports, and deliveries in kind, as required by the treaty, were to continue unabated. These demands were presented on 5 May, together with an ultimatum – the so-called London Ultimatum – requiring unconditional acceptance of the whole and payment of 1 billion gold marks within 25 days.

Before the end of the London Conference the German Chancellor Fehrenbach (who had succeeded Müller in June 1920) resigned. Another coalition was formed under the Democrat Josef Wirth, just as the conference ended. The new coalition included one of the most memorable German politicians of the early Weimar days, Walter Rathenau. The head of the *Allgemeine Elektrizität Gemeinschaft* (AEG or General Electricity Company), Rathenau had been put in charge of the Raw Materials Section of the War Ministry in 1914 and served as Minister for Reconstruction in the Fehrenbach government. A sensitive and imaginative man, he was made vulnerable in the post of Foreign Secretary by the fact that he was Jewish. Both men recognised that there was no alternative for Germany but to accept the Allied terms and succeeded in convincing their colleagues not only to accept them but to fulfil them scrupulously: a 'policy of fulfilment', designed deliberately to prove that the terms were, in the end, quite unfulfillable. The first billion marks was paid on time by selling paper marks on foreign currency exchanges, thereby accelerating the inflation that would soon dominate all other economic considerations.

Price had an enormous territory and every conceivable subject to cover as the *Daily Herald* correspondent. It was perhaps not surprising that he did not write a great deal about the first Paris and London Conferences. He concentrated instead on the research which enable him to produce a major series of articles with which the *Daily Herald* would try to counter the Northcliffe Press campaign in February 1921, which insisted that Germany was merely 'shamming dead' and could perfectly well afford to pay reparations at the level set by the Paris Conference.

2 March

In the tenement building which I visited a few days ago, over 20 families were 'housed'. Yet there was only one water closet for the lot. There were, on average, more than four persons living and sleeping in one room. And this is no exception. The same applies to over 100,000 apartment dwellings in Berlin. Moreover, no less than 3,656 persons, registered as tubercular by the Berlin State Insurance Bureau, have no sleeping places of their own ... One old woman of over 60 I found living in a cellar. She was bent double owing to a chest infection. The air was damp as in a well and she could hardly save her clothes from rotting on her back. In the rooms of the somewhat more 'fortunate' families I found seven children living and sleeping and one expectant mother ... Most of the people I met seemed to have been so steeped in the drab misery of their surroundings that it had become second nature to them. Their senses had become atrophied, their desire to see anything beautiful or good in life had vanished. Worst of all, they neither knew, nor wanted to know the cause of the conditions under which they were forced to live. Their minds could not reach beyond their immediate surroundings or probe into the real cause: the profit system, the imperialist war, and the flooding of the land with worthless paper and debt. Nor did they realise the meaning of the London Conference, where the German bourgeoisie are meeting militarists and financiers of the Entente to contrive new indemnity schemes which will rivet the chains of wage slavery still tighter on their necks.

The effect of the present housing conditions in those parts of Berlin which I visited last week is seen in the terrible statistics of the Municipal Health Board. Of the 24,971 school children who are in their first year at school, 4,277 are anaemic, 1,127 have rickets, 1,532 are scrofulous, 534 tubercular, 1,750 suffer from heart and 1,079 from nervous troubles, 854 are mentally weak, 1,287 stammer, 1,814 have throat trouble, 3,364 have eye defects and 1,921 ear defects. In other words, one child in every five is suffering.

4 March

It is not German industry that is prosperous today but German capitalism. And that prosperity is artificial – a hothouse culture which will wither away at the first blast of the March wind of revolution. What better proof of this is the fact that, while German home markets are starving for essentials, the export trade is flourishing? The extremely low value of the mark has been a godsend to the German capitalist. As was to be expected, he is using his country's misfortunes to produce goods below the world market value and rake in the difference between this and the home price. The depreciation of the mark has, of course, made all German purchase of raw materials from abroad very costly. This, combined with the growth of the Stinnes super-trusts, which are out to starve all competitors off the home markets, has made it necessary to raise huge blocks of fresh capital. Hence capital inflation is the order of the day. Once again, the superficial observer sees in this a sign of prosperity instead of a sign of decay. For the raising of fresh capital is now done by the mechanical method of printing more money. In other words, the high dividends declared in Germany during the past year have simply enabled the German capitalists to draw still further from the state printing press ... Industrial capital is being converted more and more into what Marxists call 'unfixed capital' for speculation and finance purposes, and less and less into 'fixed capital', that is plant, stocks, wages ... The patriotism of the German super-trusts is such that they have higher prices for their own government than for the foreigner. Thus the railway deficit rises and is covered by the State printing press. In other words, the German workers pay in decreasing purchasing power. Can one then honestly say that German industry is flourishing? The only thing that is flourishing in Germany today is social parasitism. And it is supported and encouraged by the Allies.

5 March

A certain section of the English capitalist press is busy proclaiming that 'Germany is shamming dead', that her industries are showing 'immense progress' and that they are well able to pay the 300 milliard gold indemnity. Incidentally, a cynical suggestion can be

read between the lines that the British working man ought to copy
the example of the patient Fritz, who is unselfish enough to work
long hours and accept low wages.

But are Germany's industries flourishing? In answering this
question it is necessary to warn readers against accepting the other
extreme view – namely that Germany's industries are on the verge
of collapse. One cannot say that without considerable qualification.
Let me give a few facts. Germany's foreign trade, as shown in a
recent Government paper, is as follows:

Years	Imports	Exports
	(in 1,000 tons)	
1913	70,669	66,155
1919	9,924	12,065
1920 (January to June)	8,406	13,018

From these figures it is clear that, as far as trade balance is
concerned, Germany's foreign trade reached the bottom in 1919
and that since then a recovery has set in. But when we examine
the figures in detail what do we discover? One would expect to
find that after the vast destruction of wealth in Germany during
the war, the bulk of her present imports would be raw material,
to enable German industry to get on its legs again. As a matter
of fact the raw materials are only 25% of the total imports, as
against 45% in 1912. On the other hand there is a colossal
increase in the import of luxuries ... Further examination will
show that a great amalgamation process is going on. Trusts are
being converted into super-trusts. Germany is becoming visibly
Americanised in this respect. The whole economic life of the
country is being concentrated into the hands of a few great
magnates, chief of whom is Stinnes. New bank buildings are
being run up and new business premises. There is talk of having
skyscrapers in Berlin. What does all this mean? Superficial
observers conclude from this that Germany is becoming a second
Eldorado, that the British working man can follow the example
of his German comrade, and that the Allied governments can
turn round the thumbscrew once more. But it is a purely 'paper
prosperity' ... It is the economic basis of that gigantic instrument
of oppression which the Allies have forged to enslave Europe: the
Versailles Treaty.

12 March

In a recent number of the *Daily Mail* I find the following passage from the 'special investigator' in Germany: 'Low wages and long hours are the rule in industrial Germany today ... But notwithstanding the cheap wages, the majority of German workers do not show any signs of distress.' If he had gone to Pankow and Lichtenberg in Berlin East, or to the side streets of the West Saxon industrial cities, or if he had even walked about in any small provincial town in Germany with his eyes open, he would have seen children with pale faces, babies with rickety limbs, women in clothes which are half rags, men wearing the old army caps and overcoats which are the last bit of clothing they possess.

Let me in this article give some figures to show the extent to which the war and post-war capitalist economy has brought about the pauperisation of the working classes of Germany. The Alliance of the German Trade Unions has just completed an exhaustive investigation of the condition of its members in 30 industrial centres of Germany. According to this, 1,444,851 organised workmen and women in these centres are now earning wages eight times more than before the war; 817,706 are earning five to eight times more, and 37,496 less than five times more. In the same areas the cost of living, together with the minimum necessities of life, have risen an average of 15.5 times. In other words, even the best paid workers in Germany receive in real wages a little more than half of what they received before the war.

After collecting material from various sources I would say that for Berlin the weekly minimum expenditure for an unmarried workman is 158 marks, for a childless married couple 238 marks, and for a married couple with two children 330 marks. Now 330 marks weekly is only earned by the skilled mechanics and by miners working overtime underground. Other grades of labour in these days of short time cannot possibly earn more than 250 marks weekly ... When I use the word 'workers' I do not refer only to the manual labourers. The headworkers are in many respects worse off, because they have to keep up appearances. Not only the intellectuals, but also the small craftsmen are becoming proletarianised through the depreciation of money values and the rise of real values. German society is reorganising itself into the few who possess everything and the many who have nothing but their muscles and brains. The middle element is being squeezed into the latter. It is upon these that the demands of the Entente will fall with crushing severity.

15 March

... The catastrophic state of affairs is nowhere better seen than in the public finances. It is true that the Ordinary Budget appears to balance ... But there was also an Extraordinary Budget, which had an expenditure of 85.3 milliard marks (45.2 milliards of which was incurred by obligations under the Versailles Treaty) and a revenue of 3.4 milliard marks. Even in the Ordinary Budget the revenue contained items, such as single-time taxes and other forms of income which were not recurring, and had no right to be reckoned as revenue at all. On paper the German budget appears the most progressive – almost socialistic – budget in Europe. There is, for instance, a capital levy. No one may possess over 172,000 marks annual income more than he possessed before the war. But in practice only a fraction of this capital levy has ever been collected ...Will Lloyd George compel the collection of the capital levy, which was passed by the National Assembly in 1919 under the pressure of the socialists and the followers of Erzberger in the *Zentrum*? I don't think. For he probably knows that if he did it would mean the beginning of the end of capitalism in Central Europe ... Therefore, Mr Lloyd George is compelled to fall back on the legend that the German public, which in this case means the German working classes, is not taxed as highly as in other countries.

On 21 March the head of the British Section of the Inter-Allied Armistice Commission at Cologne, Major-General R. Haking wrote in one of his reports to the Chief of the Imperial General Staff:

If Europe, including England and France, is to be saved from utter chaos, the Allies must abandon this insane policy of utterly crushing Germany ... A stable democratic government in Germany is the only means of obtaining peace and order in Europe ... The great statesmen of the world at the present time must surely recognise that democratic government of a pronounced socialist type is certainly coming, and they have the power of guiding it into channels which will lead to the good of the people as a whole, instead of to a condition of anarchy and barbarism.[1]

But it was not long before anarchy and barbarism once again descended upon Germany.

At its second Congress, in June 1920, the Comintern had endorsed a policy of precipitating revolution in member countries even where popular support could not be assumed. Paul Levi, Luxemburg's successor as leader of the German Communist Party (KPD), had resigned as leader in protest. Early in March 1921 the Executive Committee of the Comintern (ECCI) sent the Hungarian Communist Bela Kun to Berlin to argue that the party must immediately exploit any crisis that might arise. Only days later the news came that police reinforcements had been sent to Saxony where, it was alleged, striking miners were stealing coal. The Berlin Executive of the KPD seized on this as a suitable pretext for attempting a full revolution in Germany. Attempts were made to raise sympathy strikes in Hamburg, Berlin and the Ruhr. Price documented the failure of these attempts, consigned to history as the March Action (*März Aktion*). On 26 March he went to Saxony to be able to report at first hand.

Leipzig, 29 March

I have just spent two days going on foot through disturbed districts of the province of Saxony ... The whole mining area is experiencing the horrors of civil war. No trains are running and all the mines and factories are standing idle. Many towns show in the streets signs of bitter fighting with barricades and dynamite explosion. In the course of my journey I have crossed the fronts of the two contending armed forces. I have been with the government troops (*Sicherheitspolizei*) and I have penetrated to the Red lines and spent Easter Day in the staff headquarters of the Reds. I have tracked down and seen in the flesh the semi-mythical Max Hölz, the Robin Hood of Central Germany who strikes terror into the minds of the propertied classes in these regions. The Prussian government has put 60,000 marks on his head.

31 March

The Red Army, which has sprung up in the Mansfeld mining district in the last ten days, is of mushroom growth, the result of a spontaneous outburst among the mining population. It has no firm root and may melt away like snow in a few days' time. It is neverthless proof that the miners of Saxony mean to fight for the right to prevent their peaceful valleys from being occupied by troops on the excuse that there is an exceptional amount of stealing going on in the mines. This stealing, if it exists to any extent, is the direct result of the lowered purchase power of labour, which is particularly bad in the Saxon mining areas, where semi-feudal conditions used to prevail till right up to the 1918 Revolution. It is as if Winston Churchill sent 5,000 Royal Irish Constabulary to occupy the Rhondda Valley on the excuse that the South Wales miners refused to accept a wage reduction. The result is the mining villages have risen to one man.

But of course the Government is in position to coerce the miners, having the use of artillery and machine-guns which the miners have not. But the miners, if poorly armed, have the advantage of knowing the country and if, as is probable in the course of the next few days, the government troops succeed in occupying the mining area, it will be easy for the miners to hide their rifles in the woods between Eisleben and Sangerhausen and wait for a better occasion.

This elementary outburst of the miners has been supported by the Communist Party, which has a majority in most of the local district councils. Here comes the tragedy of the whole business. The conflict in Saxony is a local conflict, and the victory of the miners is only possible if the Government climbs down, which it won't do and can't do unless the movement spreads throughout all Germany. The Communists feel compelled to work for an immediate sympathetic movement in other parts of Germany, particularly the Ruhr, Thuringia, Berlin. It is unfortunate, however, that in the Saxon mining area the movement has got largely out of the hands of the Communists into the hands of such people as Hölz, whose love of adventure is stronger than his political wisdom and his proletarian discipline. He is not a member of the Communist Party and is really following tactics of individual terror and the blowing up of public buildings by dynamiting. Hölz was repudiated by the

Communist party upon his refusal to obey party discipline after the Kapp *putsch* last year. .

Hölz claimed to have raised an 'army', largely consisting of unemployed miners, 2,500 strong, which moved from town to town, engaging in activities of little military value.

1 April

Continuing my tour in Saxony I reached the headquarters of the Red Army in the Mansfeld district, which was in the central hall of a Prussian Junker's country mansion. A political commissar received me and briefly explained what had been happening in the theatre of war ... We then sat down in the ancestral hall of the Prussian Junker and ate a meal of black bread and drank beer, fetched from the village, out of dainty cups which were formerly used for after-dinner coffee ... Suddenly the sound of a motor was heard and all was astir. A little man with fiery eyes and a shabby coat burst into the hall, followed by armed miners. It was the famous Hölz with his staff.

A war council with the participation of the political commissar now began. Couriers arrived and reported that the government troops had retired on Halle. The attack was called off and we prepared to rest for the night. Meanwhile I got into conversation with Hölz. He is a highly-strung, nervous man but speaks quietly and gives his commands with decision. 'Yes', he said to me, 'it is true. I do plunder banks but I never touch the savings of the poor. I have 60,000 marks from banks now – the price which the Government has put on my head. In each district I get to I have a local man who tells me who are the rich and profiteers, and I go for these.' When I asked him why he adopted these tactics he replied: 'We must show the Government that the Reds are a power to be reckoned with. Tomorrow the Government shall have something to think about.' Then he became suddenly melancholy. Someone began to sing a revolutionary song with a plaintive air. Just then a courier arrived and reported that considerable government forces had been observed moving from the west. They would probably attack the positions round the mansion at dawn. *'Donnerwetter'*, (Thunder and lightning) roared Hölz, rising like a lion at bay and throwing down a beautiful eighteenth-century French chair on which he was sitting. 'Tell the comrades to get ready to evacuate at once to the south, where reinforcements are expected from the Leuna works near Merseburg.' Amid much stir and suppressed excitement the Red troops gathered in the couryard with transport motor-lorries and machine-gun detachments. Together with Hölz and the political commissar I got into a motor. We were just about to start when Hölz suddenly roared, 'Halt! We have forgotten the dynamite.' Someone came along with a big tin case and plumped it down under my seat. Feeling uncomfortable I ventured to ask Hölz if it was safe. 'It won't explode unless the car upsets', came the comforting reply.

We started out, and the car jolted and bumped over ruts, half-pulled-down barricades, half-filled trenches, while I remembered the dynamite under my seat. After two hours in company with Hölz and his dynamite we stopped. The main body of the Red troops in the lorries went off to the south and we crept stealthily towards the west ... Hölz and the political commissar disappeared into the darkness and we[2] cautiously approached Merseburg, expecting to be shot at by pickets at any moment, for we were now between the Reds and the government troops ... We lay down exhausted in the first inn in Merseburg, and next morning woke to hear that the railway line between Merseburg and Halle had been blown up. And I thought of the dynamite on which I had sat the previous night.

Agency messages printed in the *Daily Herald* on 31 March gave the impression that the so-called Communist rising in Germany was gaining ground and had spread from the Ruhr to the Rhincland and Westphalia. Rail communications between a number of important cities had come to a halt, bridges had been blown up and telephone and telegraph wires cut between Berlin, Bremen and Hamburg. Nonetheless on 1 April the Central Committee of the KPD cancelled the strike call, blaming counter-revolutionaries for their defeat. Levi wrote a pamphlet criticising the party's conduct of the whole affair. He accused the party leaders of attempting to spread the revolt outside Saxony with no regard to the realities of the situation in the rest of Germany. The German Communists, he wrote, represented only a fraction of German labour: the most conscious fraction, certainly, but one not big enough to initiate mass action. He was expelled from the party and the Central Committee was purged of his supporters. Nationally, membership of the KPD fell by nearly half. On 20 April Price reported that all important centres in Saxony had been occupied by Bavarian units of the Reichswehr and large numbers of workers, especially known Communists, had been 'shot for attempted flight'.

One month earlier, on 20 March, a plebiscite had been held to determine the future of Upper Silesia, which had been awarded to Poland in the first draft of the Treaty of Versailles and the subject of one of the German government's few successes in getting a reconsideration of any of its terms. The result found 60 per cent of the population in favour of remaining with Germany and 40 per cent in favour of union with Poland. The issues dividing the voters were not really based on linguistic or nationalistic but rather on socio-economic grounds. German was the second if not the first language of virtually all Silesians. Those who spoke a Polish dialect (*Wasser Polen*) would not have been readily intelligible to educated Poles. Where there was contention it was because most of the coalfields were German-owned and conditions were very poor. Wages in the Upper Silesian coalfields were much lower than in the other coalfields of Germany (though not worse than those in Polish mines). At the beginning of May the Poles instigated a rising under Korfanty in which the insurgents were blatantly assisted by French occupation troops. Korfanty had already been involved in an earlier rising, in August 1920, which had been harshly suppressed by the German government, thereby reinforcing resentment, where it existed, of the German presence. French support for a Polish solution was based more on anti-German than on pro-Polish sentiment. In addition the French claimed that there was a real danger of some kind of German alignment with the Bolshevik government and of a revival of German militarism based on possession of the Silesian coalfields. A Polish Upper Silesia would create a useful *cordon sanitaire*.

In the second week of May Price toured through the Polish-occupied parts of Upper Silesia and on 16 May he interviewed Korfanty, who told him that he would not be responsible for the results if the Allies did not award the whole industrial area of Upper Silesia to Poland. Price found that the local trade union leaders and socialists with whom he talked were 'whole-heartedly with Korfanty'; they insisted that the rising was backed by the majority of Upper Silesian Labour against 'Prussian officialdom and German capitalists'. But his conversations also led him to conclude that their beliefs were being 'exploited by unscrupulous Polish demagogues in the interests of Polish national chauvinism and the Paris *Bourse*, which is out to liquidate France's war debt to America by getting control of the Upper Silesian mines'.

24 May

The Polish national movement in Upper Silesia is artificial and of recent date. The original inhabitants, the *'Wasser Polen'*, had before the war no strong national attachments. They formed the bulk of the peasantry and of the miners and unskilled labourers. The skilled labour, the *intelligentsia* and the government officials were, for the most part, Germans. Then the coalowners began to import cheap Polish labour from across the Russian frontier. The German artisans began, not unnaturally, to look on the latter as blacklegs. The sharpening of the class conflict was the opportunity for the Polish nationalists, backed by the Paris *Bourse*, to divide and rule Upper Silesian Labour. From this time on the Polish miners and immigrants from over the border were to be emancipated from German capitalism by the Bank of France and Pierpont Morgan!

In the German Revolution of 1918 there was a temporary glimmer of sanity in Upper Silesia. Labour, both skilled and unskilled, began to flock to the German trade unions and to the Independent Socialist Party. A wage movement began which reached its climax in August 1919 in a strike. This strike was suppressed by the Majority Socialist Hürsing with hideous and relentless brutality. Thus during 1920 the French-subsidised Polish propaganda had good ground to work upon. Korfanty became the man who was going to deliver Upper Silesian Labour from Prussian junkerdom and from the German coalowner. The miners left the German Independent Socialist Party and flocked to the PPS [Polish Socialist Party]. They also joined the Polish trade unions. But they did this not out of any belief in Polish nationalism but because they thought that the Polish parties and the trade unions would assist them more effectively in their struggle against the rising tide of Prussian reaction and the *Orgesch*. If one looks at the social aspect of the Upper Silesian problem one finds that the quarrels over the Polish and German territorial rights lose much of their meaning. The sovereignty of this or that 'profiteer republic' in Upper Silesia is a question merely of interest to the Paris and Berlin *Bourses*.

In September 1921, on the basis of advice from the Council of the League of Nations, the Allied Supreme Council awarded the industrial area of eastern Upper Silesia to Poland. Germany received the larger – but industrially less valuable – western territory of the province. In the same month one of the few achievements of diplomacy between France and Germany was nearing its conclusion, and in the first week of October an agreement between the two countries was signed at Wiesbaden. This was the climax of discussions which had been in progress throughout the summer between Rathenau and the French Industry Minister, Loucheur. The Wiesbaden agreement set up a semi-private Germany company which was to deliver building materials to a semi-private French company, the value of which was to be credited to Germany's Reparations account. It had been the possibility of achieving a mitigation of the Allied demands by such means that had motivated Rathenau to enter the Cabinet in the first place, and it remained a unique example of a settlement negotiated rather than dictated.

The year 1921, in which the determination of the Allies to crush Germany completely became manifest, was also a year in which Right-wing patriotic and often also secret organisations flourished and proliferated. One of these was the *Organisation Consul*, to which reference has already been made, whose members were largely drawn from the former *Erhardt* Brigade which had played the leading role in the Kapp *putsch*. Its headquarters were in Munich and it had a membership of several thousands organised in 14 districts throughout Germany. Its *raison d'être* was political murder, notably the murder of German democrats. Both President Ebert and Chancellor Wirth were on its blacklist.[3] In June the Independent Socialist leader Karl Gareis was shot dead in Munich.

13 June

The murder of Gareis, the Bavarian Independent Socialist leader, has caused a revulsion of bourgeois feeling against the chauvinist and capitalist reaction. Unfortunately the proletarian parties as usual fail to find a common ground of action to take advantage of the public sentiment in order to stem the reactionary tide ... At yesterday's conference of the leaders of the three Left parties at Munich the Majority Socialists contended that any widespread action by the workmen would merely be utilised by their opponents for violence and perhaps even a *coup d'état*. The three parties could not unite on a programme. Meanwhile Kahr, the Bavarian Premier, while expressing great sorrow at the murder, continues repressive measures, forbidding workmen's public assemblies and suppressing the *Kampf*, an Independent Socialist newspaper.

Little more than two months later the Centre Party leader, Mathias Erzberger, was assassinated by Consul agents in the Black Forest. Erzberger had been the moving spirit behind the Reichstag (Peace) Resolution in 1917, the head of the German delegation to the armistice talks in 1918, foremost in arguing for acceptance of the Versailles Treaty in 1919 and, as Finance Minister in the Bauer government in 1920, responsible for introducing for the first time a capital levy.

August[4]

... When the history of contemporary Germany comes to be written, I believe that Erzberger's role will be that of Mirabeau who, while acting as the spokesman of the declining class, had neverthe-less greater wisdom and foresight than the majority of his masters ... For he possessed a keen political sense and understood, as few of his contemporaries, that concessions had to be made to save the house from falling about the owners' heads. After being an uncompromising 'annexationist' at the beginning of the war, he was one of the first to see that Germany's defeat was inevitable and foreboded the fall of the German dynasties, and he made haste to secure for the middle classes, his patrons, the sole control of the new state. In order to do this he knew that he must induce the middle classes definitely to break with the monarchists and, what was for them even harder, submit to heavy – indeed almost crushing – taxation ... And yet these very measures were carried through in the teeth of the opposition of the middle-class parties of the Reichstag and only reached the statute book with the aid of the Majority Socialist Party. Moreover their passage was a signal for a campaign of personal vilification, unknown even in German political history, from that very class which the measures were intended to save.

There were few more remarkable figures in contemporary Germany than this shrewd, far-sighted, erstwhile Catholic schoolmaster of the Rhineland who saw the day of trial and visitation coming to the class which he served, who warned, who prepared, who acted, and who, as if to prove once more the irony of history, was struck down by the very class which he tried to save.

16 September

Last night's sensational news that the Bavarian police were aware of the identity of Erzberger's murderers is followed by the statement that the assassins are members of the *Erhardt* Brigade. This notorious force, which shot down thousands of workers in 1919 and took part in the Kapp *putsch* last year, was supposed to have been dissolved, but has in reality been illegally existing under the protection of the Bavarian government. Evidence is held that the murderers, who are Munich students, were in that city until Saturday evening, evidently feeling quite safe under the wing of Herr Pöhner, the [Bavarian] government's Chief of Police. The discovery of the clues is entirely due to the Wurtemburg, Baden and Berlin police, and there is more than a suspicion that Pöhner's police have been doing everything to cover up the existence of the murder bureau which for two years past has been assassinating republicans, from Communists to Erzberger.

Ever since the Kapp *putsch* there had been a pronounced shift to the Right in Bavaria under its new premier, Gustav von Kahr. The state's already strong separatist tendency had been reinforced by a revival of monarchist sentiment. There had been threats of secession if the north 'turned Bolshevik'. Among the 'patriotic' associations based in Bavaria which began to attract attention in 1921 was the NSDAP (National Socialist German Workers' Party). Originally a small post-war association which Adolf Hitler joined in 1919, he renamed it when he assumed its leadership in the following year. After the March Action a state of emergency had been declared in Bavaria and Left-wing meetings and newspapers banned or strictly controlled. After the murder of Erzberger the Berlin government had issued a decree – 'the Republic in Danger' – making incitement to change the constitution by violent means a criminal offence and suspending nine newspapers, two of which were Bavarian. The Bavarian government refused to accept or carry it out and the decree was stigmatised as 'the first step towards a Soviet regime' in some quarters.[5] Mass meetings were held at which all blame for inflation and for the general disorder of the country was laid on the Jews. The *Einwohnerwehr* was now estimated to number 300,000, armed with machine-guns as well as rifles, and with aircraft concealed in the rural areas. The Allies had long since (June 1920) demanded the disbandment of the *Einwohnerwehr* and Bavaria had notionally complied in July 1921, but another so-called emergency organisation, *Notbann*, was set up in its stead, nominally under police control, but with the same objectives as the *Einwohnerwehr*.

In a trial of strength between Berlin and Munich in September 1921, Berlin wanted to see an end put to the Bavarian state of emergency on the grounds that it exceeded the powers of the *Landtag*, but Berlin was reluctant to exacerbate the situation by repealing it over the head of the *Landtag*, and it was hoped that the Bavarians would do it themselves. The Bavarian Chancellor, von Kahr, proposed that if the incitement decree were amended to apply equally to organisations and newspapers of the Left as to those of the Right, Bavaria would consider raising the state of emergency. But even that proposal was defeated in the *Landtag* and on 10 September von Kahr and his government resigned. A new government, more inclined to reconciliation with Berlin, was formed under Count Hugo von Lerchfeld. The incitement decree, amended to suit Bavarian political susceptibilities, was accepted and von Lerchfeld agreed to abolish the state of emergency from 15 October, although the summary tribunals established under it were to be retained. Even this was too much for the Bavarian police chief, Pöhner, who thereupon resigned.[6]

20 September

The conflict between Bavaria and the rest of Germany has taken a new turn within the last 24 hours. The Bavarian Catholic Party has suddenly veered round to the side of reaction again. Apparently the cause is to be found in the revelations of the Prussian Commissioner for Public Safety about his attempt to get at the Kapp rebels in Munich. Bavarian Catholics are always very sensitive about the interference of Prussian law officers in their country. They now demand that Bavaria shall have its own president, with large powers independent of the central Government of Germany. The Congress of the Majority Socialist Party, which is opening at Görlitz, will be important as indicating how far the largest Left party is prepared to go to force the present impossible situation between Munich and Berlin to an issue.

Görlitz, 22 September

In this Lower Silesian town, where the German Majority Socialists are holding their annual conference, the next phase of the internal struggle in Germany between Bavarian reaction and the Central Government is being decided, for it is no exaggeration to say that the course of this struggle depends on the policy of this greatest [largest] of German parties. A fortnight ago the question was how to bring Bavarian reaction to its knees in the shortest time. Today it has been: 'Shall we go into government with the Stinnes [People's] Party (DVP) and save the shadowy form of the republican constitution of Germany, or shall we stay out and save what remains of our socialist programme?' The party leaders put up a plausible case for government coalition with the Stinnes party. That party, said Hermann Müller, contained many elements besides industrial magnates, and signs of progress in its ranks had been apparent lately ... But I find these optimistic views not held by a number of delegates. Those who come from Frankfurt, Thuringia, West Saxony and Silesia have a dread that the young Majority Socialist lady who goes out for a ride on the Stinnes tiger will return from the ride in the manner well known in the story.

These views were expressed in speeches in a tone which seemed to suggest that opposition to the party officials was slowly crystallising. Nevertheless the leaders had an easy task today to persuade the Congress that the only way to save the republican form of government in Germany is to enter the government with the constitutional monarchists, and that the isolation of the Kappists on the one side and the Communists on the other is the first task of the party. The resolution in favour of entering the government with the Stinnes party was passed by 290 votes to 67. A certain number of delegates voted for this resolution, imagining that amendments imposing conditions for entry into the coalition – especially on the matter of property taxation – would be voted on. The party Executive, however, cleverly passed over these amendments, and now the party is virtually delivered, bound hand and foot, to the Executive, which is in a position to make what terms it likes with the Stinnes party.

Görlitz, 26 September

Reviewing the Congress, one may say that the party leaders managed to get their way, but not without a struggle with the opposition which, for the first time in the history of the party, is beginning to crystallise. The Majority Socialists remain the party of the German masses, and in the present state of the Left-wing parties is likely to remain so. Its great drawback is the bureaucracy, composed of men demoralised by contact with propertied classes in government offices; but against this the rank and file of the party, while maintaining reserve towards the Communists, nevertheless are ready to work with all parties who demand the serious tackling of the social problem. It may be that the decision of last Tuesday to work with the Stinnes party will bring opposition in the provinces into open conflict with the leaders and prepare the way for reunion with the progressive labour elements so tragically divided in the past.

The Majority Socialists and the Independent Social Democrats had pulled together after the murder of Erzberger and both parties had experienced a considerable increase in membership in the course of the year. The Majority Socialists now numbered 1,200,000 and the Independents 450,000. But in the event neither a reunited Social Democratic Party nor the People's Party were included in the next government. The partition of Silesia brought about the resignation of the Wirth Cabinet on

22 October. Wirth agreed to carry on until a new ministry could be formed and this he eventually achieved himself. But Wirth made no secret of his forebodings about the effect of the partition. The mark fell and the cost of living rose by 84 per cent between September and October. Thereafter price increases of 50–70 per cent a week were not uncommon. All the elements likely to lead to civil disturbance and revolution were present again in Germany, he said in a speech to the Reichstag shortly after taking office.[7]

In November 1921 Price was asked by an agent of Krupps to go the French-occupied zones in the Ruhr and Rhineland and report on the alleged atrocities being committed by black occupying troops against the local population. In a note with his own cuttings of the articles which resulted, he wrote: 'I did so, but not in the sense desired by Krupps.' (The firm of Krupps had been associated with the extreme Right wing of German politics since the 1890s, when Alfred Krupps financed the foundation of the Navy League. A later chief director, Alfred Hugenburg, would lead the DNVP into an alliance with Hitler.) The articles which Price wrote were not printed until the end of the year but are included here because they describe conditions in November.

17 December

Among the principal grievances of the Rhinelanders is the presence of coloured troops in their country. In actual fact, one of the most important arms of the French occupation force is the colonial army of Moroccans, Algerians, Berbers, Senegalese and the natives of Cochin China. Now the presence of these natives has different effects on the minds of the Rhinelanders, varying among certain classes of the population. For instance, while listening to a well-to-do German burgomaster in a Rhineland town talking about 'black and yellow beasts sent here to trample on our "kultur"' one seems to hear the voice of the hero of Amritsar discoursing on the natives of India, or a leader of an Orange Lodge on Sinn Fein ... Much more serious are the charges of brutality and rape of German women by black and yellow troops on the Rhine. I have received a considerable amount of evidence in the towns that I have visited showing that these occurences do take place wherever these troops are stationed. Exact figures are impossible to obtain, and I have no reason to believe that they are more numerous in the areas occupied by the native armies than in those occupied by whites ... but it is also a fact that a single case of rape by a black soldier arouses greater bitterness than a dozen cases by white soldiers ... On the other hand it is a fact that among other sections of the population of the Rhineland there is no hatred whatever against the coloured troops. Local Social Democratic and trade union leaders, or at least those of them who have not come under the influence of Pan-German propaganda, assured me that the workmen in several places had quite friendly relations with the coloured troops. In the villages of the Trier district the smaller peasants have asked the Moroccan soldiers to help them in the vine harvest, and often a sturdy darkie in French colonial uniform can be seen carrying a German child on his arm, and playing with him in the village street when he is off duty ... Progressive elements of German labour in the Rhineland are fully aware that the Pan-German propaganda against the 'black terror' is only a chauvinist agitation aiming at another war. They know that the black soldier is not an enemy but a friend ...

5 January 1922

In the course of a journey through the areas of the Rhineland occupied by the Allied armies I have had occasion to converse with all classes of the German population, and am thus able to record the state of feeling prevailing in these quarters. On the surface, life in the Rhineland seems fairly normal and but for the displays of the military forces of the Allies one would not observe at first sight anything out of the ordinary. But on closer examination one finds that the civil population is mentally depressed and suffering from severe physical disabilities which, when added to those prevalent at present throughout the whole of Germany, are driving many sections of the population to the verge of despair ... The grievances of the local German population can roughly be divided into two kinds – those caused by physical disabilities arising from military requisitions and from political influences aiming at a permanent change in the status of the Rhineland; and those caused by the moral effects of the presence in the Allied armies of non-European troops, with which I have dealt in a former article.

Now I have obtained a certain number of statistics, which seem to show that the Inter-Allied High Commission in the Rhineland has been unduly severe in the imposition of burdens on the population, and has in some cases gone beyond what is necessary for the satisfaction of the needs of the occupying forces ... Towns of 50,000 inhabitants, which used to have accommodation for a garrison of 6,000 now have from 10,000–12,000 soldiers quartered on them. The result is that the housing problem, acute throughout all Germany, has become catastrophic in the Rhineland ... The inhabitants, moreover, are forced to bear the cost of the occupation and to pay for the privilege of seeing their houses and public buildings taken away ... For instance I found that considerable bitterness had arisen over the fact that the French in Mainz, Coblenz and Trier had been requisitioning whole buildings for not strictly military purposes. They have settled all sorts of persons in these properties, together with their families, because they are connected with the 'section économique française' and kindred bodies which exist for the purpose of bringing the Rhineland, by devious means, within the French economic system.

On the whole I heard much less complaints against the British army of occupation ... I think it is beyond doubt that the British authorities have been considerate to the inhabitants, as far as is possible. The American Army, which used to be the most popular with the inhabitants, is now much less so, although it is more popular than the French, for the Americans are known not to have any direct political aims in the Rhineland ... But the fact that the American army has changed now from a conscript to a mercenary one, and moreover that most of the American soldiers in the Rhineland are mainly engaged in having a good time and in buying up the country, has caused demoralisation in one section of the inhabitants and indignation in another section ... The jovial if ruinous activities of the Americans, though unpopular, are not resented with such bitterness as the political intrigues and pin-prick policies of the French ... In one district of the French area the French military authorities have demanded complete statistics of the mineral wealth, present and prospective, the forest wealth, the method of exploitation of that wealth by the German Department of Forestry, the plan of work for the next ten years, the number of factories, their output, plant, and their balance sheets. It is obvious that the plan is to prepare for an economic annexation such as has virtually taken place in the Saar. In fact, there is no doubt in my mind that should the French occupation of the Rhineland continue

for a few years longer, its economic absorption into France will
become an accomplished fact.

While Price was in the Rhineland the next development in the
endemic reparations crisis was beginning to dominate public
attention. The Government declared that Germany would not
be able to pay the January instalment of 2 billion gold marks.
On 4 November representatives of all the major members of the
Alliance of German Industries held a meeting after which they
announced that they could raise the money themselves. But
their conditions included the denationalisation of the railways
and economies in public spending so severe that the Wirth
government felt it could not accept them, although it agreed to
continue with talks about credits. The Reparations Commission had sent a delegation to Berlin to make its own assessment
of Germany's ability to pay. On 19 November Stinnes went to
London, on what was officially stated to be private business, but
with the full knowledge of the Chancellor. In fact the Berlin
correspondent of the London *Times* reported (22 November)
that it was generally believed in Berlin financial circles that he
had gone 'to see what can be done by way of raising a foreign
loan' and that Wirth had, in effect, corroborated this impression. Meanwhile, the Reparations Commission decided that the
state of the German economy was due to an ever-increasing
floating debt combined with inadequate taxation, and that if the
Government would just take the appropriate steps, Germany
could perfectly well pay the January instalment. On that note
the delegation left Berlin. Stinnes remained in London until 24
November and rumours continued to circulate: he was not only
trying to raise a loan but he was trying to obtain some
mitigation of the terms of the London Ultimatum. Moreover, he
was thought to be negotiating with a group of British industrialists for co-operation in the resumption of trade relations with
Russia.

On 15 December the German government sent another
Note to the Allies declaring inability to pay, apparently in the
hope that a declaration of virtual bankruptcy would automatically relieve it of the liability. The Reparations Commission
remained unmoved.

27 December [8]

This refusal is undoubtedly due to the insistence of the French members of the Commission. A semi-official communiqué issued yesterday states that foreign values in the possession of the Government cover only a fraction of the amount needed in January. It says also that the Reparations Commission considers Germany's production and prospective taxation insufficient to cover the coming liabilities. In view of this, the Government has proposed to the Commission negotiations for an international loan. No reply has yet been given by the Commission to this suggestion. This is where Herr Stinnes comes in. It will be remembered that through the Alliance of German Industries he had offered to find the money for the reparations payment on certain conditions. These conditions include: the handing over at once of the state railways of Germany to private syndicates; the reduction of the number of state employees; subsequent transference of the posts, telegraphs and of all state- and municipally-owned works and industries to private trusts; and finally the complete independence of the trusts and industrial departments of the state from all political influences, and the abandonment of schemes for nationalisation and state control of industry. The Wirth government refused the terms. But the Wirth government has got to find the money ... The Wirth government has got to get credits from abroad. America has declared definitely against loans to Germany to enable her to pay France and Britain (which are already heavily in debt to America). Therefore, the new credit must come either from France or from Britain, though probably America would be in either case the real, though indirect source of the money. Now Stinnes' policy is one of Anglo-German financial co-operation, in opposition to Dr Rathenau's policy of eo-operation with France. Stinnes, then, has gone to London to try to arrange for a British credit that will make possible the reparations payment. And this credit arrangement is to link up with his project for capturing the German state services for private capitalism. He will try to capture the leading British statesmen for his plans to denationalise Germany's public services and control them through trusts, as a guarantee for English credit to Germany, whereby he will become broker between London and Berlin. Stinnes has the support of the British Embassy and of the British experts on the Reparations Commission. The French members are said to be nervous but they have no alternative suggestion except the usual one of the coercion and dismemberment of Germany.

30 December [9]

The German government maintains silence regarding its intentions as to the coming reparations payments. Meanwhile, it is known here that the Government possesses 200 million gold marks, foreign values, but from a trustworthy source I hear that this is being reserved for the February payments. It seems that the Government made no provision for the January payment and can only fall back on the gold reserve of the *Reichsbank* to meet this liability.

With the object of finding out how far gold reserve is available for reparations, I obtained an interview yesterday with the vice-president of the *Reichsbank*, Herr Glasenapp. 'From the legal standpoint', he said, 'the German government is not in a position to lay hands on the gold reserve, because the *Reichsbank* is a private institution. By the Bank Act of 1875 the *Reichsbank* acquired the privileges of monopoly note issue, for which concession the Government has the right of inspection: a control which, however, is vested not in the Finance Minister but in the person of the Chancellor. The rights of the Government over the *Reichsbank* are political and do not touch the private rights of the bank, which remain the property of the shareholders. To lay hands on the gold reserve for reparations would be a flagrant breach of the rights of private property. Moreover, of 180 million marks, the capital of the *Reichsbank*, 34 millions have been acquired by non-Germans since the war.'

Glasenapp's view, however, does not seem to be shared in German industrial circles. Thus last Monday Stinnes' organ, *Lokalanzeiger*, stated: 'The question of using gold reserve is receiving serious consideration in responsible quarters.' It is altogether in keeping with the policy of Herr Stinnes to weaken the German government and the Reichsbank by allowing the Entente to touch its gold reserve, thereby removing the last obstacle to his undisputed hegemony of German economic life. It cannot be too strongly emphasised that under the present conditions here the demands of the Entente for more indirect taxation, the abolition of state subsidies on bread and the denationalising of the railways would fall exclusively on the shoulders of German labour and would assist the German industrial magnates who would become economic dictators. German railwaymen are already in the throes of a struggle to secure a rise of wages to balance the rise in the cost of living. Thus the Allies' demands for 'sound finances' will be equivalent to denying an elementary standard of living for German labour, and the German government will use the Allies as the stalking horse for a campaign against this standard.

At the end of the year Price published a long article, 'The Philosophy of Indemnities', extracts from which follow, for the first volume of the newly-founded British Left-wing journal, *Labour Monthly*.

Labour Monthly, Vol. I (July–December 1921)

The Allied demand for indemnities is in direct relation to Allied financial embarrassments. The debates in the French Chamber show this also very clearly. In introducing the Budget for 1922 the French Finance Minister said: 'The financial convalescence of France depends entirely upon the punctuality of the German indemnity payment for 1922. Only then will it be possible for us to avoid new loans.'

The Versailles Treaty is thus only one aspect of the post-war attempt of the victors to throw the burden of inflation on the vanquished and to sacrifice the exchange of real values for one-sided contributions, thus upsetting still further the economic balance between countries. The vanquished in the war, however, consist not of Germany only. They include also Russia, the Baltic States, the new satellites of France arisen from the ruins of the Austrian Empire, and even Poland herself, that proud lackey of the *Banque de France* in Eastern Europe. And can even France, with her tribute yet unpaid on the war loans taken up in America and England, be regarded strictly as victorious? She is like a profligate, speculating heavily in the hopes of paying off a huge debt. Can England, with her debt unpaid from Italy and France, with America pressing her for interest, and with Germany threatening to undersell her on every neutral market, be called victorious either?

The only victors have been the bondholders, particularly in America. The vanquished have been labour and the small middle classes of all countries, particularly on the European mainland.

During the year 1921 Bavaria had come into increasingly open conflict with the Reich government and became additionally notorious for harbouring the Right-wing murder organisation, Consul. The award of the most profitable areas of Upper Silesia did little for the future of German–Polish relations. The KPD demonstrated that it was completely out of touch with political reality at the cost of many lives in the Ruhr and Saxony. The level of reparations set at the London Conference was as unrealistic as the March Action had been. The polarisation of German society continued.

1922

Inflation as an instrument of policy – the Cannes Conference sets conditions – the Genoa Conference and the Treaty of Rapallo – murder of Rathenau: the Law for the Defence of the Republic – inflation becomes hyper-inflation – the relationship of reparations and inter-Allied debt – industrialists put pressure on government – re-unification of the German socialist parties – rise of reactionary and nationalist parties – condition of working-class families – Wirth succeeded as Chancellor by Cuno – Bavaria, nationalists and Fascism

The year began, as the last one had ended, under the shadow of reparations and came to be remembered for an inflation then unparalleled in European history.

Public finance in Germany had traditionally been based on borrowing. Money was printed under the guise of borrowing from the *Reichsbank* and interest charges on borrowing were financed out of the Ordinary Budget. Until the revolution the right to impose direct taxation had been reserved to the states (*Länder*) and the Central Government drew its resources from indirect taxation and paper money. In 1922 machinery for the central collection of direct taxes had not long been in existence and did not yet function well. In any case the Germans were notoriously '*steuerscheu*' (tax shy). Taxation had supplied only 6 per cent of the cost of the war to Germany; the rest was found by borrowing, that is, by printing money. Price inflation during the war was seen as a form of taxation and, moreover, had worked quite well as a means of suppressing private consumption and thereby releasing capacity for war production. But when the war ended the level of taxation that would have been needed to pay in a non-inflationary manner (such as by direct taxes) for the running costs of the state plus reparations, would have had to be unacceptably high. Direct taxation was in any case not collected at source (except in the case of income tax on workmen's wages) but on the basis of declarations made in advance. In the interval between declaration and collection the currency had usually depreciated but the tax remained based on the old valuation and so came in at a fraction of the value originally calculated.

Furthermore, the vengeful mood of the victorious Allies ensured that reparations were far higher than anything the German government could have expected when it accepted liability for war damage on the basis of the Fourteen Points. Nothing had been said, then, about German liability for the war pensions of all the Allies. But the reparations bill was not presented for two years, and during those years Germany was already paying all the other penalties – deliveries in kind and occupation costs – which had been laid down in the Versailles Treaty and which the German government was obliged to pay. By the beginning of 1922 German credit-worthiness had effectively been destroyed, and uncertainty as to how much harder the Allies might turn the screw had destroyed the incentive of successive German governments to attempt to deal radically with successive economic crises.

The British and French Premiers met briefly in London just before Christmas 1921 in the knowledge that Germany was simply not going to be able to pay either the January or the February reparations instalments and that another conference of all the Allies would be needed to decide what to do about it. This took place at Cannes between 6 and 14 January 1922. All the Allies were represented and the USA sent an observer. Rathenau was summoned to appear before the conference. His arrival coincided with a French ministerial crisis which resulted in the replacement of the French representative at the conference, the then Prime Minister Briand, by his successor, the ominously hardline former President of the Republic, Raymond Poincaré. Rathenau succeeded in persuading the conference that Germany must at least be allowed a moratorium so far as the cash payments due in January and February were concerned. But the moratorium was made conditional on Germany calling a halt to the printing of money, on stabilising the exchange rate and on balancing her budget.

17 January

The conditions imposed by the Entente on Germany for the preliminary moratorium is likely to create a crisis in Germany's internal finances. The plan which the German government must produce in 14 days for balancing the budget is being worked out. Judging from a statement by Rathenau to a correspondent of the *Kölnische Zeitung* the German government has a simple plan of doubling existing taxation, raising the post and railway rates and abolishing the bread subsidies. Every one of these measures will fall with crushing severity on German labour ... This morning a semi-official statement announces that as the result of pressure by the Entente governments it has been decided to raise the price of bread by 75 per cent. It is an open secret here that the rise in railway and postal rates at the beginning of the month was due to the same cause ... The Majority Socialist and Independent press still seem to regard Cannes as a partial success for Germany ... At the same time both these papers are uneasy about raising the bread prices and refer to the necessity of a new campaign to raise wages ... Besides a new wage campaign it is obvious now that the German Socialist parties will be compelled by the rank and file to press for a state mortgage on German industry, which means capturing for the community through the state apparatus a portion of the profits of production.

25 January

The sands of time available for Germany to produce her plan for balancing her budget are running out. Yet no agreement is reached and the burning question still remains: on whose shoulders is the burden of fresh taxation to rest? One central point of interest during the last few days has been in the negotiations between the *Zentrum* majority and the Socialists on the question of a state mortgage on industry. Supporters of the state mortgage policy, the three socialist parties, have not sufficient votes to put the matter through without the support of the Catholic *Zentrum*. At the same time the unadulterated capitalist parties have not sufficient votes to carry through their design of throwing the burden upon the masses through consumers' taxes and of mortgaging state properties to trusts, according to the plan of Hugo Stinnes. Thus a parliamentary deadlock is reached and the usual wearisome Cabinet crisis has already begun ... The preponderating factor in the decision about to be made is the Entente; and I have strong reason to believe that British influences have been at work to secure a solution of the financial crisis by a compulsory loan to the German government. This solution has been discussed by the capitalist press here for some days past in a way which indicates that those capitalist circles in Germany which have connections with British financial houses regard the compulsory internal loan as a means of escaping 'the dangerous socialist experiment' of a state mortgage.

28 January

At the eleventh hour the crisis of the past week has been settled on lines foreshadowed in my last message. The burden of balancing the Budget, demanded by the Allies at Cannes, will fall mainly on the German labouring classes ... The Majority Socialists have agreed to the balancing of the Budget by a forced loan of one milliard gold marks (£50 million). The owners of capital must lend this sum to the state, receiving no interest in the first three years and 3 per cent later. The mere fact that the loan is to be issued in gold means, with the falling mark, that increasing amounts must be found by the taxpayers for interest and sinking fund. The Majority Socialists started out to hunt the capitalist lion in his den; they have been hunted by him instead. The defeat of the Majority Socialists on the field of finance is absolute. On the other hand their leaders seem satisfied that they have won a political victory. They have kept the Wirth government in power and they have kept their seats in it without so far having to grant any concessions to the Stinnes [People's] party.

One of the most persistent targets of the the 'Stinnes party' had been the German railway system. A bill to rationalise the financial and control arrangements for the railways had already been drawn up and was already causing uneasiness among railway workers. Sporadic strikes at the turn of the year led to a comprehensive railway strike throughout North Germany, Silesia and Bavaria early in February to save the eight-hour day and revise the wages structure. The strike was not supported by either the Majority or the Independent Socialist parties on the grounds that the men's grievances were already being discussed by a Committee of the Reichstag. Because railwaymen were technically state officials they were threatened with dismissal and some of their leaders were arrested.

15 February

The Wirth Cabinet is faced with a new crisis. No fewer than four no-confidence votes will be before the Reichstag when it meets again tomorrow. The Government is attacked from the extreme Left because it has been too hard on the strikers and from the Right because it has not been hard enough ... Three issues lie behind the crisis. The first is the policy of the Government dealing with the strike. The second is how to secure a majority for taxation compromise. The third, which is closely bound to the second, is what political concessions does the Stinnes party demand for further benevolent neutrality towards the Government? There is no doubt the Majority Socialists will do all they can to save Wirth.

Three weeks later the answer to the third question was clear.

11 March

Abolition by the Government of the last remains of public control over industry and commerce is only one of the conditions on which the People's Party has agreed to the taxation compromise ... decided upon in principle last January ... In addition to the condition above mentioned the Stinnes party laid down the following terms: moneys received from new taxes and the forced loan must not be used for balancing the railway and postal and telegraph budgets, nor for the purchase of foreign money values for reparation payments. It must be used to compensate private firms for supplying goods under treaty obligations to the Entente, also for the payment of the costs of the occupation of the Rhineland. State administration must be simplified and cheapened ... Nevertheless, these conditions were accepted by the government parties, including the Majority Socialists.

In an article, 'Germany After Cannes', printed in Volume II of *Labour Monthly* (January–June 1922) Price concluded:

Wherever one looks one sees the process at work – the liquidation, under pressure of the Entente, of social measures which tend to raise the standard of the German workers and the imposition on them of the sole burdens of balancing the Budget. If the German workers reply to this by starting a wage campaign to cover the new imposts, they will at once be met by threats of mass dismissals and the prospect of unemployment without state benefit. German labour is to pay the war indemnities, restore North France (as far as the French business interests want it restored) and create the standard of living for Europe under the international consortium. In order to do this the eight-hour day and the right to strike must go. The Versailles Treaty will then have been revised by magnanimous England, curbing the revengeful chauvinism of France.

The Allied conference at Cannes had not confined its discussions to reparations. It also concerned itself with the wider question of the economic reconstruction of Europe and decided to invite representatives of Soviet Russia to the next meeting. This opened at Genoa on 10 April, attended by delegates of 29 states, including Russia. Almost the only outcome of the official conference, which lasted until 19 May, was a non-aggression pact. But taking advantage of their first opportunity to meet, the Foreign Ministers of Germany and Russia, Rathenau and Tchicherin, concluded a Treaty of Recognition and Commerce at Rapallo, not far from Genoa. There had, in fact, been informal contacts earlier in the year. On 3 February Price had reported that conversations had taken place between representatives of the Russian government and 'influential members of the German industrial and diplomatic circles' about the possibility of Russia obtaining credit for the purchase of industrial and agricultural machinery in Germany. He had also reported that a passage in the Chancellor's speech in the Reichstag the previous week had indicated that 'Germany will not take part in the plan to reduce Russia to a colony' and that there were 'good grounds for believing that Germany will shortly officially recognise the Russian government'.

By the Treaty of Rapallo diplomatic relations between Russia and Germany were resumed, claims for indemnities and damages resulting from the war were dropped, and most favoured nation treatment adopted in economic relations. The other participants in the conference at Genoa viewed the Rapallo agreement with unconcealed dislike. A draft treaty by which normal relations between them and the Soviet government would have been re-established was dropped. And Poincaré took the occasion to make a speech in which he emphasised the fact that under the terms of the Treaty of Versailles France had the right to take unilateral action against Germany in the event of that country defaulting on any of the conditions laid down by the Reparations Commission.

The Genoa Conference was covered for the *Daily Herald* by the journalist Frederick Kuh. Price was occupied with the meetings in Berlin of the three Workers' Internationals at that time: the Second, the Vienna and the Third International, which he reported in some detail.[1] But he had spoken to Tchicherin on his way to Genoa and he later described how the Rapallo Treaty was received in Germany.

20 April

It may be said that the Russo-German Treaty is the greatest landmark in German foreign policy since the Revolution. Up till now the Republic has kept its face to the West, but now for the first time, driven to bay by fear of isolation, it looks to the West with a mask and turns its real face to the East, as the only quarter whence help may come. The Soviet diplomats played their cards with consummate skill and, as Tchicherin told me when in Berlin, have aimed at securing co-operation between the states of East and Central Europe, whose money has low exchange value against the claims of Western bondholders. The Riga agreement with Poland and the Baltic States was the first link in this chain; the Russo-German Treaty is the second.[2]

Dr Rathenau's policy has undergone a considerable change since the summer of last year when, at Wiesbaden, he laid all his hopes on France. During the winter he transferred these hopes to Lloyd George, but the latter's constant surrenders to the British diehards convinced him of the necessity of closer co-operation with Russia. At the same time, all organs of public opinion here express the firm hope and conviction that a way will be found to reconcile the new treaty with a continuance of the work of the Genoa Conference.

Satisfaction is the general tone of the press. The Democratic and Centre organs, which reflect the views of Rathenau and Wirth, hasten to explain that Germany had no other choice but to act as she has done, since from the first the Entente studiously excluded her from participation in the negotiations with Russia, thereby exposing her to the danger of being subjected to Article 116 of the Versailles Treaty (that reserving Russia's right to claim war reparation from Germany) with all its fatal consequences. Nevertheless, these circles point out that Germany has done nothing to prejudice a general European understanding on the Russia problem, particularly as she stipulated that Germany's renunciation of compensation for nationalised German property in Russia should only hold good so long as Russia withholds compensation from other countries. The Nationalist press also approves the treaty on the grounds that Germany has at last begun to act independently, though these journals make reservations about the need to take precautions against Bolshevik propaganda in Germany. Independent Socialists welcome the treaty as a victory for the idea which the Independents have been advocating for three years, while the Communist papers regard it as the greatest diplomatic victory for Soviet Russia yet attained, and advise their readers to insist that the German government, once nailed down, stick to the treaty.

For the next two months it almost seemed as if there were nothing of any consequence to report. Early in April the British ambassador to Germany, Lord D'Abernon, had written despairingly to Curzon that he blamed the German government and the Reparations Commission equally for the hiatus in German economic affairs. The former, he said, made no attempt to stabilise the currency or restrict the note issue; the latter demanded reparations in cash and kind without taking any account of their effect on the economy.[3] In fact the programme of fiscal reforms which Wirth had put before the Reichstag in January had been designed to produce economies in state administration and to improve the collection of taxes. But the unrestricted note issue had continued. Meanwhile, the Reparations Commission proposed that a Committee of Experts should be appointed to report on the possibility of the German government raising foreign loans for the redemption of part, at least, of the reparations debt. In May, independently of the

Commission, the Government was discussing the possibility of an American loan with J. P. Morgan. In June the German Trades Union Congress debated for days the respective doctrines of the three socialist parties as they affected labour organisation as if the country existed in an economic vacuum. On the day that the *Daily Herald* printed the last of Price's reports of the proceedings of the Congress – 24 June – the German Foreign Minister was murdered while driving to work.

26 June

After Erzberger – Rathenau. After Rathenau – who? Germany stands appalled today before the decrees of a secret murder organisation which made its power again felt on Saturday, when Dr Rathenau, the Foreign Minister, was shot dead in a Berlin street ... Berlin today breathes again the atmosphere of the Kapp *coup d'état* of two years ago. Half-masting of flags on government buildings gave the signal that something of moment had occurred and soon groups were to be seen everywhere in the streets discussing the news of Rathenau's murder. Indescribable scenes of passion were witnessed in the Reichstag. With cries of 'Murderers!' infuriated Social Democrats flew at the Nationalists ... Helfferich, the Nationalist leader, was gripped by the throat and in a few minutes all the latter had left the House. Intense bitterness is felt against Dr Helfferich, who yesterday made one of his periodical provocative speeches in the Reichstag, accusing the Government, and particularly Rathenau, of treachery and submissiveness to the Entente. Several socialist newspapers point to the remarkable fact that a speech by Helfferich of this nature generally takes place on the eve of some political murder, and this coincidence is too close not to be commented on by Republicans and Socialists. Chancellor Wirth, when the storm had subsided, made an appeal to all to rally to the support of the Government ... Turning to Deputy Wulle, editor of the Pan-German, anti-Semitic *Deutsche Zeitung*, Wirth declared: 'What you have written in your paper can never be atoned for. Through your agitation and vituperative articles an atmosphere of murder has been created in Germany. There is at present prevailing in Germany a state of political bestiality.' The Chancellor then announced drastic measures. Speeches against the Republic are to be punishable by not less than three months' imprisonment and regimental celebrations are forbidden.

28 June

Amid storms of rain and bursts of sunshine, Walter Rathenau was today laid to rest. The whole city was in mourning and the foreign embassies flew their flags at half mast. At midday the general strike of twelve hours throughout all Germany began. Railways, posts and telegraphs, however, stopped for ten minutes only. Throughout Berlin monarchist flags have completely disappeared. One sees only Republican-Democratic and red Socialist flags. The masses throughout the land have been stirred to their depths to stand by the republican form of government and clear out the monarchist murder nests. Shortly after midday the Reichstag assembled to give the last farewell to the dead ... Standing before the coffin President Ebert gave a farewell speech on behalf of the German nation. He was followed by a speaker from the Democratic Party. Then, while the band played the Siegfried March the coffin was slowly carried through the halls of the Reichstag to the square outside, where the Reichswehr gave a last salute.

1 July

Germany is shaken by the greatest sensation that has occurred for years. The existence of a mighty organisation for the overthrow of the Republic, long suspected, is now proved. As the immediate sequel to this discovery, President Ebert issues a proclamation of the severest penalites, not excluding the penalty of death, for association with such conspiracies. Reports by the Berlin police on the monarchist plot are followed by a more detailed revelation which caused the sensation to which I have referred. This is contained in a letter to *Vorwärts* from Felix Claus, a former member of the secret society known as 'Consul' which is centred in Munich. He relates that this society is really a continuation of the political espionage department of the notorious *Schutzen* Division which, with Noske, held Berlin under a White Terror during a large part of 1919 and which organised the murders of Liebknecht, Rosa Luxemburg and others. Since the division was disbanded the espionage department continues, under the name of 'Consul', to organise the murder of republican leaders ... He gives a whole list of names of members of the Nationalist Party and the Reichstag who gave him money to assist this work.

4 July

The German Trades Union Congress, together with the Brain Workers' and State Employees Union, the two socialist parties and the Communist Party, have decided on a joint demonstration and a twelve-hour general strike tomorrow to enforce their demands for the defence of the Republic and the democratising of state services. It is expected that this demonstration will assist the Government to carry through the new law for the defence of the Republic ... This law will alter the Weimar Constitution in several points ... hence the law will require a two-thirds majority of the Reichstag. The question arises if the Democrats and Centrists will have the courage to stand behind the united front of the trade unions and socialist parties. If so, this will give the necessary majority ... The prospects are good, for the middle-class republicans have been stirred as never before by the murder of Rathenau. The great achievement of last week has been the creation in action of a united front of all proletarian parties, which months of dreary negotiations seemed to show was unattainable.

7 July

At the Reichstag meeting yesterday the Minister of the Interior, Köster, introduced extraordinary measures for the defence of the republic ... In general the bill found support in all quarters of the House. Even the Nationalist speaker Duringer did not attack the bill in principle, but objected to certain details. He denounced the murder organisation. Stresemann, of the People's Party, even hinted with reproach at Helfferich's propaganda, which has embittered certain circles against the personalities of the republic ... In general it seems as if the parties of the Centre and Right do not intend to offer direct resistance to the bill but will let it pass through committee in the hope of rounding off the sharp edges directed against them, for everything depends on the way the bill, if it becomes law, is applied in practice.

21 July

The Reichstag has been prorogued for the summer holidays after
the passage of the Protection Bill [Law for the Defence of the
Republic], with the aid of the votes of the Stinnes party and
Independent Socialists in support of the government. The Protection Bill provides the Supreme Court with three professional
lawyers and six civilians, nominated by the Government, to try all
persons who are found guilty of plotting against the republic; also
[providing] criminal police for the whole of the Reich, thereby
striking at the root of Bavarian obstruction and clearing out the
murder gangs. It also contains clauses giving the Government
greater powers to coerce recalcitrant members of the state Executive. These points are the chief weapons in the new law against
monarchist reaction.

The murder of Rathenau and its consequences overwhelmed all
other considerations in July, but underlying everything in the
spring and summer of 1922, inflation was turning into hyper-
inflation. As a form of taxation, inflation had been an accepted
practice in Germany since before the war. People were willing to
accept rising prices with less resentment than they felt about
higher taxes, if only because the Government could not be held
solely to blame for them. Inflation – as has been noted – was an
important element in paying for the war and continued to make
a certain amount of sense in the immediate post-war period,
until the depreciation of the value of the mark holdings,
accumulated by foreigners in respect of Germany's import trade
surplus, came to be outweighed by domestic social costs. The
question of when and why inflation became hyper-inflation did
not admit of a simple answer. There were a number of
contributory causes, all of which gradually fed into the process,
but the chief among them was probably sheer lack of confidence, whether at home or abroad. The continued and paralys-
ing uncertainty about Germany's total reparations liabilities
was aggravated by, for example, the failure of the Genoa
Conference. Then Poincaré threatened unilateral military action against Germany if any of the clauses of the Versailles
Treaty remained unfulfilled despite the fact that many of them
had not even yet been quantified.

On 10 June the Committee of Experts – the Bankers' Committee – which had been set up by the Reparations Commission, recommended the postponement of any long-term lending to Germany until the entire reparations schedule had been revised, on the grounds that any loan would simply disappear with the declining mark. The crippling uncertainty was thus prolonged. The Committee helpfully suggested, however, that a short-term loan to prevent total collapse in the meantime was probably quite feasible. But the murder of Rathenau cast a long shadow: what kind of a country was this? Foreigners became increasingly reluctant to invest in the German money market and thereby rinforced the very depreciation of the mark which they were trying to escape. Thus stabilisation of the mark became a foreign policy as much as a domestic economy issue. When the revenue returns for the German Treasury for the financial year 1921–22 were published in May 1922 they were nearly 30 per cent higher than had been estimated. But the excess was entirely fictitious, caused largely by the fall in the value of the mark. And all the time the cost of living went on rising; including the cost of clothing, it rose by 71.5 per cent between August and September 1922. But real wages nowhere near kept pace with prices, let alone scarcity prices.

15 July

From the few facts that are known today, supplemented from private sources, it is possible for an observer to see the general downward tendency in the labour standard of Germany, low as it was compared with England before the war. It is known that 276 kilograms was the amount of cereal food at the disposal of each person in Germany in 1914. The head of a family of five persons, therefore, had to earn in that year by his labour 1,380 kilos, at the price of 18 *pfennigs* per kilo, or 248 marks [*per annum*]. These figures, let it be clear, refer to the period immediately before the recent collapse of the mark. As a matter of fact there are not 276 kilos, as in 1914, but only 198 kilos available today for each person in Germany, owing to the fall of cereal production and of exports. This means that in actual fact the head of a family of five must work 495 hours a year, or 82 hours more than before, in order to win 78 kilos of bread less than in 1914.

And all the time reparations were still being paid in kind, thus not only depriving Germany of badly-needed raw materials, above all coal, but also – because the Government had to pay the producers for them in cash – necessitating the continual enlargement of the note issue. An article in the *Berliner Tageblatt* on 25 July pointed out that the payments entailed in this form of reparations between 1 January and 13 June 1922 were approximately equivalent to the increase in notes in circulation during the same period. On 13 July D'Abernon forwarded to Curzon in London a paper by the Commercial Secretary to the British Embassy in Berlin, F. Thelwall, which concluded that it was literally impossible for Germany to pay any foreign debt, least of all in cash. She would only be able to do so when she could sell more in world markets, purchase and keep for herself more raw materials, and re-establish internal purchasing power by halting the depreciation of money. Germany would only be able to meet her obligations when the German nation was no longer compelled 'to live under a continual threat aimed at the very foundations of her existence'.[4] But at the beginning of August Poincaré suddenly demanded the immediate payment of 2 millions in sterling; and a Note from the British government raised the whole question of the interrelationship of Allied debts. All the European allies were in debt to the USA at the end of the war and Washington was now pressing for repayment. Far from lightening the reparations load on Germany, the Allies began to pile on the pressure in turn.

4 August

The unprecented fall of the mark in the last few days differs from the previous falls ... This time it is a general psychological panic wave, involving the Stock Exchanges of the whole of Europe. The recognition that the economic stability of Europe cannot be attained by the methods employed hitherto is the main cause of this mark ctastrophe ... The opinion is expressed that M. Poincaré is making a desperate attempt to force the pace and to create a *fait accompli* before meeting Lloyd George on 7 August, whereby he may wriggle out of the French debt payments to England and retain at the same time as much as he can of the fruits of the Versailles

Treaty ... The German course will largely be determined by developments in London. If the finance and industry groups in England which would postpone or work for a reduction of the American debt gain the upper hand, and the pressure on France is thereby reduced, then Germany would again obtain breathing space which might last until the next French financial crisis, causing another Poincaré ultimatum and mark catastrophe. If, on the other hand, the American-friendly groups in the City of London get their way, and pressure for the settlement of inter-Allied debt is increased, the catastrophe here will widen and deepen.

18 August

The arrival of the German mark at a thousand to the dollar has caused a panic in the warehouses of Berlin. Prices are soaring to unknown heights and people with paper money in their pockets are making haste to convert it into goods. The tendency is becoming more pronounced to reckon the value of goods in dollars, thus intensifing the flight from the mark. It is reported that industrial companies are commencing to draw up their balance sheets in gold marks. The Labour organisations have not yet put forward demands for payment in gold values, but the agitation among the workers, due to the violent rise in the cost of living, is becoming intensified.

In the following week the Reparations Commission sent another delegation to Berlin, when German ministers admitted that the country was completely bankrupt. Before returning to Paris the Commission concluded that sufficient guarantees for a moratorium were only possible if German heavy industries participated with the German government in making them.

29 August

The result was an arrangement whereby joint responsibility is taken over by the German government and the industries for the deliveries of coal and timber. Should the industries fail to supply the necessary amounts they will be liable in future to find the balance in cash payments either to the German government or direct to French importers ... Nobody yet knows what *quid pro quo* the industries are demanding from the German government, but everyone knows that they have for a long time had their eyes on the German railways being handed over to them as a guarantee for taking over the responsiblity from the Reich.

Indeed the most important fact in the present crisis so far is the obvious impotence of the Government to face its financial burdens, and the obvious will to power of German industrial capital ... This, incidentally, brings the German trusts one stage nearer to direct relation with the French trusts, which is the development so keenly desired for so long by the German Stinnes group and the Loucheur group in France. At the same time it cannot be said that Stinnes is alone responsible for this German proposal. The responsibility is with the Alliance of German Industries, on which Stinnes, Krupps, the AEG, Thyssen and others have their say. In spite of internal jealousies the Alliance always holds together when any question arises of securing a mortgage on the national assets of the German people ... The German proposal does not contain any offer to supply coal or timber beyond the amounts already prescribed by the Spa Agreement. The only new guarantee offered is that these deliveries shall be regular and have a material forfeit attached if irregular.

Throughout the closing months of 1922 there was a striking similarity in some of the comments on German inflation made by British and other observers: both diplomats and 'experts'. While the German government was unanimously blamed for the inflation to the extent that it went on printing money, there was widespread agreement that no permanent solution was available unless and until the pressure for reparations was abated. The Reparations Commission wrote a report on currency reform in October which called for the reparations scheme to be based solely on the consideration of 'economic possibilities'.[5] D'Abernon sent three reports to London in the first week of November alone in all of which he advocated the suspension of reparations for two years.[6] A committee of experts, which included Keynes, stated that even if the inflation was partly caused by the *Reichsbank*'s own policy, it was equally caused by the Versailles Treaty. It was essential to suspend reparations until a budget surplus could be established.[7] And the Reparations Commission itself published another report in December which quoted the opinion of the Committee of Bankers: the situation required 'a final and *bearable* [my emphasis] settlement in respect of the totality of the burdens proceeding from the Treaty of Versailles'.[8] But it was to be another year before a remedy for the German inflation was discovered, and nearly two more before the Dawes Report proposed a way of making reparations 'bearable'.

In the course of the summer of 1922 the two wings of the German Social Democratic Party were at last reunited. In reporting the process Price was liable to account for it largely as a necessary – and of course desirable – republican response to a monarchist threat. As yet he tended to regard all reactionary or Right-wing political activity as emanating from monarchists and/or Prussian Junkers and generals. It was not until towards the end of the year that he began to understand that the events he was describing were the early indications of Fascism.

18 July

An event of the greatest importance for the Labour movement in Europe has taken place in Germany, where the parliamentary parties of the German Majority Socialists and the Independent Socialists have entered into an agreement for co-operation of a far-reaching nature. In future these parliamentary parties will hold joint sittings, will appoint joint committees for the consideration of special questions, and in general will present a united 'bloc' in the Reichstag ... That it has created considerable uneasiness in the middle-class parties of the Reichstag is natural. Herr Stegerwald, Conservative leader of the Catholic Workers' Union, has been busy in beating the alarm and mobilising the faithful from Stinnes' party and his own to present a united citizens' 'bloc' against 'the Red danger'. But it is far from certain how far he will meet with success. First it is not clear if the creation of this new socialist bloc will mean that coalition between the socialist and liberal-capitalist parties is impossible ... but without doubt the possibilities of this are now nearer than ever. The difficulty is that the Independents have for some years past adopted resolutions at their party congresses against coalitions with liberal-capitalist parties, and have always stood for pure labour coalitions. But they have never faced the extraordinary situations which might arise, and in which united parliamentary action of Independents and Democrats is necessary in order to repel monarchist reaction, since the socialist parties by themselves have not sufficient votes in the Reichstag to undertake such action alone.

16 August

Now that the two Social Democratic parties are on the eve of reunion, the idea of a large republican bloc is no longer an idle dream. The monarchist reaction in Germany today is based on two elements of the population. The chief driving force and the financial source is the so-called *Landbund*, which is really an economic alliance of East Elbian Junkers together with some of the richer peasants. These people would, no doubt, like to see a return to the semi-feudal system of the Hohenzollerns' three-class electoral system, but it is doubtful if they really believe that this is any longer possible.

 They are now mainly concerned with declaring the independence of the countryside from the towns, which in effect means the holding-up of the state to ransom for necessary agricultural products. Nevertheless, this policy will not go down in the towns, nor even among the small proprietors in the villages, and therefore the *Landbund* is compelled to adopt other methods. Thus arises a second column which supports the house of German monarchism – namely the so-call *Deutschvolkische* Party. This semi-detached extreme Right wing of the Nationalist Party, while receiving financial aid from the Junkers, is engaged – not directly in backing the claims of the agrarians, which would be very unpopular in the towns, but in inciting the small shopkeepers and urban craftsmen, the small peasants of the villages, the impoverished rentier class and the needy university students, to pogrom against the Jews. From this quarter the murders of Rathenau and Erzberger came. These people can be secured for monarchism, not by singing the praises of the Prussian squirearchy but by presenting to them the Berlin government as run by Jewish speculators. There is not the slightest doubt that these two wings of the All-German Royalist movement stand behind the Bavarian government today ... In fact the power behind the Bavarian government is nothing less than the Prussian *Landbund* and the Pan-German anti-Semites, neither of whom have anything in particular that is Bavarian about them.

How far Ebert is going to succeed in his task of attracting the impoverished middle classes of the German towns away from this monarchist bloc remains to be seen. Thanks to his efforts, a compromise has been reached between the Reich and Bavaria over the Protection Law. Bavaria withdraws her decree annulling the law, and the Reich agrees only to apply the law in cases of 'exceptional importance' and only to use the special central [criminal] police in agreement with Bavaria. Over this compromise *Vorwärts* comments that the Reich has gone to the extreme limit of concession and has even overstepped it. To add to the anomaly of the situation the parties behind the Bavarian government in the Munich *Landtag* announce that the compromise does not satisfy them and that they regard the Protection Law as only a temporary force. Meanwhile, in order to show that the Protection Law is only intended by the Bavarian government to be directed against the Socialists and Republicans, the Bavarian police have just arrested the editors of the Munich Independent Socialist organ, the *Morgenpost*, on an obscure charge of high treason.

26 September

Within the walls of the old German city of Nuremberg the union of the two German Social Democratic parties took place today. The most notable figures in the German Social Democratic movement were present, chief among them being the veteran leaders Bernstein and Kautsky, who have been spending their best years in working for the reunion of the Socialist movement in a Germany broken by the war. Today's first meeting of the two parties, which had just completed their last congresses as independent parties, was a demonstration of unity under the joint chairmanship of Wels and Dittman.

C. H. Ammon spoke on behalf of the British Labour Party and the Trades Union Congress ... On behalf of the French Socialists Compère Morel brought greetings. He said that the tragedy of the war was as nothing compared with the tragedy of the disunion of the proletariat. Amid great enthusiasm Wels read the manifesto of the United Social Democratic Party. The provisional programme of the united party was then unanimously accepted ... It marks the modification of the old Majority Party's Görlitz programme of last year, in which coalition with the Stinnes party is in certain conditions permitted. The provisional programme says nothing about coalition with the capitalist parties, the question being left open. The commission set up under the presidency of Kautsky, the man who drew up the last great programme of German Social Democracy in 1891 in Erfurt, will make the new programme.

In a letter to Curzon written on 16 October Kilmarnock mentioned that in the course of a recent visit to the Rhineland the Prussian Interior Minister, Carl Severing, had professed himself to be 'not too pessimistic' about the outlook; he thought that the fusion of the Majority and Independent Socialists had had 'a steadying effect'.[9] But if it existed at all, the steadying effect did not extend to the mark, which continued to plummet.

4 November

If any elector in England wishes to get proof of the ruin which the Versailles Treaty and other acts of the late Government has wrought to Central Europe, he could not do better than enter the homes of some of the lower middle and working classes in Germany. I was in the home of such a one today. The tenant was a photographer who, before the war, used to make a nice little income in taking portraits of wedding parties, Sunday outings, local festivities ... Whereas, he told me, he used to have five or six callers a morning for portraits or orders, he is lucky if he gets one. No one is able now to spend anything on even such simple pleasures as getting a family photograph done. I know of labourers' families in Berlin who are no better off. A wage-earning acquaintance of mine with three children has now reached the stage in which he has to search the dustbins for rags in order to find something with which his wife may patch the children's clothes. He has not bought any new clothes for two years. A new suit of clothes costs about as much as he would earn in one month. Everything has to be concentrated upon all-important articles of food, so that at least the children shall not absolutely starve. Yet the food now consists mainly of potatoes and lard, with an occasional piece of meat, perhaps once in ten days. The man is working full time and sometimes overtime, and there is talk of a permanent extension of the eight-hour day to nine in the near future for his trade. The state of affairs on market days in Berlin beggars description. Despairing women rush from booth to booth and from shop to shop to find out if they cannot get something a little bit cheaper. It has been normal here for butter to rise every day for the last fortnight by fifty marks a day.

No one can keep pace with the catastrophe. Everyone has lost his head, and tradesmen simply chalk up fictitious prices on their boards, in order that they shall not be caught napping if by midday a telephone message states that the dollar on the *Bourse* has risen three hundred points. Hens lay eggs now, it appears, according to the state of the dollar. Although the food which the hen ate was bought six months ago, when the mark still had some value, the finished article acquires a value dependent upon the manipulations on 'Change [Stock Exchange] in New York and Berlin. One of the principal causes of all this, although not the only one, is the imposition of the burden of liabilities under reparations on the German State Budget. On the other hand, the big German capitalists get away scot-free and ... are already stretching out their hands across frontiers in a common attempt to impose the burden of post-war reconstruction on the masses by sweated labour conditions in Central Europe and unemployment in England.

On 29 November D'Abernon warned Curzon, not for the first time, that it was likely that there would be serious trouble in the coming winter because of the escalation of the cost of living and the fall of the mark. One of the reasons, he suggested, was that there were 'no socialists in the Government'.[10] Earlier in the same month Wirth had resigned as Chancellor, largely because the newly reunited Social Democrats had finally refused to enter into a coalition which included the People's Party, and retreated into opposition. Ebert, whose period of office as President had recently been extended without further election to June 1925, succeeded in getting Wilhelm Cuno to form a government.

23 November

The history of the Cabinet-making has been one of complex intrigue between the two big capitalist groups. Herr Cuno is, of course, associated with the Hamburg–America, Rathenau, Krupp–Haniel combination, which is the rival of the Stinnes group. In consultation with Mr Harriman, the American shipowner, and with the Hamburg Big Businessmen, Herr Cuno first endeavoured to form a Cabinet from his own group, excluding the Stinnes interests. But Stinnes' political grip was too strong. The attempt failed, and an inclusive capitalist coalition to fight Labour and parliamentarism took its place. Cuno's attitude to parliamentary institutions may be gauged from the fact that he carried on his Cabinet-making from his business office and complained bitterly of 'interference' by the parliamentary leaders. His idea evidently is – by using the economic power of the 'united front' of Big Business – to play Mussolini to the Reichstag. But he will find himself faced by the determined opposition of the Socialists, who are preparing to take up the challenge. 'We shall not pursue any policy of blind malice', says the *Vorwärts*, 'but we shall oppose where opposition is needed.' And it prophesies that there will soon be reason for using the full force of opposition. The party strength in the Reichstag will be: Government Bloc – 197; Socialists and Communists – 195; Monarchists and Pan-Germans – 68. Thus the monarchists will hold the balance.

In concluding the letter to Curzon quoted above, D'Abernon had noted that the recent success of the Fascists in Italy (where Mussolini had marched his forces to Rome on 30 October and assumed the premiership) 'unquestionably stimulated elements of disorder on the Right. Members of the various organisations ask themselves why they should not succeed as well as Mussolini.' He did not refer to the organisations he had in mind by name, but one of them would almost certainly have been Hitler's National Socialist German Workers' Party (NSDAP), now active in secret collaboration with the Bavarian army command and the paramilitary organisations which had simply ignored the orders of the Allies to disband. One such group, with which the NSDAP was working, was the United Fatherland Association (*Vaterländische Front*), which itself linked together 18 military and veterans' associations and which provided Hitler with useful contacts with the Bavarian army. Price, who had all along been keenly aware of the forces of reaction in Bavaria, wrote in the course of the late autumn of 1922 a long article entitled 'Bavaria and the German Fascisti' which appeared in *Labour Monthly* in January 1923, extracts from which follow.[11]

Of all the Teutonic lands Bavaria was the furthest removed from the big highways of land and sea traffic during the industrial developments of the last fifty years. The industrial population is sparse and scattered, and the peasants, freed by the influences of the French Revolution from the Junkers, became independent cultivators earlier than in Prussia. Shut in on their upland plateaus bordered by the Alps, the Thuringian and Bohemian forests and the Jura, the Bavarian peasant remained the boorish, superstitious, good-natured and politically backward element of Germany that he is today. Thus with a backward but landowning peasantry, with an absence of a politically effective industrial proletariat (except in the far north, Frankenland), it only required the introduction of an element which had been accustomed to rule to convert Bavaria into the Vendée of Germany. And that element was soon to be found in the emigrant Junkers and generals of the Hohenzollern army who have settled in Bavaria in recent years, in order to make it the centre from which they could work for the re-establishment of the old regime in Prussia. Prussia, in fact, according to popular saying in contemporary Germany, has migrated to Bavaria after the November Revolution.

It is not generally realised that the Kapp *putsch* of March 1920 succeeded in its object – the overthrow of a republican government based on a coalition with the Socialists – in one part of Germany, namely in Bavaria. Ever since then an undisguised dictatorship of reaction has been in power in Munich. In Bavaria one can see on a miniature scale what would be likely to happen in the rest of Central Europe if the emigrants in Munich succeeded in accomplishing their plans. But the first thing that one can observe about the Bavarian reaction is that the various elements composing it have not by any means a common policy ... During 1920 the Bavarian *Volkspartei* (Bavarian People's Party) commenced a plan of action whereby Bavaria should get back its old rights of fiscal autonomy, control its own passport and police regulations and foreign affairs, and generally undermine the strong centralist tendencies of the Weimar Constitution. In its separatist zeal it was prepared to enter into relations with the diplomatic agents of the French government and the representatives of the French General Staff, who were aiming at the re-creation of the Federation of the Rhine under French tutelage. Even the Prussian generals, including Ludendorff, began to coquet with these French agents ... They wanted a separate Bavaria for their schemes of restoration in Prussia, although of course they would not disclose this to the French. But the French got wind of Ludendorff's intentions and made conditions for their recognition of an independent Bavaria under a restored Wittelsbach dynasty, which would have left the Bavarian government a mere cipher of Paris, and so the whole plan fell to the ground. Thus ended the first phase in the history of the post-revolutionary Bavarian reaction ...

In the early part of the winter 1920–21 the Entente secured, under the terms of the Versailles Treaty, the dissolution of the Civil Guards (*Einwohnerwehr*) which had played such a part, along with units of the old Hohenzollern army, in suppressing the revolution in Prussia [the Berlin uprising] in 1919. The *Orgesch*, too, was threatened by the same fate, but by converting itself into a secret organisation it managed to save itself and to continue to keep its arms and depots, to drill its members, carry on nationalist propaganda, organise strike-breakers, break up socialist meetings and raid the bureaux of the revolutionary Left. It was, in fact, the early phase of the German Fascist Movement ...

German heavy industry had, by the winter of 1921–22, largely overcome the crisis immediately following the revolution. They had carried through their great concentration and had got large blocks of their capital out of Germany and safely invested in neutral countries. The necessity for co-operation with industry and finance capital in the Entente countries, and particularly with the French ironmasters, was becoming an urgent problem for at least one of the German trusts and consequently the existence of a potential praetorian guard in Germany which might take their nationalist and chauvinistic slogans rather too literally became a danger. For the Stinnes trust anti-French propaganda is only a means whereby better conditions may be obtained for that trust in any future amalgamation of coal, iron and steel interests in Westphalia, Lorraine and Northern France. But the [Bavarian] nationalist agrarians, with their militarist and anti-Semitic hangers-on, have no understanding of this diplomatic game. The anti-Semites in particular began to kick over the traces. These elements had got control over the so-called 'Organisation Consul' ... And this Organisation Consul, in the summer of 1921, commenced a regular campaign of terror and assassination ... The leaders of this movement began to preach the most extreme form of racial hero-worship. With them Jews are vermin, and even the Christian religion is tainted because of the racial origin of its founder. Their cult is semi-heathen, the old Teutonic gods and Wotan their symbols of greatness, the Teutonic 'Swastika' of Indian origin their sign of power. It is almost inconceivable that such views should be held in these days in a European land, but they are undoubtedly the inspirers of the murderers of Erzberger and Rathenau, as the trials of the accomplices at the Leipzig High Court showed.[12] The ills of Germany are, to these impecunious sons of former Prussian officers now gaining a precarious living, due to a universal Semitic capitalist conspiracy against a chaste Germania.

The crisis caused by the shot which brought down the head of the royal stag amongst Semitic capitalists, Walter Rathenau, shook the *Orgesch* to its foundations. The money from the heavy industries and from the economic organ of the Prussian Junkers, the *Landbund*, stopped at once and the Nationalist Party in the Reichstag [DNVP] made haste to repudiate the *Völkisch* elements [the proliferating nationalist groups and organisations] ... At the congress of the Bavarian People's Party this autumn in Munich a new party programme was worked out, demanding for Bavaria an autonomy bordering on separation and the virtual abolition of the Weimar Constitution. Other separatist groups have begun to take the initiative in Bavaria of late. The Bavarian Royalist Party (*Königspartei*) have revived the plan for a restoration of an independent Bavarian monarchy under the Wittelsbach dynasty with the assistance of French finance. The group called the 'Donau Federation' [Danubian Federation] aims also at a separation of Bavaria from the rest of Germany and at a federal union with Hungary and Austria under the Habsburgs. The financial assistance for this plan comes from the Vatican ... Another group arising out of the *Orgesch* is that centring round the so-called 'National Socialists' (NSDAP). To them have come what remains of the Organisation Consul and the *Freikorps*. As extreme anti-Semites they have reconstituted themselves under this new name and are organising terrorist expeditions against socialist industrial centres, attacks on Jewish shopkeepers and the plundering of banks and post [mail] trains. In fact even the Bavarian government has been forced to issue warrants for arrest for highway robbery against some of the leaders of this group. They represent the extreme Right of the Fascist Movement in Germany – the romantic robber barons of the Middle Ages transplanted into the twentieth century, with the self-imposed task of saving the capitalist system. The German trusts have ceased to finance them any longer. Only Hugenburg, a former director of Krupps, is known to have given them money recently, for they would undoubtedly be useful in the event of a general strike.

There remains to be considered the original kernel of the *Orgesch*, the men immediately round Escherisch himself, who still retain the old organisation after the others have split off. They retain also the connection with heavy industry trusts and are still amply supplied with funds from Stinnes, his friends and industrial rivals. The latter do this because they see in the *Orgesch* still an extra-parliamentary organisation which can force the Socialists into submission to their economic dictatorship ... the practical as opposed to the romantic Fascisti: the tame servants of industrial capital, who will break strikes or organise nationalist demonstrations whenever their masters ... require a little assistance from 'the people'. But if the rejuvenated *Orgesch* is to be the private military arm of the German trusts, it is necessary to find an intellectual arm. Stinnes, in his recent speech to the State Economic Council, has told all Germany that the eight-hour day must go, and that an extra two hours a day must be put to produce for reparations account ... This ten-hour day must, therefore, be popularised at all costs, and the Social Democrats won over to the task of persuading the German proletariat of the necessity of this ...

Up till recently it seemed as if the 'Great Coalition', from the Stinnes party to the Social Democrats, with the extra-parliamentary forces of the industrial Fascisti in the background, was going to be realised in Germany this winter. The ground had already been prepared by the union of the two wings of the Social Democrats in the congress at Nuremberg. It was no accident that the meeting place chosen was Nuremberg. The headquarters of the National Socialists and others of the romantic Fascisti type are at Munich. From here they dominate Bavaria south of the Danube ... But between the agrarian districts of South Bavaria and the industrial districts of Prussia, Socialist Thuringia and Communist Middle Germany stands the industrial district of Nuremberg in the pastoral highlands of Frankenland. The Frankish labouring population have always been staunch Protestants and upholders of the flag of reformist socialism, and the heroes of the National Socialists would have to pass through this land in order to bring their filibustering expeditions to the north. That is what Otto Wels meant when he said, at the Unity Congress in Nuremburg: 'The fate of the German Republic is in the hands of the workers of Frankenland.'

Last month [November] a crisis came. Directly after the Mussolini *coup* in Italy the Bavarian National Socialists decided also to strike. The plan was to carry out a *putsch* in Frankenland and to use this as a base to operate against North Germany. But once again the German heavy industry capitalists blocked the way. They threatened the National Socialists with the 'Great Coalition' and the Social Democrats with the dictatorship of the National Socialists, unless they agreed to the 'Great Coalition'. Dr Wirth was put up to give an ultimatum to the Social Democrats in this sense. Faced with this crisis the trade union leaders, who are always more in touch with the masses than the leaders of the Social Democrats, forced the pace and secured the rejection of the 'Great Coalition'. So the Wirth government fell. In the meantime the South Bavarian Fascisti had missed their chance.

Price left no other documentary evidence of this German Fascist might-have-been *coup*, but throughout the early years of the Weimar Republic rumours of *coups* from all quarters abounded in every quarter, and his information was usually good. D'Abernon too had obviously heard something in November. Price is certainly not the only one, in any account of these times, to lay a great deal of the blame – apart from reparations – for the apparently unstoppable decline of the mark in 1922 on industrialists and bankers who regarded it as not their problem. They regarded it, moreover, as a problem to the solution of which they were under no obligation to contribute. If anything, it was seen as an opportunity. Cuno received as little support from his erstwhile associates as any of his predecessors had done. At the end of December 1922 the Reparations Commission declared that Germany was in default on deliveries to France of timber and coal. Poincaré announced his intention, therefore, to occupy the whole of the Ruhr. Cuno's former friends could only propose a payment in lieu to the French of 20 billion gold marks, to be raised by an international loan. Even this was to be made conditional upon the restoration of equality in world markets for Germany, the evacuation of the Ruhr towns occupied by the French in 1920 and new undertakings regarding the end of the occupation of the Rhineland. At the end of 1922, it seemed that the troubles of the Weimar Republic could hardly get worse, yet the worst was still to come.

1923

The first day of the French occupation of the Ruhr – policy of passive resistance – German Nationalists in the Ruhr – French reprisals – Fascist activities in Bavaria – inflation intensifies – cost of passive resistance – Stresemann succeeds Cuno as Chancellor – strikes and unrest throughout Germany – end of passive resistance and wages support – negotiations between German and French trusts – Rentenmark *ends inflation – Saxony and Thuringia – separatism in Rhineland – Germany governed under emergency powers – the Hitler putsch – new government under Wilhelm Marx – state of Germany at the beginning of 1924*

8 January

All Germany is awaiting 15 January, the critical day when Germany must 'default' and give M. Poincaré the occasion for his march into the Ruhr. Herr Stinnes' press – it is interesting to note – is fierce in its denunciation of the French, and declares that any action by France will mean that Germany will regard the Treaty of Versailles as null and void. Now Stinnes, as I reported long ago to the *Daily Herald*, has been by no means averse to a French occupation of the Ruhr. When M. Barthou was here in November, the two of them tried to fix up a deal between the big iron groups of France and Germany: the *Comité des Forges* and the *Verein Deutsches Eisenhüttenleute*, of which a French occupation of the Ruhr was to be an integral part. But it is evident now that this negotiation has not been completed and that Stinnes fears that if the French go into the Ruhr before the deal is through, he will find himself in the position of the junior partner ... Yet he has been partly instrumental in giving M. Poincaré the excuse for action. I hear that the German failure to provide the necessary timber deliveries is due to Stinnes holding back supplies from his forests on the ground that the German government was not paying him enough since the last fall of the mark.

Essen, 12 January

At four o'clock this morning [11 January] I left Essen by car. We ran out towards Düsseldorf through a chain of mining towns. This great industrial heart of Germany was asleep and all in darkness, save where occasionally the flare from a blast-furnace lit up the sky. After a while we reached open country, where the coal seams end, and drove on through sleeping Westphalian villages. Then, as we came to a wooded valley, just beyond Kettwig, I saw the glare of lights ahead. It was the advance patrol of one of the French columns marching through the night to occupy the Ruhr coalfield.

We met the advance guard and were at once challenged and ordered to halt. My papers were examined and I was allowed to proceed, but not until the officer had asked rather anxiously if trouble was expected in Essen. It is clear that the French are nervous, as is indeed evident from the large force they are using. Three divisions – cavalry, cyclists and armoured cars leading – converged on Essen during the night. Two of them – entirely French – marched from Düsseldorf via Kettwig and Werden; the other – mainly Belgian – from Duisburg via Mülheim. I came back to Essen by side roads and waited until the slow-moving columns were approaching the town. Just before ten I went out again and met the advance guard. An hour later the cavalry were riding through the silent streets of this great engineering town. Only a small detachment is to remain here. The rest of the troops are moving to their allotted positions in a half circle around the town. Martial law, I gather, will be proclaimed at once. The whole industrial area is in a state of suppressed excitement. There is great bitterness among the population and assaults on innocent foreigners have occurred. Last night, after a huge demonstration outside the town hall, a nationalist crowd tried to break into the Hotel Kaiserhof under the impression that French officers were already there. The *Oberbürgermeister* however succeeded in quietening them and sending them home. French troops have occupied the offices of the coal syndicate and a rigid censorship has been established.

Essen, 13 January

France's dramatic military coup was made yesterday but the industrial struggle is only just beginning. The question is, will France be able to run the whole complicated apparatus of coal production and distribution in this, the industrial heart of Germany. The Germans have withdrawn their Coal Syndicate and have, I hear, burnt most of the vital documents dealing with the coal distribution apparatus. The French told the Prefect that the Coal Syndicate and the miners, according to the order issued, must take orders not from Berlin but from the French Coal Commission just set up; secondly that the first charge on the coal production of the Ruhr is reparations coal, the coal required on the left bank of the Rhine, and then what is left over can go to Germany. The German Prefect replied that he had no authority to obey this order. Everything seems to indicate that the German industrialists intend to start a policy of systematic obstruction to French attempts to secure dictatorial control of the German coal and metal industry. How far they will succeed it is impossible as yet to say, but if obstruction is carried on long enough it will be two-edged sword-hitting. Not only the French but the Germans too will suffer, and before long the German railways will be without coal and industries outside must cease.

The German Cabinet had been remarkably unanimous in deciding to oppose the French occupation of the Ruhr with a policy of passive resistance. All officials, railwaymen and factory workers were ordered to refuse to co-operate with the French. The French thereupon put in their own managers: men who were generally completely unfamiliar with the services they had been sent to run. On 17 January the British ambassador reported to London that the German response to the occupation had shown great solidarity, and 'workmen are even more furious than mineowners'. The attitude of the latter, he went on, could be judged by the fact that some of them – including Thyssen – had returned to Essen with the idea of courting imprisonment by the French, in achieving which they were soon successful.[1]

19 January

Germany, it is quite clear, is preparing to carry on her passive resistance to the French whatever the consequences may be. 'Whatever the French do we shall not give way. Nor will the coalowners give way', said a high official to me this afternoon. And there was no mistaking the tone in which he said it. It will be a long and a hard struggle. If the French carry out their threat of cutting off the Ruhr coal from the rest of Germany the consequences may be terrible. But the Germans are preparing to face them. In Essen six of the big coalowners – Herr Thyssen among them – are facing a French court martial today. But their imprisonment – which will be a gross breach of all law and of the definite provisions of the Treaty of Versailles – will not end the resistance. Their subordinates will equally refuse to obey General Degoutte's illegal orders. And they will have the support of the workers ... For Germany considers that this is a new war, deliberately provoked by a French invasion. It is a new war and of a new type. The French are not to be opposed by arms. They have already crossed the frontier of the neutral [that is, unoccupied under the terms of the treaty] zone and are approaching the garrison town of Münster. To that new violation of the Treaty the German Government has replied by withdrawing the garrison in order to avoid all danger of an armed clash. That, I understand, is part of a general policy. As the French advance, the German troops will retire. But the German resistance will not weaken. 'The French may come to Berlin', said the high official I have already quoted, 'but we will pay no reparations until they have withdrawn.'

20 January

The financial outlook in the Ruhr is causing the French great anxiety. Wages were somehow paid to the workers yesterday but the banks are all on semi-strike. Meanwhile, the workers in the Ruhr are being driven by the French display of force to make common cause with their employers. The whole capitalist press of Germany is mobilising for a general strike campaign against France, and an atmosphere is being created hostile to those who doubt the wisdom of sabotage tactics. Undoubtedly the situation is grave, and M. Poincaré can reflect that by his action he has poured oil on the flames of German chauvinism ... The Socialist Party and the Federation of Trade Unions have unanimously resolved that it is the duty of Labour to do everything possible to support the resistance offered to the Franco-Belgian invasion. But it adds that the fight against the reaction and against the Jingoes who are exploiting the situation in order to inflame nationalist feelings will be energetically continued ... Undoubtedly there is a real danger that some of the German Labour leaders will succumb to the pressure which the Nationalists are exerting on them for their own ends.

Essen, 24 January

This morning a new trouble confronts the French authorities in the Ruhr. The Thyssen and Stinnes miners had demanded the release of Herr Fritz Thyssen and Herr Spindler.[2] The French general had refused. And the men – over 100,000 in number – have now struck in protest. The miners' attitude is precisely that of the railwaymen. They are not impressed by the attempts to represent the arrested coal magnates as national heroes. They know too well how these gentlemen made their fortunes. But they will not have military interference in their industry. 'We have no intention', said their leader to me, 'of working so long as French bayonets are seen on the mines, just as we would not work if German troops were seen there.' That is the principle on which they acted yesterday. At Recklinghausen, where a small body of French troops tried to occupy the state mine, they were forced by the hostility of the miners to take refuge in a shed, where they were locked up for two hours. But if the French troops keep away the miners will work. They realise that their main interest is to keep the industrial machine on which their livelihood depends working. Today's events follow what appeared yesterday to be a tendency to improvement. The French had released two directors of state mines. They had withdrawn their troops from the Reichsbank at Essen. And they had conceded the demand of the Dortmund railwaymen that they should withdraw the troops from the station and agreed not to interfere with the normal working of the railways. On this the railwaymen have resumed work, though traffic is still by no means normal. The production of coal has also, of course, fallen off considerably. What is being produced is still going mainly to Germany. The French announced with great pride that one coal train has already arrived at Trier with 600 tons of coal. In view of the fact that the normal production of the Ruhr is 360,000 tons daily and that even the present production is probably half of that amount, this is not very encouraging from the French point of view. From the economic standpoint, the French raiding expedition is a complete failure.

Düsseldorf, 31 January

The entire Council of Essen postal workers was arrested yesterday during a sitting at which they were discussing a strike to secure the withdrawal of French military pickets from the Post Office buildings. The immediate effect of this coup was to produce a complete postal, telegraphic and telephone strike. To this the French retorted by declaring an 'accentuated state of siege' under which – amongst other things – everyone must be indoors after ten o'clock ... The attitude of the Ruhr workers remains passive and strikes only occur only when the French interfere in normal business. There is not the same feeling of confidence among the German upper classes as last week and in Berlin one or two voices are heard hinting at the possibility of negotiation. Undoubtedly the working-class support given to the Cuno government is not so strong as it would have been had Herr Cuno or his predecessor had the courage to make the magnates disgorge some of the wealth they have accumulated during the past few years. To sum up: The Germans have certainly won the first round by making the French ridiculous. But in the second round it will need more evidence of sacrifice on the part of the powers behind the Cuno government if the Ruhr is to be saved for Germany.

Düsseldorf, 2 February

I ran down to Cologne by car yesterday and talked with some of the British officials there. Their position is an extrordinarily difficult and thankless one. 'We have', said one of them to me, 'to avoid appearing to the Germans as French agents and to the French as German agents.' For the moment the British have given it to be understood that they will not tolerate any further arrests of German officials in their zone because – the military mind puts it – 'it ruins our prestige'.

In fact British diplomats and the officers of the British zone were, to judge from their reports to London, privately highly critical of the French action, but felt bound to say nothing openly hostile to it. The policy laid down by the British Foreign Secretary (Curzon) was that in the British zone no proceedings should be taken against any German national who was acting in accordance with the orders of the German government, but neither were they to obstruct the French and Belgians from enforcing their decisions so long as no British troops or officials were involved.[3] While disassociating themselves from the French, in other words, they would not actually break with them, a policy characterised by a phrase then current: *la rupture cordiale*.

Essen, 17 February

Throughout the Ruhr, and particularly at Essen, the situation is becoming increasingly critical ... I find a feeling amongst the men that the fight against French imperialism must be carried on by themselves, independently of their employers, whom they secretly fear may at any moment come to terms behind their backs. This attitude is all the more strengthened by the fact that a secret circular has come into the possession of the Metal Workers' Union, which I have seen, and which was written by engineering employ-ers since the French occupation to their members. It advises the latter to take advantage of the present situation to initiate wage cuts, extension of hours, and depletion of union funds through inciting local strikes. Meanwhile Nationalist bands are being formed in the Ruhr out of thugs imported from Munich. The latter are terrorising shopkeepers to make them refuse to sell anything to the French.[4] The wretched tradesmen are in grave difficulties, threatened with ruin from both sides. At night these German Nationalist bands smash windows and wreck the shop of anyone who displeases them. Against these bands the workmen in a number of mines and metal factories have formed themselves into guards, armed with rubber batons and wire coils, to defend themselves from their own Nationalists, as they have no confi-dence in the German police. Several cases have occurred, to my knowledge, where French soldiers have come quietly to miners and asked them to do everything to avoid conflict with soldiers, since they did not wish to shoot and are in the Ruhr against their will. In general the situation is becoming as complex as it is grave, and everyone has the suppressed feeling that an explosion is at any moment possible.

Price was not the only one to report the increasing activity of so-called Nationalist gangs in the Ruhr. The presence of extreme Right-wing groups containing a large element of students and ex-soldiers from all Germany was a cause for concern in a debate in the Reichstag. The French ambassador in London drew the attention of the Foreign Office to it on 10 March.[5] Two weeks later the British ambassador in Berlin was reporting that the population in the Ruhr was being 'worked by the Nationalists, who seek to impose by terror the introduction into the Ruhr of Fascist elements, and by Communists who endeavour to win the mass to their cause'.[6] Not long before, D'Abernon had discounted rumours of illegal organisations in the Ruhr preparing for civil war. The time was too unpropitious, he thought, for such an attempt 'even by Right-wing fanatics'. Characteristically, he thought that the Communists in the Ruhr posed a greater threat.

In the course of February the French pursued a policy of increasing harshness towards the population of the Ruhr.

Essen, 16 February

Everywhere, but especially at Recklinghausen and Gelsenkirchen, the rule of the whip and the rifle-butt is law. The people invariably answer with a boycott and the French seem to have given up the idea of maintaining order. At Osterfeld food trains have been plundered by the people and the French have not interfered. Indeed they drove away the special guard appointed by the German trade unions to protect the trains. The reply of General Fournier to the boycott in Essen has been to invite his troops to help themselves. And so the population is full of fear and resentment.

Cologne, 19 February

Two *Bürgermeisters*, Herr Havenstein of Berhausen and Dr Schafer of Essen, together with Dr Büssmann, manager of the *Rheinische-*

Westfalisch Electric Works were sentenced by court martial at Bredenay on Saturday. The *Bürgermeisters* were sentenced to three and two years' imprisonment respectively, the former for cutting off the electrical supply from the railway station occupied by French troops at Oberhausen, the latter for refusing to carry out the requisitioning order for the French. The manager of the electrical works was fined 5 million marks. The court martial convicted upon French law. It rejected the arguments of the defence that a military court was not competent to judge cases in the Ruhr, since M. Poincaré had declared that the occupation was a purely economic measure.

Essen, 3 March

The *Essener Arbeiterzeitung*, a Social-Democratic newspaper, has been forbidden by the French general to appear for 14 days because of 'defamation of the character of the occupying troops'. The journal published a list of street robberies by French troops in Essen. During last Saturday night alone, 25 cases were noted, and the names of the citizens who had been robbed by armed soldiers were given ... These actions are increasing the people's anger and contempt for the French, but nevertheless the workers are maintaining discipline and are carrying on a purely economic struggle. The central organisation of the struggle is the working class of the Ruhr – the miners, the railwaymen and the metal workers. The orders of the capitalist government at Berlin are only followed insofar as they do not harm the economic life of the region. Thus the Minister for Railways, Herr Gröner, forbade the supply of water, gas and electricity to the French. The Ruhr workers have declared that this order cannot be generally carried out because it is harmful to the economic life of the Ruhr, and they reserve to themselves the right to decide in what cases they will supply the French. The instructions of the Government have been altered to this effect.

By the end of March a German transport strike, which included Rhine river traffic, was wrecking French plans to get coal out of the Ruhr. Trade unionists in France and Belgium began to show some solidarity, or at least sympathy, with the Ruhr workers. In a series of articles during this month Price reported on negotiations which were going on between German, Belgian and French railwaymen under the auspices of the Amsterdam International, and on the fact that most Dutch transport workers were refusing to handle Ruhr coal. The French Transport Union declared all work in the Ruhr to be blackleg work. The occupying French continued to seize any stocks of coal and coke which they could find on the surface at the state mines, but this amounted to only 5 per cent of what they had been getting before the occupation. The British did not allow any trains over and above the originally agreed number to pass through their zone. The Ruhr mineowners negotiated an agreement with the miners to bring no coal to the surface except for immediate household use. Coke ovens and blast furnaces were progressively damped down and work underground was confined to technical improvements and modernisation. 'As far as the workers are concerned', Price wrote on 16 April, 'there is reason to believe that they will support all measures of passive resistance to the French which do not involve the destruction of the instruments of production by which they get their living.'

In Bavaria the initial reaction of all the parties to the French occupation of the Ruhr had been moderated at first by the firmness of Berlin's response. Protest meetings were held, but significantly neither Hitler nor Ludendorff were invited to address them. But it was not long before reports began to circulate that the Nationalist activities in the Ruhr (which Price had begun to note in early February) were in large measure being instigated and carried out by members of illegal paramilitary organisations from Bavaria, including members of the supposedly outlawed *Orgesch*. After the compromises achieved between the Reich and the Bavarian governments over the application of the Defence Law (see p. 135) the last remaining Right-wing extremists in the Bavarian government had withdrawn from the coalition, leaving them free to operate outside the constraints of government. On the other hand the moderate Premier, Count Lerchfeld, had resigned in November 1922, to be succeeded by a nominee of the People's Party, Dr von Knilling. In the same month Hitler had become the official leader of the National Socialist Workers' Party (NSDAP). In April 1923 Price returned to Bavaria and found abundant evidence of his increasing influence.

Munich, 5 April

Iron crosses. Armed Reichswehr troops wearing steel helmets and with a hint of the goose-step in their marching gait. A cluster of young *Hakenkreuzler* (Swastika-wearers) roaring 'To Hell with the French beasts!', 'Down with the Jews!', *'Deutschland über Alles!'* Flaming placards on every street corner announcing another Fascist meeting at which Hitler, Mussolini's mimic, will speak on Germany's Hour of Revenge. Police, troops, civilian White Guards and more police. These are a few of the random sights that greet the visitor in Munich. I was walking across one of this city's magnificent parks and paused before a lavish brown mansion. 'Is this the ex-king's palace?' I asked a passer-by. 'That', he corrected me, 'is the next king's residence.'

There is little in Munich to indicate that Bavaria belongs to the republic. Flags of the old monarchy are more frequent than the republican colours. To be a republican in Munich is to be indiscreet if not foolhardy. There is, indeed, nothing to suggest that anyone except the Bavarian worker has paid the price of stubborn militarism. The war has left plentiful traces in the topsy-turvy of Bavaria's economic life. But the fanatical chauvinism, the hatred of democracy and the martial tunes to which Munich's tired feet are shuffling along – all imply that Bavaria is dominated by men who have learnt nothing and forgotten nothing since 1914.

Bavaria is seething with hatred – hatred of Protestant North Germany, of the French, Jews, Republicans, Liberals and, above all, Socialists. All are anathema. All will get short shrift when the hour of reckoning strikes. At least, so they say. Adolf Hitler, a native Austrian and a locksmith by trade [sic] has pushed his way to the leadership of the Bavarian counter-revolutionary movement. A skilful demagogue, who wins converts to Fascism by drinking beer with the common people, he has mastered the routine of whipping up popular passions.

'How can we help the Fatherland?' I heard Hitler ask his audience. 'I'll tell you how. By hanging the criminals of November 1918!' (These criminals are, of course, the republican workers of Germany.) 'By punishing the worthies of the Republic we shall gain the respect of foreign nations', cried Hitler. 'If we had resorted to arms two years ago, we would never have lost Silesia and there would have been no Ruhr problem.' At this point in his harangue a company of Hitler's 'shock troops' paraded across the platform beneath the banner of monarchist Germany. Such scenes are daily occurrences in Munich.

The reaction in Bavaria is intricate. It consists of numerous groups, all united in their determination to overthrow the republic and trample upon Labour, and yet divergent in the means which they propose to employ. One speaker will shout loudest when denouncing the French, another when excoriating the Jews and a third when damning the German constitution. But all are openly agreed that their common purpose is to fight organised Labour.

Three groups dominate the rising Bavarian reaction. First, there is the separatist movement led by ex-Crown Prince Rupprecht, the former Bavarian Premier von Kahr and the clerical-farmer deputy, Dr Heim. Briefly summarised, their policy demands greater autonomy for Bavaria within the Reich, restoration of the Wittelsbach dynasty in Munich, union with Austria (except Vienna) and a reinforcement of clerical (Roman Catholic) influence in the Government. Second, there are the Fascists, guided by Hitler, for whom the Roman Church and the monarchy are minor details, and who are mainly concerned with the forcible subjugation of Labour, suppression or explusion of Jews, and a Fascist dictatorship with its roots in Bavaria but extending throughout Germany. Third, there is the Ludendorff element, anti-clerical and anti-separatist, relying upon the ex-officers and the Prussian Junkers for a revival of Pan-German militarism. All three factions are busily preparing civil war, storing up arms and munitions and building illicit White Guard armies. A steady stream of funds pours into their treasury from German industrial magnates. Well-informed citizens forecast a counter-revolutionary uprising in Bavaria within a few weeks. They say this will be the signal for a 'White' offensive in all Germany.

On his return to Berlin Price appeared to have looked for – and found – indications that his informants in Munich were, indeed, well-informed.

10 April

Signs are not wanting that another reactionary *coup d'état* is being planned in Germany. As usual Bavaria is the centre of the movement, but the Pan-German Fascisti who are preparing to

move are only using Bavaria as a stalking horse. The Fascist
organisations are standing by, ready to threaten the Cuno government if it shows signs of listening to the demand throughout the
country for a reasonable solution to the Ruhr problem, which
might involve sacrifices for the oligarchy of capitalists who control
German industry. That these Fascist organisations have spun their
webs from Munich all over the country is becoming clearer every
day. Last week the so-called United Fatherland Alliance, at a
meeting in Berlin, demanded of the Cuno government that it
should carry on the struggle in the Ruhr by new economic
measures, including 'making labour in Germany free by abolishing
the eight-hour day, creating the open shop in the factories,
imposing a compulsory labour service, and suppressing the Communist Party'.

Following upon this comes news of a bloody conflict between
Fascisti and workmen in Regensburg (Bavaria). Yesterday the
correspondent of *Vorwärts* in Munich was arrested on the charge of
having communicated information to Berlin about the activities of
secret Fascist organisations. In other words, it is now treason to
examine the activities of those who are flouting the Weimar
Constitution. This morning the *Rote Fahne*, the Berlin Communist newspaper, has been suppressed for two weeks on the ground
that it has insulted the Government by accusing it of sacrificing the
interests of German workers in the Ruhr to the industrial
oligarchy. This last event indicates that the Bavarian Fascisti have
their agents right inside the Prussian police service, which uses the
law – passed last summer – for the protection of the Republic, only
against the Left-wing movements while it leaves the Fascisti
severely alone.

As the Ruhr situation develops more and more into a deadlock,
the Fascist organisations are certain to become more active.

The flight of the mark from inflation to hyper-inflation was now
beginning. Passive resistance was expensive. Workers rendered
unemployed as the result of it were still paid two-thirds of their
normal wage in unemployment benefit. Employers still able to
offer work were subsidised. Figures illustrating the situation
which now developed are so abundant that it is hard to know
how to choose between them. In an article published in *Labour
Monthly* later in the year Price wrote: 'Paper money began to

flow like water. Seven billion marks were printed in less than two and a half months. It was a paradise – of paper and on paper.' The article continued:

> ... During May an understanding was reached between prominent members of the *Reichsverband der Deutschen Industrie* [Alliance of German Industry] and the Minister of Finance of the Reich, a nominee of the former, that no further credits would be forthcoming for the payments of increased wages for the next two months. Having secured this the Stinnes group at once began to force down the mark by buying large amounts of foreign currency. In a few days the dollar rose from 40,000 to 80,000 marks, and was quickly followed by the prices of food and necessaries, which in the Ruhr rose 100 per cent in ten days. The heavy machine of the trade union bureaucracy began to work, and negotiations dragged on in Essen and Berlin with the employers and members of the Government. Meanwhile the *Reichsverband* was preparing its 'offer' of reparations guarantee to the Government, the acceptance of which was to be the condition of permitting a rise in wages to cover the collapse of the mark. The game, however, was spoiled by the metal workers and miners in a number of towns, spontaneously and together downing tools and electing a strike committee to enforce unconditionally their demands for an adequate rise. At the same time a number of control committees sprang up in the strike areas to supervise the prices on the local markets and punish by confiscation local profiteers. In this way some acts of plunder were committed. The employers got their Fascist organisations to work at once and bands of *Bürgerwehr* [citizens' police] began to clear the streets, arrest strike leaders and reinforce the police. The strikers replied by creating a local labour militia of organised trade unionists who disarmed the Fascists and took over the responsibility for local order ... The disarming of the Fascists by the labour militia however so put the wind up the representatives of the trusts that they quickly patched up a truce and agreed to an immediate advance of 50 per cent in wages as from 1 June. At once the order went out from the strike committees to return to work.[7]

On 7 June the German government despatched a Note proposing to end passive resistance in return for the resumption of civil administration in the Ruhr; and the appointment of an impartial Committee of Experts to determine Germany's capacity to pay reparations and to advise the Reparations Commission on the question of how these could best be guaranteed. But Poincaré ignored the Note, merely demanding the unconditional abandonment of passive resistance before any other proposal would be considered. The result was, predictably, the reinforcement of German will to continue resisting. France replied by reinforcing the economic blockade of the Ruhr and the complete militarisation of its railways. Then food was only allowed to be transported after the payment of freight in francs. This was forbidden by the German government so that food could only be transported by road and shortages developed. Moreover, the French encircled the Ruhr with troops, protected with wire entanglements and trenches, and forbade the population to enter or leave the area.

21 July

The French meanwhile are busily engaged in taking stock of materials at hand in the Ruhr industries. Coal, of which some 2 million tons are still at the pitheads, has been requisitioned and is being slowly taken to France. Seventy per cent of the heavy industry is lying still, a large part of the coking ovens and smelting furnaces have gone cold and most of them are not worth rebuilding. There is reason to believe the German trusts are not shedding tears at this development. The coking and smelting plants in the Ruhr are more than are needed to cover any possible consumption in the German and world markets, which have been reduced since the war. The trusts are getting paid for the furnaces cooled down by the Reich in gold values, which they immediately invest abroad, thus further assisting the collapse of the mark.

23 July

There are now two rates for the mark, one in Germany and one outside. Thus yesterday the dollar in Berlin was 218,000, in Danzig 300,000. The *Reichsbank* and the Cuno government, which are making half-hearted attempts to bolster up the shadow of German currency independence, have to fight against enemies both at home and abroad. In the Rhineland General Degoutte

forbids transactions in, and publication of, the German official
mark rate and finds willing supporters in the German private banks
and industries, for whom nothing is more welcome than freedom
to plunder the coffers of the Reichsbank at will ... The *Reichsbank*
is becoming less and less able to supply the foreign currencies for
purchase of necessary foods from abroad, especially for the Ruhr.
This again will have the effect of making passive resistance more
and more difficult which, in view of the secret transactions going
on between the French and German heavy industries at the present
time, is not altogether undesired by the latter.

The negotiations to which Price refers here were to become common knowledge in the late autumn of 1923 and will be referred to
again below.

27 July

Prices are rushing upwards in a way that once would have seemed
incredible, but to which we are now becoming accustomed. Food
prices in the shops are higher at noon than in the morning, higher
in the evening than at noon. And nobody thinks of tomorrow.
Under these circumstances the centre parties are losing their hold
and their morale. The drift is more and more to the extreme Right
or to the extreme Left, because nobody sees any room for hope in
the existing order.

28 July

... The crash of the currency is confronting Berlin with a serious
food shortage. Queues reminiscent of London in wartime or –
perhaps even more significantly – of Petrograd on the eve of the
Revolution, are forming outside the food shops. There have been
no disturbances so far. But the authorities are nervous. And
yesterday, in the City Council, speakers urged that unless the
Government took immediate steps, the storm might break at any
moment. The Government has made one move. It has summoned
the Reichstag to reassemble on 10 August.

Price was misinformed about the date. The Reichstag in fact
reassembled on 8 August and by then the storm had already
broken. In his last address to the Reichstag Cuno began by sum-

marising some of the effects of the seven-months' occupation of the Ruhr. France and Belgium 'had obtained less than a fifth of the amount of coal and coke which voluntary German labour would have delivered'. More than 100 people had died, ten had been condemned to death in the Ruhr, and terms of imprisonment amounting to 1,200 years had been handed down. One hundred thousand people had been evicted from their homes and 95,000 transport workers dismissed. But Cuno had nothing new to offer in terms of policy and the measures which he proposed to deal with inflation were derisory. On the very day of his speech to the Reichstag the printers' union voted to strike and a shortage of even paper money threatened. On 11 August Price reported that not only the printers but also railwaymen, shopkeepers and those working in the municipal services in Berlin were on strike, and that 'even graver reports' were coming in from the provinces. On 12 August, the *Daily Herald*, in a column announcing the resignation of Dr Cuno and the whole German Cabinet on the previous evening, went on:

All Germany, with the exception of the extreme east and south, is in the throes of a big spontaneous movement of millions of half-starved workers and middle classes clamouring for bread and for a wage which will not melt in the hand of the receiver in an hour, wires our Berlin correspondent. The power stations of Berlin have closed down and no trains are running. Gas and electricity are cut off in many parts of the city ... In the provinces the situation is equally desperate.

The article went on to summarise their correspondent's report of rioting near Breslau and Silesia, Hanover, and Stettin; miners' strikes in Saxony; looting near Erfurt, and 'explosive incidents' in Krefeld, Aachen, Bottropp, Düsseldorf and 'elsewhere'. The strike movement had even spread to the occupied area and near Gelsenkirchen the workers had hanged effigies of Cuno and Stinnes.

The new German Chancellor, Gustav Stresemann, was to become one of the most stable figures in German post-war politics and was to hold office, either as Chancellor or as Foreign Minister, for the next six years. Himself now a member of the People's Party, Stresemann's first coalition Cabinet also

contained members of the Centre Party, Democrats and Socialists. He appointed Hilferding as Minister of Finance. In a
dispatch summarised in the *Daily Herald* on 15 August Price
noted that Stresemann had, until recently, been associated with
Stinnes in determining the policy of the People's Party, but that
if his past record was any guide, this would not deter him, in his
efforts to save capitalism in Germany, from courting the
opposition of his 'powerful erstwhile associate'. And it did not.
Stresemann immediately proposed to double the income tax of
certain categories of taxpayers and more than double that of
others, to increase corporation taxes and taxes on business,
industry, trade, commerce, forestry, horticulture and motor
cars. He introduced a compulsory gold loan. The loan was
graduated in proportion to income. For large holders of foreign
currency, it was specified that payment had to be made in
foreign currency or foreign investments. In this way Hilferding
had hoped to break the obstruction of the trusts which had
hitherto succeeded in escaping taxation by keeping their money
outside the country. In a second article printed on the same day,
Price wrote:

> The coming into power of the new government, with a
> programme of taxation which is supposed to be paid mainly by the
> rich, has had a soothing effect. The Communists have decided to
> advise the workers to break off the strike and concentrate on
> demanding from the new government a minimum hourly wage of
> 8d. (gold standard), food price control and a state mortgage on
> industry. The next move, therefore, lies with the Stresemann
> government, and great responsibility rests on the Finance Minister,
> Hilferding, who has attained the long-desired position from which
> he can carry out his finance programme and end inflation.
> Everything now depends on whether Hilferding seriously intends to
> tackle the trusts and impose a state mortgage on industry to
> balance the budget and stabilise the mark, and whether he is strong
> enough to break the sabotage of the trusts. The experience of
> coalitions between the Social Democrats and the capitalist parties
> during the last four years is not very promising, but *Vorwärts* today
> is confident and calls on the opposition element within the
> Social-Democratic Party to give Stresemann and Hilferding full
> support in their difficult task.

On 20 July the British government had cautiously modified the *rupture cordiale* with a Note to the French government suggesting steps for resolving the Ruhr conflict which differed very little from the German proposals of 7 June. They made as little impression on Poincaré as the German proposals had done but Curzon was persistent. On 11 August he sent another Note. He again insisted that an impartial enquiry was essential to establish Germany's capacity to pay, but this time he drew attention to the dangers as well as to the failures of French policy and concluded with a hint of menace. The British government was 'reluctant to contemplate the possibility that separate action may be required in order to hasten a settlement which cannot much longer be delayed without the gravest consequences to the recovery of trade and the peace of the world'. A Foreign Office memorandum outlining events since the fall of the Cuno government records that on 13 August Stresemann had told D'Abernon privately that passive resistance could not continue indefinitely. On 3 September he declared publicly that he would accept the British Note of 20 July as the basis of negotiations with France and Belgium. Poincaré still replied that there would be no negotiations before a complete cessation of passive resistance.

By now the cost of passive resistance included the trebling of the number of people receiving public relief. Only 29.3 per cent of the entire German labour force was now fully employed due to the deprivation of raw materials from the Ruhr. The excess of government expenditure over income had doubled (since 1920) and the dollar quotation for the mark had risen from 17,972 in January 1923 to 4,200 trillion in November. The gold loan had indeed produced $11 million by the end of August and daily revenue had increased tenfold.[8] But government expenditure on the Ruhr continued to outpace all resources. At the end of September the total gold reserve of the Reichsbank had diminished by three-quarters and in the previous week the average daily output of paper had been 907 billion marks. Hilferding's project for currency reform based on the values of rye and establishing a new independent currency bank with capital subscribed equally by agriculture, industry and trade was never tried.[9]

On 26 September Stresemann announced the end of passive resistance in the Ruhr and the resumption of reparation payments. The former Minister of Defence, Otto Gessler, was appointed Dictator for all Germany and an Enabling Law drafted which provided that subject to the approval of the Reichstag he could suspend the constitution if necessary to maintain order. Executive power was vested in regional military commanders. The Social Democrats in the coalition Cabinet resigned in protest and on 4 October Stresemann resigned as Chancellor. Asked to form a new government, he succeeded in reappointing all his former ministers except two (one of whom was Hilferding). A condition of their appointment was agreement to abandon the eight-hour day. On 24 October the new government requested the Reparations Commission to investigate Germany's ability to pay reparations on the basis of the current assessment and on 30 November the Commission appointed a committee under the American financial expert, Charles G. Dawes.

As D'Abernon had noted on 30 October: 'The Government have on their hands no less than five major crises, viz., Bavaria, Saxony, Rhineland, the resumption of work in the Ruhr and the financial position.'10

In the late summer of 1923 the von Knilling government in Bavaria, aware that the end of passive resistance was possible and that this might lead to some kind of Right-wing *coup*, decided to appoint a state commissioner with special powers in relation to public security. The man selected for the post was the former premier, Gustav von Kahr, who already had strong ties with the local Reichswehr commander, General von Lossow, and the head of the police, Colonel von Seisser. All three were close to Bavarian monarchist and Pan-German movements and it was not long before they became involved in Bavarian politics. This was a crisis in waiting, but the problems of the Ruhr lay even closer at hand. On the very eve of the abandonment of passive resistance Price had been in Essen.

Essen, 25 September

After a week of walking about in this great industrial city, covering an area as big as Middlesex, I have the feeling that the working man, composing the overwhelming part of the population, is filled with contempt of the government in Berlin and with hatred of the government in Paris ... This settlement will, it is felt by the Ruhr miner, dispose of the mineral wealth by which he gets his livelihood to a combine of international financiers, and he will be left to his fate ... Small wonder that the feeling is widespread that the Berlin government thinks more of making propaganda out of the 'French robbery' than of providing the workers of the Ruhr with fuel for the winter ... The financing of the passive resistance in the Ruhr bids fair to become one of the scandals of capitalist plundering of public funds. I find that, of the 89 blast furnaces in the Ruhr, only four are now working. The rest are cold, and most have fallen in and will have to be built up again. The same applies to coking ovens, most of which were of the old type. These will be rebuilt for the trusts, at the expense of the German state, on the modern type. Now the German trusts have already received the cash for the rebuilding of the plant in foreign currency – when the mark stood at 20,000 to the £ sterling – from the *Reichsbank*, and have got it safely tucked away in some corner of the world. Some have paid the *Reichsbank* back in marks at 1 million to the sterling. Others are in no hurry and will wait until the mark falls a little further.

From Essen, Price went on to Cologne.

Cologne, 27 September

At present many hundreds of thousands of miners, engineers, railwaymen and professional men are receiving wages and salaries from the German government in accordance with its policy of financing passive resistance. But now that passive resistance is to end, the money will be withdrawn ... What is to become then of those who received the subsidies up to now? That is becoming the vital question for the Ruhr workers, even more pressing, perhaps, than the question of wages vanishing through the flight of the mark. The worker has become the victim of the economic anarchy in Germany today.

Price went on to summarise the views of the Left-wing 'Union of Hand and Head Workers' in Cologne, who believed that

Neither the German trusts nor the Comité des Forges nor any international regime in the Ruhr would tolerate a reduction of the profits of capital. If the German trusts have to give up a share of their interests in the Ruhr industries in lieu of reparations then, say these people, the class consciousness of the French capitalists and of Poincaré will be strong enough to allow the German trusts to take it out of the Ruhr workers in a ten-hour day and an army of unemployed kept at the starvation level.

This prediction was not far out. The mineowners and industrialists in the Ruhr had been negotiating privately and secretly both with individual French trusts and with the Inter-Allied Mission for the Control of Factories and Mines (MICUM). Several agreements were nearly achieved but broke down, usually over French intransigence. Early in November it was agreed that arrears of coal tax owed to the German government by the mineowners and all future demands for coal tax would be paid by the mineowners to the French in francs. Reparations (18 per cent of coal and 35 per cent of coke produced) and the requirements of the Regie (the Inter-Allied Commission in control of the railways) would account for nearly three-quarters of total output in any case, but anything left over was to be allowed to be sold outside the occupied territory, that is if it could be moved. The disastrous state of the railways under Regie – in effect French – control had virtually brought goods traffic to a standstill. In return a proportion of existing stocks of coal, steel and pig iron were allowed to be retained in the Ruhr in order to keep a modicum of industry going, but on the basis of a ten-hour day, to reduce the costs of production.[11]

The measures taken by the Government to end inflation constituted one of the few success stories of 1923. The man who succeeded Hilferding as Minister of Finance, Hans Luther, found an ally in the new president of the Reichsbank, Hjalmar Greeley Schacht, whose co-operation did much to bring about the stabilisation of the mark. On 15 October Luther established a new bank, the *Rentenbank*; a month later a new currency, the *Rentenmark*, was issued, guaranteed by a mortgage on industrial and agricultural property and limited as to amount. The exchange rate of the paper mark against the dollar was allowed to fall for five days, when it reached the level of 1 billion paper marks to 1 gold mark. At this point its value held. Confidence began to return and people no longer rushed to spend the money in their hands before its value disappeared. Government credits, which the industrialists had been using to buy foreign currency and delay repayment until the mark had further depreciated, were cut off. Speculators were compelled to sell their foreign currency holdings to the *Reichsbank*, thus virtually doubling the bank's gold and foreign currency reserves.

The third of D'Abernon's crisis areas was Saxony, where a Socialist government supported by the Communist Party had been in power since March 1923. Saxony lay directly in the path of any move which the Bavarian Fascists might be thinking of making to spread their doctrines in North Germany, and the Minister President of Saxony, Erich Zeigner, decided in October to strengthen his position, as he thought, by inviting three Communists into his Cabinet. In Thuringia a Socialist government with Communist support had held on to power despite an attempt by the Reich government in May to make the army responsible for maintaining order in the *Land*, which only succeeded in reinforcing the coalition of the Left parties. At some point in August Price had visited both these states.

17 August

Thuringia and Saxony are now spoken of as the 'Red heart of Germany' ... Quite apart from the strategic importance of Thuringia and Saxony in the event of a Fascist coup is their importance as a centre in Germany where Labour is definitely in the saddle and where, within the framework of the Weimar Constitution, Labour can and does hold important administrative posts by virtue of the democratic franchise. My visit here has enable me to gain an idea of what has been done in the short time that Labour has been in power, and I may say from the first that, within the rather narrow limits which the constitution imposes, advances have been made. The police force has been transformed into a kind of militia, in which at least 70 per cent are organised trades unionists. A very capable Social Democrat and former soldier has been put at the head of this force in Thuringia. A clean sweep has been made of all the secret Monarchist and Fascist organisations both in Thuringia and Saxony and such arms as they had, during 1920 and 1921, been collecting in these two lands have been seized. In each factory the workers have been allowed to form 'hundreds' for the purpose of watching and preventing any reactionary agents getting into posts in the administration ... Social Democrats with whom I have talked say that their main differences with the Communists are that the latter are forcing the pace too fast and are laying Thuringia and Saxony open to the danger of the intervention of the Reich, which is a coalition of capitalist parties and which views the events in Middle Germany with great suspicion. While leaving Bavaria severely alone, the Central Government has been writing long epistles to Dresden and Jena, lecturing the Saxon and Thuringian governments and threatening them with intervention for breaches of the Weimar Constitution.

On 23 October, fearful of the influence of the Communists in Saxony, the Reich government sent in the Reichswehr, as permitted under the state of emergency. When Zeigner refused to carry out the orders of the regional Reichswehr commander to dismiss his Communist ministers he was deposed under the terms of the Weimar Constitution. Tragically, during the period of the Socialist–Communist coalition in Saxony the Executive Committee of the entire German Communist Party had moved from Berlin to Dresden, where it was on the immediate receiving end of Comintern pressure to take advantage of the economic chaos in Germany to launch a Communist revolution throughout the Reich. Plans were accordingly laid. The intervention of the Reichswehr in Saxony and a sudden abatement of popular support for Zeigner caused the plans to be cancelled, but the message announcing that the revolution would not now take place did not reach Hamburg in time to prevent a totally futile uprising there on 23 October.[12]

The Rhineland, the fourth of D'Abernon's five 'crises', had no serious tradition of separatism until 1918, when latent anti-Prussianism focused on the centralising tendencies of the Weimar Constitution. A separatist movement surfaced in the Rhineland after the French occupation of the Ruhr both despite the occupation and because of it. The French supported the separatists with food, money, transport, arms and general protection and a Rhenish republic was proclaimed, in the last ten days of October, in Bonn, Coblenz, Mayen, Duren, and Kaiserslautern. But the separatists had little popular support, the British refused to recognise them and the movement gradually dwindled. Price had made his last tour of the Ruhr and the Rhineland at the end of September. He was not impressed by what he found.

Frankfurt-on-Main, 2 October

Life in the Rhineland, though not so hard as in the Ruhr, is still hard enough. But the rural population is still not much touched by the developments of this year. Living on their vineyards, their main consideration is the wine harvest, and doubtless they feel that they will be able to find as good a market for their wines in France as they did in Germany. On this the French authorities are speculating. On this the Rhineland separatist movement is partly built up. The leaders of this movement are mostly broken-down existences [sic], former German officials who got the sack for one thing or another – men with a grievance. The money comes from the French, who use these people. But the economic background is a section of the small bourgeoisie, who want a settlement at all costs, and the peasants of the distant valleys, who want to sell wine and pay no taxes.

A few days after the establishment of the *Rentenbank* and three weeks before the first *Rentenmarks* were issued the *Daily Herald* printed the last dispatch which Price wrote in 1923.

18 October

The condition of Germany now literally beggars description. That is no exaggeration but naked truth. I have lived through some very critical times during the Russian Revolution in 1917–18, but I do not remember a time quite as bad as this which has now befallen Germany. Even in the worst times in Russia one always had a feeling that the suffering was for some ideal which would make it all worthwhile. Today in Germany the economic catastrophe is worse than in Russia then, and in addition to that there is scarcely a ray of light on the horizon ... In Germany today there is a complete breakdown of the capitalist mechanism of distribution and exchange, and there is no sign yet that any of the would-be dictators are in a position to set up any state machinery which can do what the Communist Party did for Russia in 1917–18 – namely, hold the nation together by making everyone bear the same burden to achieve a common end. The government of the Reich is bankrupt. The mark has ceased to be currency and is merely a vast mass of paper packets representing so many dollars or pounds. The number of packets to the dollar varies every day ... Those who are lucky enough to have foreign currency can get along, but even then with difficulty. If anyone were to be asked how much it costs to live in Germany today he could only reply: 'It cost me at ten o'clock this morning so much, and at five o'clock this afternoon so much' ... The new currency, if it is going to be stable and backed by some material asset, will, under the present relation of classes in Germany, be dependent for its stability on the trusts. A percentage of their property will become the gold guarantee, and they have put their conditions for this 'sacrifice': the abolition of the eight-hour day. The Bavarian government, as the advanced guard of the trusts, is pressing for this. The government of the Reich and of Prussia still has Social Democrats in it who are pledged to resist the conditions of the trusts, and the trade unions will keep a watch on them. But the Franco-German industrial combine is on the march and its slogan is: 'Down with the eight-hour day, no more unemployment benefits and "open shop".' ... The volcano is smouldering; there are eruptions here and there, and it may continue for a long time yet in this state of suppressed activity.

In late October Price returned to England to take part in the forthcoming general election. His last assessment of the state of the Weimar Republic (which appears below) was written in January 1924, at the end of five years during which he had been an almost continuous observer of German affairs. He was not in the country at the time of the Hitler *putsch* on 8 November, although it would probably not have surprised him. Shortly before leaving he had written, on 8 October:

One thing is certain. Fascism in Germany is bound to assume a German form, not so spectacular as that which exists in Italy and Spain[13] but nonetheless a definite force to be reckoned with. The fact is that in Germany today the constitutional rights of the German people, set down with such care in Weimar in the summer of 1919, have almost imperceptibly disappeared. As in 1919, during the Noske dictatorship, the full executive and administrative power in the Reich has passed into the hands of the War

Minister. The government is considering measures for 'temporarily' restricting the rights of the Reichstag till 31 March of next year. No Labour newspaper can appear and no meeting of any nature can be held without the permission of the general commanding the Reichswehr in the locality. The excuse, of course, is plausible. The Bavarian government has threatened the sovereignty of the Reich by, in effect, putting the Weimar Constitution out of force in Bavaria. The government of the Reich has answered by setting up the generals to defend the Weimar Constitution, which reminds one of a German saying that it is not wise to appoint the goat as a gardener.

The following account of the first overtly Fascist *coup* in Germany is derived almost entirely from Foreign Office archives. It may have been noted that the information reaching London from British diplomats and the members of British military personnel serving on Allied Control Commissions at posts throughout Germany during the years under review – from which many quotations have already appeared – corroborated to a remarkable extent the purely factual information contained in Price's dispatches. This may be considered remarkable since Price was at this time an avowed Marxist, and it was perhaps even more remarkable that he was not taken in by Hitler's early, if spurious anti-capitalism. It may also be considered regrettable that so little notice was taken in Whitehall of the reports of the men on the spot. One of the consuls in Bavaria, William Seeds, had been particularly observant. Early in January 1923 he described, in a long memorandum addressed to Curzon, how popular attitudes to Hitler had changed in Bavaria in the course of 1922. From being an object of amusement he had begun to be considered 'the man who was always in the right'.

He gathered round him a most businesslike collection of young men whose discipline and aggressive action against Socialists and Communists (as enemies of the nation) impressed those classes which have most to fear from the Bolshevik bogey. There seems no doubt that Hitler has been able to raise considerable funds from industrial circles and his organisation is at least looked to for assistance in dealing with strikes. Consequently, long before the

Mussolini *coup d'état* in Italy, Herr Hitler's name was in everybody's mouth as that of the only possible saviour of the people, and
now his fame is so great that he was able recently to fill to
overflowing no less than ten meetings held simultaneously in
Munich one evening. He has as yet produced no constructive
programme; his aim is the creation of a strong government or
dictatorship, not necessarily entailing a restoration of the monarchy, but he has not worked out the details, and has hitherto
resisted every temptation to plunge into precipitate action.

Seeds went on to give a detailed account of events in Bavaria in
1922 and to account for the fact that, as the economic situation
deteriorated, the thoughts of the population turned increasingly
away from pure politics.

This applied specially to those middle classes who had hitherto
been the backbone of the militant reactionaries; their loyalty to the
various monarchist and war veterans' societies became tinged with
the conviction that economic salvation was the most pressing need
and was not to be looked for in those quarters. The star of Hitler
seemed to outshine the medals of Ludendorff ... Much was still to
be made out of Germany's sufferings under Entente aggression, but
the minds of the population were at least equally occupied with
building up an edifice of hope on the somewhat vague Hitler
programme of a dictatorship and a business government. As Hitler
himself would not positively come out either as a monarchist or as
a militarist, the patriotic societies accepted, with certain reservations, the inclusion of his group into their general league, and the
extremists' leaders worked out schemes for using Hitler as at least
a pawn in their own game.[14]

In *The Times* of 12 May 1923 'a correspondent' in Germany[15]
described Hitler's following as 'one of the most important
factors in the political situation of Bavaria' and professed
himself amazed 'by the number of men wearing Swastika badges
to be seen during a walk through the streets of Munich'. He
went on to summarise the '25 Articles of Faith'[16] of the Fascist
movement (which included the denial of the rights of German
citizenship to any 'individual of the Jewish faith'). But even so
he concluded that the politicians, monarchists and veterans'

organisations which supported him regarded Hitler as 'a useful tool, to be discarded in case of success and disowned in the event of failure'.

In June Seeds summarised for Curzon an article in the *Münchner Post*, a leading socialist paper which had been suspended for five days as a result of its appearance. This gave the names of eight patriotic associations associated with Hitler's National Socialists, numbering some 200,000 men, and stated that it was additionally proposed to form 50 regiments of 10,000 each in Prussia, Saxony, Upper Silesia, Baden, Wurtemburg, Pomerania, Thuringia and the North Sea provinces, for which arms and equipment had been assured.[17] On 24 September D'Abernon reported to Curzon:

> In East Prussia and Bavaria organisations exist which openly threaten to overturn the Government if they venture to give in to the French demands. So far as to rumours. Report from reliable source predicts that present regime will be overturned about 10 October. The Reichstag will be dismissed and a dictatorship established ... who the dictator or dictators will be has not yet been decided or if decided, not stated.[18]

D'Abernon's 'reliable source' was not far out. On 8 November a meeting of patriotic associations was held in the *Bürgerbraükeller* in Munich. The theme of the meeting had been advertised as 'Marxism and the danger to the state of socialist influence'. Most of the members of the Bavarian government were there, as were also Colonel von Seisser and General von Lossow. In the middle of a speech by von Kahr, Hitler leapt on to the platform, revolver in hand, and announced that the place was surrounded. He retired into an adjoining room with von Kahr, von Lossow and von Seisser and returned to state not only that the von Knilling Cabinet had been deposed but that the President of Germany and the entire government of the Reich were to be deposed. A German national government would be formed in Munich, with himself as political leader and a national army under Ludendorff, with von Lossow as Army Minister and von Seisser as Police Minister. As soon as the meeting had broken up, which it did peacefully enough, and Hitler had disappeared into the night, von Kahr, von Lossow and von Seisser ordered the immediate mobilisation of the Reichswehr and the police, broadcast their repudiation of the attempted *putsch* and ordered the arrest of Hitler and Ludendorff 'wherever they may be found'.

The next morning von Lossow and von Seisser placarded the city with denunciations, declaring that they had acted under duress the previous night. Hitler, apparently unaware that they had disassociated themselves from him, marched into the centre of the city with himself and Ludendorff at the head of his storm troops. Confronted by the Reichswehr they continued to advance. The soldiers fired. Hitler was slightly wounded but got away. Ludendorff gave himself up. Hitler was later caught, tried for treason and sentenced to five years' detention but released after eight months. The NSDAP was proscribed, but reformed in February 1925.

When, on the morning after the *putsch*, von Kahr had complained to the press that Hitler's action had been a breach of faith he was unconsciously confirming the predictions both of the British Consul and of *The Times* correspondent, that the triumvirate (von Lossow, von Seisser and himself) had been planning to use Hitler and then discard him. Less than a week earlier, von Kahr alleged, Hitler had promised to take no action 'without previous warning'.[19] The truth was that all three men had been close to leading an open rebellion against Berlin. At the beginning of November von Lossow had blatantly disregarded orders from Berlin. President Ebert himself had wanted to send troops to Bavaria but von Seeckt, as usual, was reluctant to set units of the Reichswehr against one another. However, he had warned the triumvirate that they had better put a little space between themselves and the Hitler–Ludendorff axis. Having thought they had done so by extracting that promise from Hitler, they felt betrayed. And now Stresemann, in Berlin, handed the executive power of the entire Reich to von Seeckt, who remained in that position until the state of emergency was ended, which was not to be until 13 February 1924.

On 23 November Stresemann lost a vote of confidence in the Reichstag. The Socialist members of his Cabinet had already resigned (3 November) in view of the apparent inconsistency between the Government's reaction to events in Saxony and in Bavaria. But on 23 November all the Socialist members of the

Reichstag voted against the Government. Stresemann resigned as Chancellor but retained a position in the Government as Minister for Foreign Affairs. The new Chancellor was a member of the Centre Party, Wilhelm Marx.

When Price returned to Berlin in January 1924 the emergency powers provided for at the time of the abandonment of passive resistance (see p. 164) were still in force. Although his last articles were not printed in the *Daily Herald* until late January and early February, they are included here as representing his concluding thoughts on the state of the country in which he had worked, lived, indeed married, for almost exactly five years. They were sent by surface mail and the date of publication is no guide to the date on which they were written, but it is doubtful that he would have wanted to write anything substantially different only two or three weeks earlier.

21 January

It can truly be said that the only thing which has been stabilised up to now in Germany is poverty. Some people still seem to believe that the mark is stable at last, but a large part of the population have their doubts, although they only express themselves under their breath, for fear that the ubiquitous spies of General von Seeckt should overhear them. Should this happen they might find themselves housed for an indefinite period without trial, within the four walls of one of the 'Republic's' prisons, under the so-called *schutzhaft* or *lettres de cachet* [emergency powers] for having 'spread unrest among the people'.

Fascism here is of a peculiar northern, Teutonic kind: not flashy and dramatic, as in Italy, but thorough, quiet and efficient. A change there certainly has been in the last three months. The unwholesome swarm of East European speculators who have been engaged, along with the Teutonic variety, in plundering the German public while inflation was going on have disappeared ... When I went into a bank last week, for the first time in Germany for three months, I discovered that I was the only member of the public there. The bank clerks were standing idly behind the counter and looked very pleased to see someone come in, as if it was a rare occurrence. Last year it took one often several hours to get a cheque cashed. Now it takes as many minutes ... Today half the bank staffs are dismissed and the rest have little to do. And it is the same with most of the other branches of industry and exchange in Germany.

A familiar sight for all Englishmen is the unemployed man standing at the street corner or outside the Labour Exchange. This can now be seen in Germany. And yet the streets of Berlin are piled high with snow, which has been lying there since the middle of December. But the thousands of unemployed cannot be put on to clear it away because the municipality cannot find the money. Taxes do not come in, and the pleasant method of printing paper money has now been, in true Prussian style, 'verboten'. Everyone is contemplating what the streets will be like when the thaw sets in.

There is dire hunger in the working-class quarters of all German towns and cities today ... In Berlin there have been nearly 50 deaths through complications resulting from underfeeding in the last three months. The highest category of skilled engineer now gets a wage amounting to no more than 30s. a week. The average wage is 20s. and the highest woman's wage is an equivalent of 15s. And yet, if you stroll round the food markets you will find that prices, reckoned in gold currency, are at least double the pre-war prices and in many cases treble. This brings the German workers' real wage down to at the most one-quarter his pre-war level.

1 February

Will the *Rentenmark* remain stable? There is no doubt that wide sections of the German public believe that it will, or rather, they are made to believe it by the joint aplication of judicious propaganda and martial law ... No one seemed to see that the *Rentenbank*, through the Government, had simply inflated the paper mark to a point which it would probably have reached, if left to itself, at some future date, and had merely struck off the noughts from the billion paper marks and called it a *Rentenmark*. Undoubtedly, the government of Herr Marx has taken measures, as no other government in Germany has done hitherto, to balance the budget of the Reich. The efforts are, however, solely at the expense of the working classes and of the lower middle classes. Dismissals have been made wholesale from government offices and more are pending. Wages and salaries are being stabilised at starvation levels and the eight-hour day is gone. Taxation is being raised all round, but it is being so raised that those in receipt of wages and salaries bear the brunt of it ... A financial juggle is made which puts the coal, steel and territorial magnates in the position of economic dictators and profiteers out of the circulation of the currency. In order to stave off the day when the *Rentenmark* will fall, as the paper mark did before, and gain time for the flotation of an international loan which will stabilise the mark for a long period of time, the German government is making serious efforts to balance its budget. But these efforts boil down to making another twist of the thumbscrew on the working classes of Germany and on what is left of the *rentiers* who have not been ruined by inflation.

5 February

The tremendous pressure on the standard of living of the German workers is simply killing the home market, for the purchase power of the community is reduced to a minimum. At the same time, the enormous prices are ruining the export trade. As a consequence, the production of industrial and agricultural products in Germany has dropped to about two-thirds of the pre-war value. This corresponds also, roughly, with the number of unemployed, which is registered at 5,000,000. This, with the dependents, would make 20,000,000, or one-third of the total population of Germany. The policy of the dictators on the board of the *Rentenbank* is to use this surplus of unemployed population, who are living on doles of from two to six gold marks a week (2s. to 6s.) as a constant threat to those who are fortunate to have work at from 20 to 25 gold marks a week. Of course this economic dictatorship must have military and executive power to enforce its will and, if possible, to clothe its actions with the fig leaf of legality. And so it is. The President, according to the Weimar Constitution, is only entitled to hand over power to the military as a temporary emergency measure, until such time as the Reichstag is summoned to take charge of the Executive. But probably, [even] if the Reichstag had been allowed to meet at once [that is, in September 1923] it would not have done much. For when, two months later, Herr Marx summoned it to ask it to abdicate its legislative powers to his Cabinet, it obeyed like a whipped dog, the Social Democratic Party voting with the majority in favour of abdication ... General von Seeckt can order the arrest and imprisonment of any person to whom he objects without trial, for as long as he likes. Thousands are sitting in jail for mere criticisms of his regime. Not only Communist but moderate Social-Democratic papers are being suppressed, their printing machines smashed, their bureaux broken up and their editors thrown into jail. After 1 April the Government is graciously pleased to allow juries to sit and decide on cases, together with specially selected members of the legal profession. It may be taken for granted that these will be reliable.

Thuringia, the only place now left in Germany where a Socialist government elected by parliamentary vote is being allowed to exist – at least on paper – is being badgered by the minions of General von Seeckt, who interfere in the administration and do what they like. They have issued a proclamation, which declares that for the coming general election no party may hold a meeting without the permission of the military, who shall have representatives present and shall close the meeting if anything is said which shall cause 'unrest among the people' ... If they are strengthened in their positions by an international loan there is no knowing how far they may not develop their terror over the working classes of Germany.

Price's choice of words may have been apocalyptic, but they were also prophetic. By the end of 1923 the Weimar Republic had survived, if barely, the French Occupation of the Ruhr. It had averted attempts to overthrow it by extremists of the Left and the Right. Both the German Communist Party and the National Socialists lived to fight another day, the former enjoying a surge of popular support in 1928 and 1931. The Republic survived to experience the cultural renaissance by which is now chiefly remembered. But it was the National Socialists who won in the end.

EPITAPH: 1924–33

In February 1924 von Seeckt relinquished the special powers which had disturbed Price on his last visit to Germany and the Reichstag refused to prolong the Enabling Law which had made it possible for the then Chancellor (Stresemann) to appoint him in the first place. Marx, who had only held office since November 1923, dissolved the Reichstag and elections were held in May. The parties of the discredited coalitions of 1923 lost ground and the parties of the Right gained ground, but Marx remained Chancellor.

Meanwhile, the Dawes Committee had reported (April) and its recommendations were immediately accepted by the German government.[1] Ironically, Stinnes died in the same month. The legislation necessary to put the recommendations of the Dawes Report into effect was approved in a free vote at the end of August. But the parties of the Right, more interested in securing an end to reparations of any kind or under any conditions than in stable government, subsequently withdrew support from the Marx coalition. The Reichstag was dissolved again in December 1924 and new elections held. The SPD made significant gains but true to their habit of avoiding the responsibilities of government, would not enter the next coalition, which was formed by Luther – the man who had stabilised the mark – in January 1925. As usual it contained members of the Centre and People's Parties, but also, for the first time, four members of the conservative, nationalist DNVP. Stresemann remained in the Government as Foreign Minister and the year 1925 was marked by perhaps his greatest initiative and achievement: the Treaty of Locarno.

The treaty bound the contracting powers (France, Germany and Belgium) to renounce the use of force and confirmed the inviolability of their existing frontiers and of the demilitarised zone of the Rhineland. It was signed in London on 1 December, guaranteed by Britain and Italy, and supplementary arbitration conventions were signed by most of the governments of

Western Europe. But the DNVP members of the coalition Cabinet resigned in protest even before the treaty was signed. It was ratified by 300 votes to 174 in the Reichstag, the SPD voting with the Government, but the Government fell anyway. On the eve of the Locarno conference the French finally evacuated the Ruhr. Two other events earlier in the year 1925 were to prove significant, if not ominous. The first President of the Weimar Republic, Ebert, died on 28 February and his elected successor was Germany's more or less untarnished war hero, Hindenburg. But, as Lord D'Abernon warned the first British Labour Prime Minister, Ramsay MacDonald, 'The danger is not with Hindenburg himself, but with those behind him.' In the same month that Ebert died, Hitler, barely two months out of prison, refounded the NSDAP.

In January 1926 Luther reconstructed his coalition Cabinet but it lasted only four months and in May Marx returned as Chancellor with another composed on more or less the same lines, the SPD again excluding themselves. In April his government signed the Treaty of Berlin with Soviet Russia. Designed to compensate for the western orientation of Locarno, it did little more than confirm the provisions of the Treaty of Rapallo, but it was seen by the Allies as providing yet another reason not to curtail the occupation, and by the Nationalists as yet another betrayal. The NSDAP held its first national congress at Weimar in July, and the Storm Troopers (*Sturmabteilung*, or SA) which had figured so prominently in Hitler's earlier rallies in Bavaria were recognised as being an integral component of the party. Since his premature release from prison Hitler had been concentrating on party organisation rather than membership, and the number of local NSDAP groups outside Bavaria had grown from 71 to 262. Hitler now turned his attention to the winning of support from specific areas of the population: the professions, farmers, youth groups, students.

The year 1926 saw changes in the role of the great industrialists. Since the death of Stinnes there had been a noticeable decline in their overt interference in politics, although their influence continued to be exerted in an authoritarian, anti-demcratic sense. As though their energies had returned to their proper channels, they also engaged in a series of amalgamations. Thyssen, Rhein-Elbe, Phoenix and Rheinstahl came together to form the gigantic *Vereinigte Stahlwerke* (United Steelworks); most of the chemical industries combined to form *I.G. Farben* and there were more amalgamations in electricity and petroleum production.

At the end of the year the British evacuated Cologne and at the end of January 1927 the Inter-Allied Military Commission was withrawn, but 60,000 Allied troops remained, despite the fact that Germany had been admitted to the League of Nations in September. The Marx government fell again in December, brought down by a vote of no confidence moved by the SPD, and rose again in January 1927, after which it managed to survive until February 1928: a bloc in which the Centre Party, the BVP, the DVP and the DNVP were all variously represented. But a new element now entered the political scene, personified by the appointment, in October 1926, of General von Schleicher to succeed von Seeckt as head of the Reichswehr. Until now the reactionary instincts of the military had been, for the most part, subordinated to the habit of obeying the orders of the Reich government even when they disagreed with them. But Hindenburg, although sincere in his profession of loyalty to the Weimar Constitution, was known to prefer governments of the Right and was quite prepared to intervene in politics himself to help them along. Von Schleicher now began to use his influence with Hindenburg to increase the participation of the Nationalist parties in government, under the influence of the old elites: the army, the bureaucracy and big business.

After the fall of the fourth Marx government, in the first elections to take place after von Schleicher's appointment (May 1928) the parties of the Left made considerable gains. The SPD achieved nearly one-third of the total of seats in the Reichstag, the KPD gained 54 while the NSDAP polled only 800,000 votes nationally. The main losers had been the Centre parties, as voters transferred their allegiance to the many small splinter parties with sectional interests which continued to proliferate. The DNVP swung heavily to the Right under the leadership of the former Krupps director and newspaper magnate, Hugenburg. The SPD was now obliged to come out of opposition and in June the veteran Hermann Müller formed a non-party coalition with Gröner as Defence Minister. But von Schleicher remained head of the political bureau of the Ministry. It was under a Socialist-led government that German rearmament began. The Versailles Treaty had authorised the construction of four armed cruisers. These were now laid down and the budget for the Reichswehr was considerably increased.

In August 1928 Stresemann persuaded the French to agree to review Germany's ability to pay reparations at the level set by the Dawes Report. In February 1929 another committee was appointed under the American banker Owen D. Young. It reported in June and the Allies discussed it at The Hague in August. The Young Report proposed a substantial reduction in the annual amount of reparations to be paid (from 2,500 million to 2,000 million marks) but also proposed that the liability should continue for another 59 years. If Germany accepted the plan, the Allies would evacuate the whole of the Rhineland in June 1931, five years earlier than the date set in the Treaty of Versailles. The Müller government accepted the Young Report and this was used as the pretext for a violent agitation on the Right. The NSDAP, the DNVP and the Stahlhelm joined together to force the government to hold a referendum on a so-called Freedom Law calling for the repudiation of the war guilt clause of the Versailles Treaty and the immediate evacuation of the occupied areas. The referendum was held in December. In the event only 13.8 per cent of the population supported the proposal, but the campaign created a propaganda opportunity for the NSDAP, which gained ground in autumn local elections, doubling their vote in Prussia.

The consequences of the collapse of the New York Stock Exchange in October 1929 soon began to be felt in Germany. At the beginning of the year only 1.3 per cent of the population had been unemployed; in the course of the year the number out of work began to approach 3 million. There had been a bitter industrial dispute and lockout in the Ruhr during the previous winter, and labour relations were already sour. Unemployment insurance became the focus of added conflict, since the state insurance fund was found to be insufficient and it became necessary for the government to add to it out of revenue. As they usually did in such circumstances the Alliance of German Industries called for a decrease in social benefits and for increased indirect taxes.

Rising unemployment was accompanied by rising public disorder. The government was obviously foundering and there was little sense of collective responsibility among the members of the Cabinet, who shared few if any common interests. In December von Schleicher, acting now on behalf of Hindenburg and in conjunction with Gröner, began to sound out the leader of the Centre Party, Brüning, with a view to his succeeding Müller as Chancellor once the legislation to implement the Young Plan had passed through the Reichstag.

The Müller coalition, held together largely by the necessity to get that legislation through, broke up in March 1930. Brüning was ready and waiting with a Right-wing coalition, excluding the SPD. However it was defeated in the Reichstag in July over a bill which would have implemented the regressive fiscal and social welfare policies advocated by the Alliance of German Industries. The new Chancellor had the bill promulgated by decree, and when the Reichstag voted against the decree, Brüning dissolved the Reichstag and reissued the decree. The destruction of democratic government in Germany had begun in earnest. In the election which followed in September the NSDAP won 107 seats, an increase of 95, and became the second largest party in the Reichstag with 18.2 per cent of the poll, but the SPD, with 143 seats, was still the strongest party. Germany now began to be systematically governed by decree and the SPD began literally and deliberately to 'tolerate' the situation, mainly by refusing to support votes of no confidence. In 1930 the Reichstag sat on 94 days, passed 98 laws and 5 decrees. In the following year it sat on only 42 days, passed 34 laws and 44 decrees.

Brüning now concentrated on getting an end put to reparations, no matter what that might cost in terms of unemployment. He refused foreign credits to ease the state finances rather than forfeit his freedom of action. In July 1931 he announced that reparations payments would soon be suspended. A flight of capital took place, followed by a number of bank failures. The American President, Hoover, offered a moratorium and Brüning asked that yet another committee of experts should be set up to report on Germany's capacity to pay once the moratorium had come to an end. In December the experts gave it as their opinion that Germany would never be able to resume payments and they proposed that not only German reparations but also all inter-Allied war debts should be cancelled.

In March 1932 presidential elections were due to be held. Hitler stood against Hindenburg and did well enough to force a run-off, but Hindenburg won in the second round. In the following month Brüning banned by decree both the SA and Hitler's newest and even more sinister paramilitary formation, the SS: one of 66 decrees as compared with only five laws passed in the entire year. But Hindenburg, despite his predilection for authoritarian government, refused to assent to any more government by decrees necessitated purely by Brüning's weakness. On 29 May he dismissed the Chancellor, regardless of the parliamentary situation, using the very powers upon which Brüning had been depending. Von Schleicher now succeeded in getting rid of both Brüning and his Defence Minister, Gröner. His plan was to use Hitler – by involving him in government – before getting rid of him too and installing an anti-parliamentary presidential regime underpinned by the Reichswehr. His, and therefore Hindenburg's, nominee as interim Chancellor was the vain and aristocratic von Papen, who notionally belonged to the Centre Party. Von Papen formed a non-party coalition government composed of conservatives and aristocrats. The decree banning the SA and the SS was rescinded, and in the summer of 1932 the country was torn apart by street fighting, especially in Prussia. In July von Papen deposed the Prussian government on the grounds that it was incapable of keeping public order, and instituted direct rule. This was damaging to the prospects of democratic government throughout the Reich, since Prussia accounted for three-fifths of its total area and population, and had succeeded in maintaining stable coalitions, even including the SPD, throughout the Weimar period.

Later in the same month (July 1932) elections to the Reichstag were held. The NSDAP won 230 out of 608 seats. Surprisingly, the KPD won 89 seats, which made these two parties unlikely partners in operating a blocking majority in the Reichstag. Hitler now demanded the Chancellorship for himself, the Ministries of the Interior, Justice and Agriculture for his party, and an Act enabling him to rule by decree. This Hindenburg refused, and refused in a manner calculated to humiliate. Von Papen was reappointed, but his second government did not last long and was defeated by an unprecedentedly massive vote of no confidence – 512 to 42 – in September. New elections were held in November. The NSDAP popular vote fell by 2 million, but even so it was the largest party in the Reichstag. At the same time, the numerical results for the other parties offered no obvious possibilities for another coalition. Von Papen was briefly commissioned to form a new government. His plans would have involved the suppression of all the existing parties and the imposition of radical constitutional changes. But he now began to lose the support both of Hindenburg and von Schleicher, and on 3 December Hindenburg appointed von Schleicher as Chancellor. The last act of the Weimar Republic had begun.

Von Schleicher began to show signs of unexpected and unwelcome independence of mind. He dismayed the military establishment which had supported him by making overtures to trade unionists and proposing land settlement schemes for the rural unemployed (unemployment now stood at over 6 million). The army called it 'agrarian Bolshevism'. The establishment withdrew its support and suddenly became more sympathetic to Hitler. When von Schleicher discovered that von Papen had been holding secret talks with both Hitler and Hindenburg, he resigned. Two days later, on 30 January 1933, Hitler was appointed Chancellor and von Papen Vice-Chancellor. Von Papen deluded himself that with only three members of the NSDAP in the Cabinet, including Hitler, he had Hitler 'framed in'. He soon found out how wrong he was. In February the Reichstag mysteriously burned down. In new elections the following month the NSDAP got 43.9 per cent of the vote. And in the same month – March 1933 – the Weimar Constitution was abrogated.

During the last ten years of the Weimar Republic (1923–33) there had been ten general elections, eleven governments and ten different Chancellors. Until 1932 the SPD, except for a few months in 1924, had been the largest party in the Reichstag but had been unable or unwilling to find any way of making its strength felt. It clung to the rhetoric of revolution while abandoning the substance, finding no reason why it should compromise with the old-fashioned liberal-democratic ideals which had informed the founders of the Weimar Constitution. These were years of unstable coalitions in which the key role was generally held by the Centre Party, but it too began to lean to the Right after 1928, and refused to enter any coalition containing the SPD. What had passed for parliamentary government under the Hohenzollerns had not created any tradition in favour of compromise. A contemporary observer had remarked, in 1929, 'What we have today is a coalition of ministers, not a coalition of parties. There are no government parties, only opposition parties.'2

The only real successes that could be claimed for any German government during this period were in the field of foreign policy, and even here the seeds of future conflict were germinating. The humiliations of the Versailles Treaty, above all the occupation of the Rhineland and the creation of the Polish Corridor, created an atmosphere in which irridentism thrived. Germany's eastern frontier was not covered by the terms of the Locarno Treaty. German failure to comply with the disarmament clauses of the treaty were perfectly well known to the British officers of the occupation, but they were hard to prove when the Reichswehr complained that inspections impugned their honour and insisted that the armaments in question were being produced for export. Moreover the fear of Bolshevism was still common both to Allied and to German military leaders. In 1931 Germany spent three times more on war materials than Britain.

Despite the superficial appearance of stability, the years between 1924 and 1932 chiefly demonstrate the fragility of the Weimar settlement. But Hitler's coming to power was not inevitable, despite all the work that had been put into building up the structure and membership of the NSDAP. What made it relatively easy for him were the consequences of the collapse of the New York Stock Exchange in October 1929. The social devastation of the Depression hit Germany harder than it did the other former belligerents. An atmosphere of insecurity and fear was created in which people began to look for 'scapegoats and saviours'.3 When unemployment stood at 33 per cent, as it did at the beginning of 1933, it was not surprising that the existing institutions of government did not command confidence. Hitler's oratorical gifts, combined with the simplicity of his solutions, did. Everything would be all right if Germany could just acquire more space (*Lebensraum*) and get rid of the Jews. By then the polarisation of the political parties had undermined the possibility of carrying on governing by democratic means. The parties of the Right, backed by the old elites, became increasingly authoritarian while the parties of the Left were disabled by the Comintern's doctrine forbidding any kind of collaboration between the KPD and the 'social Fascists' of the SPD. The increasing use of presidential power after 1928 made nonsense of the constitution itself. Perhaps, given the handicaps with which it was endowed from the very beginning – defeat, humiliation, the absence of a democratic tradition in politics and a tendency to look for extreme and authoritarian solutions – it is all the more remarkable that the Weimar Republic lasted as long as it did. The last, understated words go to Price, written a few years before his death in 1973:

My years in Germany enabled me to see and report about the weakness of parliamentary and democratic institutions existing there after defeat in the First World War. The Majority Social Democrats allowed themselves to become prisoners of the military reaction and of the Officers' Corps. The Communists lost their best and wisest leader, Rosa Luxemburg, by murder, and deteriorated into a rabble which accepted orders from Moscow, and Moscow was quite ignorant of German affairs. The whole history of Germany during this time was one frightful tragedy which led to Armageddon Number Two.[4]

BIOGRAPHICAL NOTES

von BADEN, Prince Max (1867–1929). President of the Upper House of the Baden *Landtag* from 1907, he concerned himself during the war with the welfare of prisoners of war. As Imperial Chancellor called in to end the war, he began the dialogue with President Wilson and later took it upon himself to announce the Kaiser's abdication although he had not yet secured his final agreement. After the war he founded a progressive school at his home, Salem.

BAUER, Gustav (1870–1944). He began to work in the central Secretariat of the Free Trade Union, joined the Social Democrats (SPD) and was elected to the Reichstag in 1912, retaining his seat in the elections to the National Assembly in January 1919. He became Chancellor in June 1919 but retired after the Kapp *putsch* in March 1920 and thereafter held no further office.

BERNSTEIN, Eduard (1850–1932). A Social Democrat from 1872, he spent many of his early years abroad and was Engels' literary executor as well as the author of many historical and theoretical works. He was much involved in the revisionism debates within the SPD. First elected to the Reichstag in 1902 he was for a while a member of both the SPD and the USPD and was a figurehead of the reunification of the parties in 1922.

BRIAND, Aristide (1862–1932). A deputy since 1902, in his early days he associated with the group of socialists around Jaures and helped to found the daily newspaper, *Humanité*. As Minister of Public Instruction and Worship from 1906 he completed the separation of Church and State in 1909. In the next 20 years he was a minister in eleven governments and was a champion of Franco–German reconciliation. He was awarded the Nobel Peace Prize in 1926.

BRÜNING, Heinrich (1895–1970). After active service in the war he worked with the Christian Trade Unions. He entered the Reichstag as a member of the Centre party in 1924 and became its financial expert and, from 1929, its leader in the Reichstag. In 1930 he was Chancellor in a non-party coalition. His opposition to the policies of the NSDAP drove him into exile. From 1939 to 1950 he was a Professor of Politics at Harvard and he held the same post at Cologne after his return to Germany at the end of the war.

CRISPIEN, Artur (1875–1946). He was a painter by trade. He joined the SPD and worked as a party functionary in a variety of posts from 1902. He opposed the war and was elected co-chairman of the USPD in March 1919, remaining in that post until its reunification with the SPD, when he became third co-chairman of the united party. He emigrated to Switzerland in 1933.

CUNO, Wilhelm Carl Josef (1876–1933). After ten years of public service, which included parliamentary drafting and (during the war) work in the departments of food control and war economy, he became in 1917 a director of the Hamburg America Line (HAPAG). He continued to be consulted on economic matters by the government during the armistice and peace negotiations. As Chancellor from November 1922 to August 1923 he had to deal not only with the French occupation of the Ruhr but with the worst period of the German inflation.

DAÜMIG, Ernst (1866–1922). With a background in socialist journalism and education, he became editor of *Vorwärts* in 1911 but was dismissed in 1916 for his opposition to the war. A leading member of both the Revolutionary Shop Stewards and the USPD, he was a member of the Reichstag from 1920 to 1922 and co-chairman of the reunited Communist Party (VKPD) in 1922, rejoining the USPD shortly before his death.

EBERT, Friedrich (1871–1925). He joined the SPD as a young man and was elected to the Reichstag in 1912. Chairman of the parliamentary party from 1913, he was largely responsible for getting the SPD to vote for war credits. He was both the last Imperial Chancellor (as a member of Prince Max's Cabinet) and first President of the Weimar Republic, a post which he held until his death.

EICHHORN, Emil (1863–1925). A metal worker, he joined the SPD in 1881 and was elected to the Reichstag in 1903. He was head of the USPD press bureau after the party split from the SPD. He was police president of Berlin from November 1918 to January 1919 and joined the KPD. He was a member of the National Assembly and then of the Reichstag (1920) until his death.

EISNER, Kurt (1867–1919). He wrote for various democratic publications until he joined the staff of *Vorwärts* in 1898, becoming effectively its principal editor until 1906. He then ran a private news service in Bavaria specialising in cultural and parliamentary affairs. Although not himself a revolutionary, believing in co-partnership between Councils and parliaments, he was the main inspirer and creator of the Munich Soviet. He was assassinated in February 1919.

ERZBERGER, Matthias (1875–1921). A former schoolteacher and editor of the Catholic *Deutsche Volksblatt*, he was elected to the Reichstag as a member of the Centre Party in 1903. Initially an annexationist, he changed his views on the war and was the instigator of the Reichstag resolution in favour of negotiated peace in 1917. As Minister without Portfolio in Prince Max's Cabinet and again in the Provisional Government, he was put in charge of the armistice negotiations. He favoured acceptance of the Versailles Treaty and as Minister of Finance in the Bauer Cabinet he produced a strongly redistributive budget. Hated by the Right wing in politics he resigned from the Reichstag after the failure of a libel action against Helfferich, but was re-elected in June 1920 and was planning to resume his political career when he was murdered.

FEHRENBACH, Konstantin (1852–1926). He was a member of the Centre Party in both the Baden *Landtag* (from 1885) and the Reichstag (from 1903). He was president of the last Imperial

Reichstag and of the National Assembly in 1919. In June 1920 he succeeded Müller as Chancellor and attended both the Spa and the London Conferences in that capacity. From March 1924 until his death he was leader of the Centre Party in the Reichstag.

GESSLER, Otto (1875–1955). He served as mayor of Regensburg and then of Nuremberg before the war. He was a co-founder of the German Democratic Party (DDP) in 1918. He succeeded Noske as Minister for the Army after the Kapp *putsch* in 1920 and remained in that post during 13 successive Cabinets until 1928. After 1932 he left politics but maintained his political contacts. He was arrested after the attempt on Hitler's life in June 1944. At the end of his life he was made president of the German Red Cross.

GRÖNER, Wilhelm (1867–1939). He was the son of an NCO in the army of Würtemberg. He entered the army aged 18 and rapidly proved himself a brilliant staff officer, outstandingly successful in securing the co-operation of both sides of industry for war production. He succeeded Ludendorff as First Quartermaster General in October 1918 and played a key role in persuading the Kaiser to abdicate and subsequently retaining the influence of the army in the Provisional Government.

HAASE, Hugo (1863–1919). A socialist lawyer who had made his name as defence attorney in political trials, he was elected to the Reichstag in 1897. He opposed the SPD's attitude to the war and was involved in the formation of the USPD, of which he became co-chairman in 1917. He was one of the three USPD members of the Provisional Government in November–December 1918; he was assassinated at the end of 1919.

HAKING, General Sir Richard Cyril Byrne (1862–1945). A career soldier since 1881, he served in the Boer War, but his greatest talents appear to have been in the diplomatic and intellectual areas of military service. He was a professor at the Staff College from 1901 to 1904, Chief of the British Section of the Armistice Commission in 1918, and then commanded British Military Missions in Russia, the Baltic Provinces, and the Allied troops in the plebiscite areas of East Prussia and Danzig.

HELFFERICH, Karl Theodor (1872–1924). Economist and author, he joined the Colonial Section of the Foreign Ministry in 1904 but went into banking in 1906 and in 1908 became a director of the Deutsche Bank. In 1915 he returned to government service as Minister for Finance and in 1919 joined the DNVP, becoming increasingly nationalistic and Right-wing in his ideas. He was singled out in the Reichstag as 'the enemy' by Chancellor Wirth after the murder of Rathenau.

von HERTLING, Friedrich, Graf (1843–1919). A member of the Centre Party, he was in the Reichstag from 1875 to 1890 and again from 1896 to 1912, specialising in Church affairs. As president of the Bavarian *Landtag* he was a key figure in the relationship betwcen Bavaria and Berlin before the war. He succeeded Michaelis as Chancellor of the Reich for the last year of the war.

HILFERDING, Rudolf (1877–1941). Viennese-born, he first qualified as a doctor but made his name as a Marxist economist. By 1914 he was the leading political editor of *Vorwärts*. He was conscripted into the medical service of the Austrian army during the war but returned to Berlin to edit the socialist paper *Freiheit* from 1918 to 1922. He went with the Right wing of the USPD at Halle and was Minister of Finance in 1923 and again in 1928–29. He emigrated in 1933 but the Gestapo killed him in Paris.

HÖLZ, Max (1889–1933). He joined the USPD in 1918 and the KPD in 1919. He organised guerrilla activity in the Ruhr following the general strike which defeated the Kapp *putsch*. After the March Action in 1921 he ran his own 'Red Army' until driven out and over the border into Czechoslovakia, where he was captured. He was imprisoned in Germany, released in 1928 and emigrated to Russia, where he is believed to have died in the Stalin purges.

JOGISCHES, Leo (1867–1919). He was active in the under-ground revolutionary movement in Lithuania and met Rosa Luxemburg when they were both in exile in 1890. They founded the Polish Social Democratic party together and became and remained close friends and colleagues for the rest of their lives. Jogisches believed that the foundation of the KPD was prema-ture but he joined it out of solidarity. He opposed the Berlin uprising in January 1919 but was murdered three months later.

von KAHR, Gustav (1862–1934). A jurist with experience of local government, he held conservative, nationalist and monar-chist views extremely inimical to the Weimar settlement. He was president of Bavaria for 18 months after the Kapp *putsch* and returned as state commissioner after the end of the passive resistance to the French occupation of the Ruhr in September 1923. His ambivalent role in the Hitler *putsch* of November 1923 led to his assassination in the 'Night of the Long Knives' (1934).

KAUTSKY, Karl (1854–1938). A Viennese-born socialist writer, he spent some years in exile under Bismarck's Socialist Law and studied Marxist theory. He led the attack on revisionism, but after 1917 he began to argue against uncritical admiration of Bolshevism. He worked for the reunification of the German socialist parties and was held in great esteem but without political position. After 1925 he returned to Vienna and played no further part in German politics.

von KNILLING, Eugen (1865–1927). After spending a great part of his life in public service, he held the post of Minister of the Interior in Bavaria from 1912 to 1918. He succeeded von Lerchfeld as Bavarian premier in 1922, representing the Bavar-ian People's Party, but not its Right wing. In 1924 he became president of the state.

KILMARNOCK, Victor Alexander Sereld Hay, Lord (1876–1941). He entered the diplomatic service in 1900, and after various other European postings was sent to Stockholm, where he acted as chargé d'affaires on many occasions between 1909 and 1913, first secretary in Tokyo (1913), chargé d'affaires again in Copenhagen (1918–19) and in Berlin (1920–21). In 1919 he was promoted Counsellor and posted as High Commissioner on the Inter-Allied Rhineland High Commission in December 1921, but resigned the service soon afterwards.

KORFANTY, Wojciech (1873–1939). He was a Polish Silesian and a member of the German Reichstag in 1903. In August 1919 and again in May 1921 he led an army of partisans who claimed the whole of Upper Silesia for Poland. After the partition of Silesia which resulted from the League of Nations settlement he went to live in Poland and was was elected to the Polish Parliament (*Sejm*). He played an important part in the organisation of Polish industry, especially mining, and is still venerated as a great patriotic leader.

KUN, Bela (1886–1934). He was captured by the Russians while serving with the Hungarian army in the First World War. He returned to Hungary in 1917 as a Communist agitator and founded the Hungarian Communist Party. In March 1919 he set up a Soviet government which overthrew the democratic republic of Count Karolyi and carried out radical reforms indiscriminately and with great ruthlessness. In August 1919 he fled to Russia, thence to Germany as a Comintern agent. After the failure of the March Action, which he actively promoted, he returned to Russia and was executed in the Stalin purges.

LEDEBOUR, Georg (1850–1947). He joined the SPD in 1891 and was elected to the Reichstag in 1900. Although primarily a writer and lecturer, in 1917 he became co-chairman of both the USPD and the Revolutionary Shop Stewards. After the Berlin uprising of 1919 he was imprisoned. When the USPD split at Halle he was elected co-chairman of its Right wing, but he resigned in 1923. From 1933 until his death he lived in Switzerland.

LEGIEN, Carl (1861–1920). A Right-wing Social Democrat and trade union leader, he nonetheless took the lead in calling for a general strike against the Kapp *putsch* and afterwards proposed a coalition government to include all three parties of the Left.

von LERCHFELD, Hugo, Graf (1871–1944). After experience in the army, local government and law, he entered the German Foreign Office in 1919. In September 1921 he was called upon to take the presidency of Bavaria at a time of strained relations between Bavaria and the Reich government. Politically opposed to extremism in any form, his life was characterised by his open-mindedness. In 1924 he entered the Reichstag as a member of the Bavarian People's Party (BVP). He retired from public life in 1933.

LEVI, Paul (1883–1930). A socialist lawyer and writer, he joined the Spartacists and became leader of the German Communist Party (KPD) after the death of Rosa Luxemburg. He resigned the leadership because of the interference of the Comintern resulting in the March Action of 1921. After the reunification of the two wings of the Social Democrats he rejoined the party and was elected to the Reichstag in 1924. He committed suicide in 1930.

LIEBKNECHT, Karl (1871–1919). He was a Social Democrat member of the Reichstag from 1912 to 1916, when he was imprisoned for his opposition to the war. Although a close friend and colleague of Rosa Luxemburg and co-founder with her of the German Communist Party (KPD) he was perhaps the more impulsive and less the thinker of the partnership.

LOUCHEUR, Louis (1872–1931). An industrialist with Left radical leanings, he was a deputy from 1919 to 1931 and a minister six times between 1916 and 1931, his progressive housing legislation in 1928 being especially well remembered.

LUTHER, Hans (1879–1962). He came into government first as Minister for Food (1922–23), then as Finance Minister (1923–25) and finally as Chancellor in 1925. The stabilisation of the mark was accomplished during his period as Finance Minister. He was president of the Reichsbank from 1930 to 1933 and ambassador to Washington from 1933 to 1937. After the war he worked as an adviser to the German government on economic reconstruction.

LUXEMBURG, Rosa (1870–1919). She was active in the Polish revolutionary underground before coming to Germany in 1895, where she identified herself with the Left wing of the German socialist movement. She was imprisoned throughout the First World War. A committed internationalist, she wrote voluminously, pamphlets and articles as well as books, of which probably the best known is her *Accumulation of Capital* (1913).

MALCOLM, Lieutenant-General Sir Neil (1868–1953). As a regular army officer he served on the North West Frontier, in the Boer War and in the First World War, being severely wounded in March 1918. He was head of the British Military Mission in Berlin from 1919 to 1921. His dispatches to the War Office and his private letters (deposited at St Antony's College, Oxford) provide a lively source of information about German politics in the immediate post-war years.

MÜLLER, Hermann (1876–1931). After editing a provincial socialist newspaper, Müller began to work in 1906 in the SPD Press Bureau in Berlin. He represented the Left wing of the party at meetings of the Second International. In 1918 he was a member of the Executive of the Berlin Workers' and Soldiers' Council and was elected to the National Assembly in 1919. As Foreign Minister in the Bauer Cabinet he was one of the signatories of the Versailles Treaty. He was Chancellor for a few months in 1920 and again between 1928 and 1930, when he resigned due to illness.

MÜLLER, Richard (1880–?). A metalworker by trade, he opposed the war and became a prominent leader of the Revolutionary Shop Stewards and president of the Executive of the Berlin Workers' and Soldiers' Council. He opposed the January uprising in Berlin, later served in the trade union section of the reunited Communist Party, but was opposed to the policies of the Moscow Trade Union International, and was forced out of the party in 1922. He then abandoned all political activity and nothing more has been recorded about him.

NOSKE, Gustav (1868–1946). He entered politics via journalism and as a member of the SPD was elected to the Reichstag in 1906, where he became the party's specialist on military and naval affairs. He was sent by Prince Max to restore order after the Kiel Mutiny, and became Minister of Defence in the Provisional Government in December 1918. During 1919 he became notorious for his suppression of the parties of the Left. After the Kapp *putsch* he abandoned politics but continued in public life as president of Hanover until 1933, when he was deposed and more than once imprisoned by the Nazis. He survived the war and died as he was about to begin a lecture tour in the USA.

von PAPEN, Franz (1879–1969). Although nominally a member of the Centre Party, von Papen was by nature an extreme Right-wing monarchist with ties by marriage to important industrialists. During the war he was Chief of Staff to the 4th Turkish Army in Palestine. He supported Hindenburg in the presidential election of 1925 and broke with the Centre Party. As Chancellor in the interim government which followed Brüning's dismissal in May 1932 he governed with the so-called 'Baron's Cabinet' but lost a vote of confidence in September and resigned. He then began to intrigue with the NSDAP. He was Hitler's vice-chancellor in 1933–34 but lost Hitler's confidence and was sent as ambassador to Vienna and then Turkey for most of the war years. Cleared of war crimes at Nuremberg, he was nonetheless given a nominal sentence of hard labour by a German court.

POINCARÉ, Raymond Nicolas Landry (1860–1934). A deputy since 1887, he was Minister of Education in 1893, a senator in 1903, prime minister in 1911–13 and president of France from 1913 to 1920. His state visit to Russia in 1914 greatly fortified the Franco-Russian alliance. From 1922 to 1924 he simultaneously held the posts of Prime Minister and Minister for Foreign Affairs – years marked by his unbending determination to exact the maximum retribution from Germany for the destruction caused by the war.

RADEK, Karl Bergardovich (1885–1939). An extremely able writer and propagandist, he worked with Rosa Luxemburg in Poland and Lenin in Switzerland before the First World War. He joined the Bolsheviks when he returned to Russia in 1917 and was made head of the Central European Department in the

Soviet Ministry of Foreign Affairs, and later head of Sovprop, the ministry's propaganda organisation. He came to Germany illicitly in December 1918, was present at the founding of the German Communist Party, and was soon after arrested and spent nearly a year in the Moabit Prison, where he conducted a kind of semi-official diplomatic mission cum political salon. For a while, after his return to Russia, he was critical of Comintern policies. Although he later conformed he was a victim of the Stalin treason trials.

RATHENAU, Walter (1867–1922). Son of the founder of the *Allgemeine Elektrizität Gemeinschaft* (AEG), Rathenau was its president by 1915. Before then he had set up the Raw Material Section of the Ministry of the Interior, which ensured the supply of materials for war production. In 1918 he was an adviser on economic matters during the armistice negotiations and at Spa in 1920. He served as Minister for Reconstruction in the Wirth Cabinet but resigned in protest against the partition of Upper Silesia. In January 1922 he represented Germany at the Cannes Conference on reparations, and in February accepted the role of Minister for Foreign Affairs. While at the Genoa Conference he negotiated the Treaty of Rapallo with Soviet Russia. He was the object of fanatical hatred by the extreme Right, both for his political activities and because he was Jewish, and he was assassinated by zealots in June 1922. One of his anonymous German lexicographers described him as a man who represented, in himself, the ideals of the Weimar Republic.

REINHARDT, Colonel Wilhelm (dates not known). After serving for 30 years in the army of Prussia, he became one of the first commanders of the Freikorps. As an unrepentant monarchist he was heavily involved in the suppression of the Berlin uprising in January 1919 and in many of the other actions subsequently undertaken by the Freikorps. He later supported Hitler.

SCHACHT, Hjalmar (1877–1970). A banker by profession, he was co-founder of the German Democratic Party (DDP) in 1918. In 1923 he played a key role, as head of the Reichsbank, in supporting Luther's policy for stabilising the mark. He later began to co-operate with the National Socialists and was Minister for Economic Affairs under Hitler from 1934 to 1943. Tried at Nuremberg, he was sentenced to eight years' imprisonment but after his release in 1950 he returned to banking.

SCHEIDEMANN, Philipp (1865–1939). A socialist journalist, he was elected to the Reichstag in 1903. He was co-chairman of the parliamentary party of the SPD in 1914 and was appointed a member of Prince Max's Cabinet in October 1918. In February 1919 he became the first prime minister of the Weimar Republic, but resigned rather than sign the Versailles Treaty and retired from politics.

von SCHLEICHER, Kurt, General (1882–1934). On Gröner's staff during the war and then in the Ministry for the Army, he succeeded Gröner as head of the armed forces in 1926 and as such enjoyed, for a time, considerable influence with Hindenburg. He was instrumental in getting von Papen installed as Chancellor and followed him in that position in December 1932. He attempted to interest the Left wing of the NSDAP in his ideas for unemployment relief, thereby incurring the wrath of Hitler, who conspired with Hindenburg and von Papen to get rid of him. When von Schleicher learned of this he resigned and retired into private life, but Hitler had him murdered all the same, in the 'Night of the Long Knives' (June 1934).

von SEECKT, Hans (1868–1936). He headed the military contingent in the German peace delegation at Versailles and in 1920 was made chief of the army command. He was responsible for the reorganisation of the Reichswehr and wielded emergency powers after the end of passive resistance. After leaving the army he entered politics as a Reichstag deputy (People's Party) from 1930 to 1932.

SEEDS, William, Sir (1882–1973). He entered the diplomatic service in 1904 and progressed through postings in Washington, Peking, Athens and Lisbon to Berlin, where he briefly preceded Lord Kilmarnock as chargé d'affaires. He was then appointed Consul General with the rank of Counsellor in Bavaria. In May

1928 he was British High Commissioner on the Inter-Allied Rhineland High Commission after which he was ambassador to Brazil (1930), when he was knighted, and finally to the Soviet Union (1939–40).

SEVERING, Carl (1875–1952). He joined the SPD in 1893. A shop steward in the Metal Workers' Union, he was elected to the Reichstag in 1907. From 1920 to 1933 he was again a member of the Reichstag and also of the Prussian *Landtag*, in which he was Minister of the Interior from 1920 to 1926 and again from 1930 to 1932. He was imprisoned by the Nazis but survived the war to become active again in German socialist politics after the war.

STINNES, Hugo (1870–1924). Educated as a mining engineer, he entered his grandfather's firm in 1890, but soon began to increase and diversify the family's coalowning business to include both internal and international transport concerns and iron and steel factories. In 1920 he entered the Reichstag as a member of the German People's Party and began to buy up newspapers, the politics of which quickly began to reflect his own. He profited enormously from the inflation, which enabled him to acquire interests in Austria, Sweden, Denmark, Italy, Spain, Hungary, Romania and the Dutch East Indies. At the time of his death his holdings amounted to some 1,500 concerns, including 389 commercial and transport companies, 83 railway and shipping companies, 37 oilfields and petroleum factories, 69 construction companies and 57 banks and insurance companies. After his death, his empire rapidly disintegrated.

STÖCKER, Walter (1891–1939). He became a prominent member of the Cologne Workers' and Soldiers' Council after being demobilised at the end of the war. He was elected to the Prussian *Landtag* in January 1919 and was a member of the first delegation to Moscow of the German Communist Party. He was a member of the Central Committee of the party from 1924 to 1932 and chairman of its Reichstag delegation. He died in a concentration camp.

STRESEMANN, Gustav (1875–1929). He was elected to the Reichstag in 1907 as a member of the National Liberal Party. During the war he was friendly with Ludendorff and hoped for victory until the last minute, but after defeat he distanced himself and supported the Republic. He founded the People's Party (DVP), becoming its parliamentary leader in 1920. He was Chancellor of the so-called Great Coalition from August to November 1923 and was in office at the time of the Hitler *putsch*, but after his resignation as Chancellor was appointed Foreign Minister in the new government and remained in that post through successive governments until he died. He re-established Germany as a European power with the Treaty of Locarno in 1925, and in the following year shared the Nobel Peace Prize with the French premier, Aristide Briand.

THYSSEN, Fritz (1873–1951). He inherited a coal and steel empire in the Ruhr and was an early supporter of and major contributor to the NSDAP, but broke with the Nazis on the eve of the war. He was caught by them in Vichy France, imprisoned first by them and then (as a minor war criminal) by the Allies, and died in Argentina.

VINCENT, Edgar, 1st Viscount D'Abernon (1857–1941). He held a variety of diplomatic posts between 1889 and 1897, most of them in different parts of the Ottoman Empire. From 1899 to 1906 he was Conservative MP for Exeter. His interests were wide-ranging, and the list of organisations of which he was a trustee or chairman covered most aspects of public life in Britain. From 1920 to 1926 he was the first fully-accredited post-war British ambassador to Germany. Although very much a British Establishment figure, his dispatches from Berlin were free from prejudice and full of common sense. See also his book: *An Ambassador of Peace: Pages from the Diary of Viscount D'Abernon – Berlin 1920–1926* (three volumes, 1929–30).

WELS, Otto (1879–1939). He was a Right-wing member of the SPD. He was military commander of Berlin during the uprising of January 1919, but he later strongly opposed the National Socialists and died in exile in Paris.

WIRTH, Joseph (1879–1956). He served in the ranks during the war despite having been a Centre Party member of the Reichstag since 1914. He was Minister of Finance from 1920 to 1921 and succeeded Fehrenbach as Chancellor from May 1921 to November 1922. With Rathenau as Foreign Minister he adopted the 'policy of fulfilment' whereby Germany tried honestly to meet the Allied reparations demands. After the murder of Rathenau he brought in the controversial Law for the Defence of the Republic. He occupied ministerial posts in the coalition governments of 1929 and 1930–31, but went into voluntary exile in 1933. He returned to Germany after the war and tried to re-establish Centre Party politics. In 1955 he was awarded the Stalin Peace Prize.

NOTES

References FO (Foreign Office), WO (War Office) and CAB (Cabinet Office) are to documents held at the Public Records Office, Kew.

1918

1. Lloyd George, *War Memoirs* (1936) p. 3257.
2. The Fourteen Points included the renunciation of secret diplomacy; freedom of the seas; reduction of armaments; the restoration of all occupied territories; detailed proposals for the adjustment of frontiers; self-determination for the peoples of the Austrian and Ottoman Empires; and the creation of an association of nations (the League of Nations).
3. Epstein K., *Erzberger and the Dilemma of German Democracy* (Princeton 1959) p. 20.
4. On 19 July 1917 the leader of the Centre Party, Matthias Erzberger, succeeded with 214 votes to 116 in getting the Reichstag to pass a resolution which contained the words: 'The Reichstag desires a peace of conciliation and a lasting reconciliation of all peoples.'
5. The quotation is from an article by Rosa Luxemburg in the journal *Kampf* (Struggle) in March 1917 and is quoted by Price in *Germany in Transition* (1923) p. 236.
6. The Hamburg Points were concerned with the socialisation of industry, the destruction of militarism and the democratisation of the army, the bureaucracy and the economy.
7. Haase was probably referring here to the Polish Silesian, also known as *Wasser Polen*, see pp. 100–1.
8. The Kornilov rebellion was an unsuccessful attempt by the Tsarist General Lavr Georgievich Kornilov (1870–1918) to overthrow the Provisional (Kerensky) Government of Russia in August 1917.
9. M. Philips Price, *My Three Revolutions* (1969) p. 160.
10. M. Philips Price, *Germany in Transition* (1923) p. 239.
11. M. Philips Price, *Germany in Transition* (1923) p. 19.

1919

1. Price was referring to what Daümig had said at a press conference on 4 January, a transcript of which was found among his papers.
2. Levi's statement is quoted by Price in his review (*Labour Monthly*, Vol. 1, July–December 1921, pp. 90–2) of Levi's book *Was ist das Verbrechen? Die März Aktion oder die Kritik darum* (Which is the crime? The March Action or the criticism of it) (Berlin 1921).
3. FO 608.129, Military Intelligence Report giving information allegedly emanating from Rotterdam.
4. FO 371.4357, Directorate of Military Intelligence Summaries, dated 6, 11 and 24 January 1919
5. Lloyd George, *The Truth About the Peace Treaties* (1938) p. 404.
6. In March 1919 Bela Kun overthrew Hungary's first democratically elected government under Count Karolyi, and established a government by Soviet which lasted until August of the same year.
7. FO 371.4357.
8. Report No. 14 to War Office from Lieutenant-General Sir Neil Malcolm, 23 July 1919, in WO 114.23.
9. *Soviet Studies* Vol. III No. 4, April 1952. E. H. Carr, 'Radek's Political Salon', pp. 411–42.
10. Summary of Intelligence, 14 January 1920, in WO 106.349.

1920

1. Report by Lieutenant-Colonel C. E. Maude, British Military Mission, Berlin, 31 December 1919, in FO 371.3779.
2. *Documents on British Foreign Policy 1919–1939* First Series Vol. IX (1960) eds Butler Rohan, Bury J. P. T. and Lambert M. E., p. 81, Kilmarnock to Curzon.
3. Report by Lieutenant-General Sir Neil Malcolm, 29 August 1919, in FO 371.3777.
4. *Documents*, Vol. IX, pp. 40–6, Memorandum by General Staff, 5 February 1920.

5. Memorandum by Churchill (Secretary of State for War) on the military situation in Germany, 8 January 1920, CAB 24.96.

6. *Documents*, Vol. IX, pp. 40–6, Memorandum by General Staff, 5 February 1920.

7. *Documents*, Vol. X, pp. 146–52, Memorandum by Brigadier General Morgan, 25 June 1920.

8. The article appeared in *Vorwärts* on 27 March 1920 and was referred to by Kilmarnock in his report of 30 March 1920 in FO 371.3782.

9. Summary of Intelligence, 15 December 1919, in WO 106.349.

10. Report dated 4 September 1920, in FO 371.4357.

11. The dates given for all articles by Price are normally the dates of publication. Occasionally the only copies to be found are pasted in his album of press cuttings, giving the dateline but not the date of publication. Sometimes articles appear in only the first edition of newspapers, and it is usually the last edition which is deposited at the British Newspaper Library. That would appear to be the case in this instance.

12. *Documents*, Vol. IX, pp. 252–4. Kilmarnock's account of the Kapp *Putsch*, sent to Curzon on 25 March 1920, is the source of all the information on this page.

13. FO 371.4357.

14. Telegram from the Foreign Office, London, to Lord Derby, British Ambassador in Paris, 8 April 1920, FO 371.3783.

15. In the summer of 1920 the Austrian Social Democrats resigned from the coalition government which had been formed after the abdication of the Emperor Karl and, in the elections that followed, they were defeated. This was widely believed to reflect the unpopularity of a government perceived as having been composed mainly of socialists and Jewish intellectuals. In the same summer the excesses of Bela Kun's Soviet-style government in Hungary forced him to resign.

16. Price referred throughout his dispatches from Germany to the 'Alliance of German Industries'. That organisation is more commonly known as the 'National Federation of German Industries', but his texts have been left as they were written.

17. Robert Williams was a member of the National Executive Committee of the Labour Party and represented it on the joint Labour Party/TUC delegation to Russia in May 1920. He was one of the sponsors of the joint meeting of the TUC and the Labour Party which set up a Council of Action, threatening a general strike if Britain joined in a war against Russia in August 1920.
18. In 1901 an International Federation of Trade Unions was formed, with an office in Amsterdam.
19. *Documents*, Vol. IX, pp. 393–4, letter to Curzon from the Consul at Munich, Robert Smallbones, 2 October 1920.

1921

1. FO 371.3782.
2. Price mentioned elsewhere that his companion on this journey was a Dutch journalist, but he did not name him.
3. *German History*, Vol. 14, (1996) No. 2, p. 262, review by F. L. Carsten of Sabrow, Martin: *Der Rathenaumord. Rekonstruktion einer Verschwörung gegen die Republic von Weimar* (Munich 1994) (The Murder of Rathenau. Reconstruction of a Conspiracy against the Weimar Republic).
4. See above, 1920, note 11, p. 206.
5. Inter-Allied Military Commission, Berlin, September 1921, Intelligence Notes, in FO 371.5989.
6. William Seeds, Consul General, Munich, to Curzon, 28 and 29 September 1921, in FO 371.5976.
7. Report from Berlin Embassy, 2 December 1921, in FO 371.5979.
8. See above, 1920 note 11, p. 206.
9. *Ibid.*

1922

1. There were four organisations commonly referred to as Internationals. The First, founded in London by Karl Marx in 1864, broke up in 1872 over the issue of anarchism. The Second, formed in Paris in 1889, was distracted for years

around the turn of the century by sectarian arguments about 'revisionism'. The Third, also known as the Comintern, was established in Moscow in 1919 to work for world revolution. The Vienna Union, or 'Two and a Half' was an attempt by socialists from 13 countries who could not identify with either the Second or the Third, to find common ground. It lasted only from 1921 to 1923. The Comintern was dissolved in 1943.

2. The Russo-Polish war was formally ended by the Treaty of Riga in March 1921.
3. FO 371.7516.
4. FO 371.7517.
5. FO 371.7518.
6. *Ibid.*
7. FO 371.7519.
8. *Ibid.*
9. FO 371.7518.
10. FO 371.7519.
11. *Labour Monthly*, Vol. 4, No. 1 (January 1923) pp. 31–41.
12. The murderers of Rathenau were caught and tried at Leipzig. Two were acquitted, one fined a small sum and the fourth sentenced to a short term of imprisonment.

1923

1. FO 371.8703.
2. Herr Spindler was probably one of the other coalowners arrested with Thyssen.
3. *Documents in Foreign Policy*, Vol. XXI, p. 51, Curzon to Kilmarnock, 22 January 1923.
4. The Nationalist 'bands' referred to by Price are also sometimes known as the Black Reichswehr. They consisted of Right-wing Nationalists from all over Germany, who were tacitly allowed by von Seeckt to undertake guerrilla operations against the French during the occupation of the Ruhr. Virtually an underground section of the Reichswehr, they were trained by the army and the money needed to pay for it was widely believed to have been provided by the big industrialists. See also pp. 152, 154 and FO 371.8670 and 8724.

5. FO 371.8670.

6. FO 371.8724.

7. *Labour Monthly*, Vol. V, (July–December 1923) pp. 9–18.

8. FO 371.8817.

9. FO 371.8666.

10. FO 371.8817.

11. FO 371.8784 contains a summary of the report published in *Le Matin* on 5 November 1923 giving the essential points of the agreement believed to have been made between Stinnes and MICUM.

12. The Hamburg rising took place on 23 October 1923, in the belief that it was part of a co-ordinated national plan and in ignorance of the fact that the plan had been cancelled. A few hundred Communists seized twelve outlying police stations and advanced to the centre of the city, where they were easily stopped. The event was widely regarded as a tragedy, especially in the literature of the Left.

13. In September 1923 the Spanish General Primo de Rivera, with the approval of King Alfonso XIII, seized power and established a Fascist dictatorship for the next two years.

14. FO 371.8769.

15. This was probably George Eric Rowe Gedye, who was certainly *The Times'* correspondent in Germany in September 1923, see the photograph of him with Price near Bonn (Plate 10). He was later the *Daily Telegraph* correspondent in Austria and Czechoslovakia, and was the author of the book *Fallen Bastions. The Central European Tragedy* (1939).

16. The Articles of Faith were summarised in *The Times* of 22 May 1923. They contained a number of points common to any movement purportedly directed towards social reform, such as the nationalisation of industry and the confiscation of war profits. But they also included the repeal of the Versailles Treaty, the expulsion of all foreigners who had taken up residence in Germany since 2 August 1914, the acquisition of new colonies and the deprivation of German citizenship for any 'individuals of the Jewish faith'.

17. FO 371.8754.

18. FO 371.8816.

19. FO 371.8818.

1924–33

1. The Dawes Report, published on 9 April 1924, accepted by Germany on 16 April, and by the Allies at the London Conference of July–August 1924, was approved by the Reichstag at the end of the month. The report proposed annual reparations payments of 1,000 million gold marks rising to 2,500 million within five years, to be met from a budget surplus and scaled according to the size of that surplus and the purchasing power of gold in any given year. Among the means whereby the surplus was to be achieved were: the establishment of a Central Bank of Issue entirely independent of the Government; the stabilisation of the currency to deter speculation and attract investment, and a mortgage to be held by the Reparations Commission on all railway plant and industrial and agricultural property. Certain revenues from indirect taxation were also attached to the Commission. The report contained no proposals on direct taxation, but recommended that prices be raised, wages lowered, railway and state employees dismissed, and unemployment benefits reduced.
2. Gustav Stolper, economist, member of the DDP, quoted by Kolb, Eberhard, in *The Weimar Republic*, translated by Falla, P. S. (1988) p. 67.
3. Kolb, Eberhard, *op. cit.* p. 99.
4. Price, M. Philips, in *My Three Revolutions* (1969) p. 202.

BIBLIOGRAPHY

ARTICLES

Bessel, Richard, *German History*, Vol. 6, No. 1, 1988 'The Great War in German Memory: the Soldiers of the First World War, Demobilisation and Weimar Political Culture'.

Buse, D. K., *Central European History*, Vol. V, No. 3, September 1922, 'Ebert and the German Crisis 1917–1920'.

Carr, E. H., *Soviet Studies*, Vol. III, No. 4, April 1952, 'Radek's Political Salon in Berlin in 1919, with an Appendix by M Philips Price'.

Carsten, F. L., *German History*, Vol. 14, No. 2, 1996, review of Sabrow, Martin *Der Rathenaumord. Rekonstruktion einer Verschwoerung gegen die Republik von Weimar* (Munich 1994).

Friedlander, Henry E., *International Review of Social History*, Vol. VII, 'Conflict of revolutionary authority: Provisional Government versus Berlin Soviet, November–December 1918' (Amsterdam 1962).

Grüber, Helmut, *Survey*, Vol. 53, 1964, 'Paul Levi and the Comintern'.

Hallgarten, G. W. F., *Journal of Modern History*, Vol. XXI, No. 1, March 1949, 'General Hans von Seeckt and Russia 1920–1922'.

Hopwood, Robert F., *German History*, Vol. 10, No. 2, 1992, 'Mobilisation of Nationalist Community, 1919–1923'.

Howard, N. P., *German History*, Vol. 10, No. 2, 1993, 'The Social and Political Consequences of the Allied Food Blockade of Germany, 1918–1919'.

Kollman, Erich, *Journal of Modern History*, Vol. XXIV, No. 2, June 1952, 'Walter Rathenau and German Foreign Policy: Thoughts and Actions'.

Newton, Douglas, *Australian Journal of Politics and History*,

Vol. XXXVII, 1991, 'The British Power Elite and the German Revolutions of 1918–1919'.

Price, M. Philips, *Labour Monthly*, Vol. I, No. 1, July 1921, 'The German Revolution' (Review).

—— *Labour Monthly*, Vol. I, No. 2, August 1921, 'Europe's Coolie Plantation'.

—— *Labour Monthly*, Vol. II, No. 2, February 1922, 'Germany after Cannes'.

—— *Labour Monthly*, Vol. II, No. 4, April/May 1922, 'The Real Power behind the German Government'.

—— *The Communist*, 6 May 1922, 'England and Genoa'.

—— *Labour Monthly*, Vol. II, No. 5, June 1922, 'Capitalist Concentration in Germany'.

—— *The Communist*, 14 October 1922, 'The New German Social Democratic Party'.

—— *Labour Monthly*, Vol. IV, No. 1, January 1923, 'Bavaria and the German Fascisti'.

—— *Labour Monthly*, Vol. IV, No. 3, March 1923, 'The Coal War in Europe'.

—— *Labour Monthly*, Vol. V, No. 1, July 1923, 'A New Phase in the Ruhr Struggle'.

—— *Labour Monthly*, Vol. V, No. 2, August 1923, 'The Hamburg Congress and the New Labour International'.

—— *The Plebs*, Vol. XVI, No. 17, July 1924, 'The Experts Report: Enter the International Bankers I'.

—— *The Plebs*, Vol. XVI, No. 18, August 1924, 'The Experts Report: Enter the International Bankers II'.

Books

Angress, Werner T., *Stillborn Revolution* (Princeton 1963).

von Baden, Prince Max; Mann, Golo and Burckhardt, Andreas (eds) *Errinerungen und Dokumente* (Memoirs and Papers) (Stuttgart 1968).

Bessel, Richard, *Germany after the First World War* (Oxford 1993).

Bessel, R. and Feuchtwanger, E. J., *Social Change and Political Development in Weimar Germany* (London 1981).

Braunthal, Julius, *History of the International* Vol. 2, (London 1966).

Carsten, F. L., *Revolutions in Central Europe, 1918–1919* (London 1972).
—— *Britain and the Weimar Republic* (London 1984).
Craig, Gordon A., *Germany 1866–1945* (London 1981).
D'Abernon, Lord, *An Ambassador of Peace. Pages from the Diary of Viscount D'Abernon, Berlin 1920–1926*, 3 Volumes, (London 1929, 1930).
Dockerill, M. L. and Goold, J. D., *Peace without Promise: Britain and the Peace Conferences 1919–1923* (London 1981).
Edmonds, Sir James Edward, *The Occupation of the Rhineland* (London 1987).
Epstein, Klaus, *Matthias Erzberger and the Dilemma of German Democracy* (New York 1971).
Harman, Chris, *The Lost Revolution: Germany 1918–1923* (London 1982).
Holtferich, C.-L., *The German Inflation 1914–1923*, translated by Theo Balderson (Berlin, New York, 1986).
Keynes, Maynard, *The Economic Consequences of the Peace* (London 1919 and 1971).
Kaes, Anton; Jay, Martin and Dimendberg, Edward, *Weimar Republic Sourcebook* Vol. 3 (Los Angeles and London, 1994).
Kolb, E., *The Weimar Republic*, translated by P. A. Fall (London 1988).
Lerner, Warren, *Karl Radek: The Last Internationalist* (Stamford 1970).
Luxemburg, Rosa, *The Russian Revolution* (Reprint, Ann Arbor 1970).
Mayer, Arno J., *Politics and Diplomacy of Peacemaking. Containment and Counter-revolution at Versailles 1918–1919* (London 1968).
Mitchell, A., *Revolution in Bavaria 1918–1919: the Eisner Regime and the Soviet Republic* (Princeton 1965).
Morgan, David, *The Socialist Left and the German Revolution: a History of the German Independent Socialist Party* (Ithaca NY 1975).
Mowat, R. B., *A History of European Diplomacy 1914–1925* (London 1927).
Newton, Douglas, *British Policy and the Weimar Republic 1918–1919* (Oxford 1997).

Nettl, J. P., *Rosa Luxemburg* (London 1966).

Price, M. Philips, *My Reminiscences of the Russian Revolution* (London 1921).

—— *Germany in Transition* (London 1923).

—— *My Three Revolutions* (London 1969).

Ryder, A. J. *The German Revolution of 1918: A Study of German Socialism in War and Revolt* (Cambridge 1967).

Tampke, Jurgen, *The Ruhr and Revolution: the Revolutionary Movement in the Rhenish–Westphalian Industrial Region 1912–1919* (Canberra 1978).

Waite, Robert G. L., *Vanguard of Nazism: The Freikorps Movement in Post-War Germany, 1918–1923* (Cambridge, Mass. 1952).

Wheeler, Bennet J. W., *The Nemesis of Power: the German Army in Politics, 1918–1948* (London 1967).

INDEX